Keeping Things Whole

Keeping Things Whole

Readings in Environmental Science

Foreword by Crispin Tickell

Selected and Edited by

Joseph Coulson

Donald H. Whitfield

and

Ashley Preston
College of the Humanities and Sciences

Published by the Great Books Foundation
with support from the College of the Humanities and Sciences

Published and distributed by

The Great Books Foundation

A nonprofit educational organization

35 East Wacker Drive, Suite 400
Chicago, IL 60601
www.greatbooks.org

Shared Inquiry™ is a trademark of the Great Books Foundation. The contents of this publication include proprietary trademarks and copyrighted materials, and may be used or quoted only with permission and appropriate credit to the Foundation.

9 8 7 6 5 4 3 2

Library of Congress Cataloging-in-Publication Data

Keeping things whole : readings in environmental science / selected and edited by Joseph Coulson,
Donald Whitfield, Ashley Preston.
    p. cm.
  Includes bibliographical references.
  ISBN 1-880323-90-7 (alk. paper)
    1. Environmental sciences. I. Coulson, Joseph. II. Whitfield, Donald. III. Preston, Ashley L.

GE105.K44 2003
363.7—dc21
                                                              2003041770

Book cover and text design: William Seabright & Associates

Keeping Things Whole

In a field
I am the absence
of field.
This is
always the case.
Wherever I am
I am what is missing.

When I walk
I part the air
and always
the air moves in
to fill the spaces
where my body's been.

We all have reasons
for moving.
I move
to keep things whole.

—Mark Strand

Sir Crispin Tickell is the chancellor of the University of Kent at Canterbury; director of the Green College Centre for Environmental Policy and Understanding, University of Oxford; chair of the International Council of Scientific Unions Advisory Committee on the Environment; and chair of the board of directors of the Climate Institute in Washington, D.C.

The College of the Humanities and Sciences is a great books distance-learning college established in 1998 that offers undergraduate and graduate education in the humanities with concentration in imaginative literature, natural sciences, philosophy and religion, and social science. The College of the Humanities and Sciences promotes student-faculty scholarship through research, discussion, and the development of collaborative publications. For more information go to www.chumsci.edu or call 1-877-248-6724.

About the Great Books Foundation

What is the Great Books Foundation?

The Great Books Foundation is an independent, nonprofit educational organization whose mission is to help people learn how to think and share ideas. Toward this end, the Foundation offers workshops in Shared Inquiry™ discussion and publishes collections of classic and modern texts for both children and adults.

The Great Books Foundation was established in 1947 to promote liberal education for the general public. In 1962, the Foundation extended its mission to children with the introduction of Junior Great Books. Since its inception, the Foundation has helped thousands of people throughout the United States and in other countries begin their own discussion groups in schools, libraries, and community centers. Today, Foundation instructors conduct hundreds of workshops each year, in which educators and parents learn to lead Shared Inquiry discussion.

What resources are available to support my participation in Shared Inquiry?

The Great Books Foundation offers workshops in Shared Inquiry to help people get the most from discussion. Participants learn how to read actively, pose fruitful questions, and listen and respond to others effectively in discussion. All participants also practice leading a discussion and have an opportunity to reflect on the process with others. For more information about Great Books materials or workshops, call the Great Books Foundation at 1-800-222-5870 or visit our Web site at www.greatbooks.org.

Contents

Readings and Questions

Foreword

Wholeness is the key theme of this anthology on the environment. We are one with the natural world, not just with the millions of other living species with whom we share it but also with the elements of air, water, and earth of which we are composed. Sometimes we need to stand back and view our world in perspective—from the beginnings of the universe to the littleness of our affairs.

The English novelist and philosopher Olaf Stapledon once wrote:

> I perceived that I was on a little round grain of rock and metal,
> filmed with water and with air, whirling in sunlight and darkness.
> And on the skin of that little grain all the swarms of men, generation
> by generation, had lived in labor and blindness, with intermittent joy
> and intermittent lucidity of spirit. And all . . . was but a flicker in one
> day of the lives of stars.

It is that "lucidity of spirit" that this book celebrates. Over the centuries and from many vantage points, people have tried to understand and make sense of their lives and circumstances. There is indeed increasing illumination—from creating an intellectual methodology to seeing the interconnectedness of the whole earth system, living and nonliving, in its measureless complexity.

Where do the humans fit in? Physicists point out that our bodies, which look so solid to the eye and touch, are mostly empty space at the atomic level, and that atoms themselves are mostly space as well. Then look at our prized sense of individuality. Are we each of us one person or many? Our individual decision-making process has been described as a boardroom of quarrelsome directors, some apparently rational but others pushing deeper agendas. Is self-awareness a convenient illusion, changing as often as the cells that make up our bodies?

Perched on our little round grain, we forget that inside as well as outside us there are countless billions of mites, all profoundly connected in mutual dependencies. Without them, or their ancestors now embedded within us, we could not move, breathe, or eat. The dry weight of a human body is 10 percent bacteria. Charles Darwin put the point very well when he wrote, "We cannot fathom the marvelous complexity of an organic being; but . . . each living creature must be looked at as a microcosm—a little universe, formed of a host of self-propagating organisms, inconceivably minute and as numerous as the stars in heaven."

From these insights, well explored in this book, comes the increasing realization of the damage that humans can do, not just to themselves but to the earth system as a whole. Indeed, our proliferation in the last couple of centuries can be seen as a case of malignant maladaptation in which a species, like infected tissue in an organism, multiplies out of control, affecting everything else. As the physician Warren Hern notes in a 1994 paper, there has been rapid growth of one such species—our own—leading to its invasion and destruction of adjacent ecosystems, colonization of all available niches, and, in terms of its behavior as well as biology, increasing similarity of appearance, function, and social structure. In terms of factors of increase within the last century, human population rose by four, air pollution by around five, water use by nine, sulfur emissions by thirteen, energy use by sixteen, carbon dioxide emission by seventeen, marine fish catch by thirty-five, and industrial output by forty.

These points were brought out by John McNeill in his book on the twentieth century entitled *Something New Under the Sun* (2000), and put forth in the Amsterdam Declaration on Global Change made by more than one thousand scientists from four international, global change research programs at Amsterdam in July 2001. The declaration states:

Human activities have the potential to switch the Earth System to alternative modes of operation that may prove irreversible and less hospitable to humans and other life. . . .

. . . The Earth System has moved well outside the range of the natural variability exhibited over the last half million years at least. . . . The Earth is currently operating in a no-analogue state. . . .

. . . The accelerating human transformation of the Earth's environment is not sustainable. Therefore the business-as-usual way of dealing with the Earth System is *not* an option. It has to be replaced—as soon as possible—by deliberate strategies of good management that sustain the Earth's environment while meeting social and economic development objectives.

It is no wonder that the present geological epoch, usually known as the Holocene, may have to be subdivided so that following the industrial revolution it becomes known as the Anthropocene, or the epoch of human impact.

Nothing is more important in public education than understanding the challenges posed by environmental science, and *Keeping Things Whole* presents a wealth of contributions that together lay out a basis for looking forward as well as back. As always, part of the problem is to ask the right questions, and then, with minds as open as possible, to discuss priorities, to see how present trends might be redirected, and to look for new social, economic, and scientific values to guide us in the future. Environmental science is still in its infancy, not least because so many of the interconnections between biological and physical processes have yet to be put together. An interdisciplinary approach is never easy, but never more necessary. This book shows us the way.

Crispin Tickell

Introduction

We live, we are told, in an age of specialization. In newspapers and self-help books, on television and in schools, experts seek the counsel and repeat the wisdom of other, more specialized experts. We defer to the authority of the specialist while a whiff of suspicion surrounds the person who professes a broad range of knowledge and skills, and we underscore this bias when we refer to the elementary teacher or the medical internist as "just a generalist."

Modern science is in large part responsible for this emphasis on specialization, this breaking down of information into component parts in hopes of better understanding the whole. We have learned a great deal by dismantling our world in this way, but the separation and isolation of smaller and smaller parts can lead to difficulties. Problems begin when the specialist loses sight of the greater whole or fails to reconnect the discovery and understanding of an isolated part to the larger whole that it supports. Even more confounding is the realization that understanding how each part works does not enable the specialist to then understand how the parts work together; the whole, in effect, may be greater than the sum of its parts.

Environmental science presents a refreshing and essential challenge in resisting both our predilection for specialization and our faith that all problems can be solved through simplification and reduction. The field of environmental science, though essentially science based, eschews a simple disciplinary approach; instead, it is interdisciplinary and holistic, combining natural science, social science, the arts, and the humanities. Agriculture, anthropology, biology, chemistry, ecology, economics, engineering, geology, history, literature, mathematics, philosophy, physics, political science, religion, and sociology compose an incomplete list of the disciplines involved in environmental science. As residents of the biosphere and students of environmental science, we must range over vast amounts of information and consider the interplay between habitats, economies, and cultural beliefs, between all that constitutes the biosphere itself.

In addition to being overtly interdisciplinary and holistic, environmental science is also atypical of most traditional, objective sciences in that it is explicitly prescriptive. It begins with the premise that the earth's living and nonliving systems are in grave danger from human activities, and ends with the demand that we act in such a way as to stop and, where possible, reverse those harmful effects. Precisely what we should do, where we should do it, how much we should do, and how it should be done are the difficult questions, and in seeking answers we directly confront issues of ecological and social justice. Do we save individuals or populations? Do we focus on whole ecosystems or on parts? Do we give preference to indigenous species or colonizers? To live, humans consume resources and produce waste. At what point do our consumption and waste become profligate? If we accept the premise that the world and its resources are finite, and if we accept that both population and consumption are rising exponentially, then we must ask ourselves where we will continue to get the resources we consume. How will we decide who gets what and how much? Where will we put the waste? If we seek to protect the natural environment, at whose expense will such protection come? Who will have to forfeit some basic freedom and who will receive the benefit of such a sacrifice?

But before we address these questions, we must ask ourselves what we mean by the term *environmental science*. How is *environment* the same as or different from *nature*? And how are both of these terms related to *wilderness* and the *wild*? These are not easy questions to answer definitively and conclusively, but as with the question of "What should we do?" our answers have more than semantic importance. How we understand and differentiate between nature, wilderness, and the environment will have profound consequences on how we choose to act.

The nature-wilderness-environment debate is as old as the distinction between human/built environments and natural/found ones, between domesticated nature and wild nature. And those distinctions, it turns out, are largely defined by culture and history. For example, the North American landscapes that European immigrants categorized as wilderness were the results of millennia of management and settlement by Native Americans: to the immigrants this land was wild, to Native Americans it was home. It is ultimately perhaps a question of whether we consider ourselves, and our activities, to be *a part of* nature, or whether we consider ourselves to be *apart from* it. Are human works natural or artificial? Are some natural and some artificial? Which ones? Where do we draw the line? Is it only a question of degree? It all depends upon how one defines nature and the natural, and the place of humanity in the world. Each person, each culture, understands the relationship differently.

In the United States, we have a legal definition of wilderness. We spell it out in the Wilderness Act of 1964: "an area where the earth and its community of life are untrammeled by man, where he himself is a visitor who does not remain." However, it is not clear, given the global nature of pollution and the ubiquitous effects of human activities, if any such place remains. How are we to understand this kind of wilderness in a world where man-made chemical compounds are found at the outer limits of the atmosphere and in the bodies of fish that live in the depths of the oceans? Where the peak of Mount Everest is littered with oxygen tanks, and the ice pack of the South Pole is cluttered with supply dumps? Where grizzly bears and wolves, salmon and whales, are tagged and tracked, measured and probed? Even outer space is not beyond our reach: defunct satellites and the waste from space flights float forever over our heads. Where have we not left our mark? Where is the Wilderness Act's place that is "unimpaired for future use," where "the imprint of man's work [is] substantially unnoticeable"? There is good reason to suspect that there are no untrammeled places left.

Perhaps we define wilderness too simply, too narrowly, or, if you will, too grandly. Might wilderness and nature be found in a crack in the sidewalk, in a backyard garden, or, as Terry Tempest Williams notes in her essay, in a marsh on a stretch of polluted shoreline in New York's South Bronx? By what process of thought, by what aesthetic judgments, do we relegate wilderness and nature to somewhere far outside the human/built world? Do we need to rethink our definitions of nature and the wild? Or do we need to strengthen our commitment to the original definition of wilderness and restrict our activities even more? Are nature preservation and environmental quality issues of survival, quality of life, or aesthetics?

And what about the environment? Today, the term *environment* is often used as a synonym for *nature*. An environmentalist, for example, is generally considered one who seeks to preserve nature. And yet we have a host of environmental laws promulgated and enforced by environmental agencies, such as the Environmental Protection Agency (EPA), that are concerned with spaces that seem to have little or nothing to do with the *natural* environment. The EPA is concerned about the interior air quality of buildings, the presence of lead-based paint in and around older homes, the quality of the drinking water that comes out of our taps, and the safety of the food supply. In this understanding of environment, the built world is clearly as important as the found one. If we understand environment to include the built world, is it still synonymous with nature? And if we understand nature this way, is it still synonymous with wilderness?

It turns out that environmental science takes a holistic view of its subject matter as well as its methods of knowing that subject matter: the environment includes pretty much everything—built or found, wild or domestic, human or animal—hence the necessity of the interdisciplinary approach. Such an approach does little to resolve the problem of drawing boundaries between spaces, but that is, perhaps, the point. Perhaps nature and culture are not separable in any real, practical, or meaningful way, and our environmental knowledge must somehow take this interdependence into account when framing issues and offering solutions.

Which brings us to our consideration of the second part of the term *environmental science*. What kind of science is it? How should it be conducted? Can it be conducted at all with an object as large as the environment? What is its role in "knowing" the environment? If the scientific method works best when one can control the variables and manipulate them at will, can it work with something as irreducible, unbounded, and indeterminate as the environment? Environmental science, as we noted above, is inherently interdisciplinary. It brings together ecologists, botanists, soil scientists, wildlife biologists, foresters, physicists, biogeochemists, riparian and aquatic scientists, geneticists, biologists, and a multitude of others who have an intimate understanding of the minute details of their particular disciplines. What makes environmental science unique is that it attempts to weave all of this particular knowledge into a broader scientific framework of the environment as a whole. Environmental scientists are equally concerned about the social and political contexts of environmental issues. This broader focus makes environmental science somewhat different from the traditional sciences.

Questions about the limits and uses of science are thus an explicit part of this book. We have included selections that push the limits of what we typically understand to be scientific. Some of the theories you will read about were not considered scientific when they were introduced; several have been reconsidered in light of new knowledge and evidence. Others were widely accepted and based on what was considered solid science, but have since been rejected as inadequate or inaccurate. Some of the selections are highly scientific. Others are without any scientific pretense at all, and yet, they are not unscientific: the authors use information gained from complex and sophisticated scientific research, and they contribute to our understanding of the world we live in by integrating this knowledge into narrative frameworks that tell stories. In some instances, it is simple, but careful and precise, observation of the workings of nature that underpins the narrative. The author has no particular expertise in the profession of science; the "research" is not sanctioned by a large corporation, a university, or the government; and the tools, skills, and methods are those practiced by all humans at every moment of their waking lives. In this sense, environmental science is available to all of us. It is something we each can, and must, do every day as we walk around on the planet.

The selections in this book offer no definitive resolutions to any of the issues raised here. Instead, they will challenge your ideas about what is meant by environment, nature, and wilderness, as well as extend your understanding of what constitutes scientific knowledge. Environmental issues are ultimately human issues, and the choices we make will have profound consequences for the life of someone, somewhere, at some time.

Exploring environmental science through shared inquiry discussion promotes the unity inherent in the subject because the give-and-take of discussion encourages readers to think about ideas that cross myriad disciplines. The selections in this book provide a coherent introduction to the concerns of environmental science and demonstrate the depth and scope of a field that is vital for the stewardship and survival of the biosphere and all that lives in it.

Theme Notes

The readings in this anthology were chosen in part because they correspond to the six major themes the College Board uses to organize its Advanced Placement Program Environmental Science curriculum. In the pages that follow, you will find an explanation of each of these themes, along with a table indicating which themes are addressed by which selections.

I. Science As a Process

Science is generally understood to be cumulative. Year after year, the quantity of knowledge increases as scientists make observations, conduct experiments, and formulate theories. The ongoing result of this activity guides continuing work and sometimes makes possible the accurate prediction of future events. At any given time in history, the approach to understanding the natural world in a way that can be called scientific is based on deeply embedded assumptions about what kind of knowledge of the world is possible and how it can be acquired. Each age, including our own, cherishes its scientific ideas about the way things are. In addition, each age has its own ideas about what procedures to follow in investigating the natural world.

However, all the sciences have changed profoundly again and again throughout history—including those that compose what is now called

7

environmental science. This process of change happens not simply because more knowledge is acquired, but because new knowledge continually raises new questions, sometimes at such a fundamental level that the entire set of assumptions underlying science shifts to a new pattern of understanding.

Because environmental science is a synthetic, field-based discipline that combines many different sciences, theoretical principles, procedural methods, and knowledge from disciplines not typically considered scientific, it presents a challenge to our traditional understanding of what counts as science. It also asks us to reconsider our traditional notions of science as objective and value neutral.

Each of the selections in this anthology deals with a specific set of questions or issues in environmental science, while at the same time saying something—directly or indirectly—about science as a process. Therefore, science as a process should be kept in mind as an overarching theme.

Many of the investigative procedures set forth in these selections exemplify this theme. In 1619, René Descartes proposed a radically new method for seeking knowledge about the world; that method has been the standard of practice in Western science for nearly 300 years. Frederic Clements successfully applied Descartes's method of reduction and isolation in his groundbreaking studies of plant succession on the Great Plains of North America. A. G. Tansley extended the method to the study of entire ecological systems, but his holistic approach begins to test its limits. These limitations prompted the search for alternative approaches that are more able to deal with complex phenomena as wholes; one such alternative is that outlined by Vladimir Vernadsky.

It is sometimes the case that individual theories or models of how the world works also offer challenges to the underlying patterns of understanding that direct scientific research. James E. Lovelock's controversial Gaia hypothesis is one such example: it challenged long-accepted assumptions about the nature of the world. Lovelock's efforts to phrase his intuitions in scientifically verifiable ways lend invaluable insight into the practice and culture of science. And finally, Gordon Miller builds on insights from the study of the history of ideas as well as the philosophy and sociology of science. He suggests that our choice of experimental methods and investigative techniques arises from the complex interplay between the original thinking of scientists and the cultural and social practices through which we see the world.

The writers in this anthology who deal most explicitly with science as an investigative process are Descartes, Vernadsky, Clements, Tansley, Leopold, Lovelock, and Miller.

II. Energy Conversion

The concept of energy, or the capacity for doing work, is fundamental to the understanding of all natural phenomena. One of the most important insights in the development of life and environmental sciences is that the basic laws of thermodynamics govern the processes of living and ecological systems. According to the first law of thermodynamics, energy can be neither created nor destroyed; that is, energy must come from somewhere and go somewhere—it is conserved. But the second law of thermodynamics states that the effect of physical and chemical changes *in a closed system* increases the disorder (entropy) of the system. In other words, as energy flows through a system, even though it is conserved, at each step more of it becomes unusable. These basic laws form the core of our understanding of how environmental systems work.

However, living systems, like living organisms or ecosystems, are preeminent examples of orderliness, complexity, and self-organization in nature. Plants capture radiant energy from sunlight and transform it into chemical energy, a form useful for life on earth. Animals eat plants or other animals that have eaten plants. Each stage in the food chain produces growth as well as heat waste, which joins the pool of energy released back into space. Thus, the small portion of the sun's energy that is temporarily captured and stored in the various life forms through which it travels sustains all ecological systems.

Understanding the inextricable connection between life, energy, and order is essential to environmental science. Lovelock's "improbable distribution of molecules" becomes a measure of the expenditure of energy necessary for its assembly, and this in turn becomes an indicator of life. The odyssey of Aldo Leopold's particle X demonstrates the power of life to slow the inexorable slide of atoms to death, disorder, and entropy. Vernadsky's wonderfully organized biosphere is the product of and a participant in an intricate, self-perpetuating cycle of energy exchanges between living and nonliving matter. And Lewis Thomas's organized, self-contained live creature is marvelously skilled in holding out against equilibrium—the thermodynamic equivalent of entropy.

But this intricate web of energy is easily disrupted. Humans, in pursuit of life, well-being, and wealth, intervene in this cycle, appropriating and converting for their own use energy previously destined for other systems and processes. Understanding the ecological as well as sociological and economic effects of this conversion is a primary concern in environmental science.

Among the readings in this anthology, those by Vernadsky, Leopold, Boulding, Commoner, Thomas, Dillard, and Lovelock probe different aspects of energy conversion.

III. Earth's Interconnectedness

Perhaps the single most important principle of environmental science is the insight that the earth's systems are interdependent and interconnected. We may speak of or treat ecological systems, plant communities, animal populations, or human social systems as if they were somehow independent, autonomous entities, but in reality these systems coexist only within a complex web of interrelationships with a host of other living and nonliving systems. The interconnectedness of the environment is largely responsible for the interdisciplinary and synthetic character of environmental science.

The fundamental insight into the earth as an interconnected system has profound implications for human actions. Natural systems always have and always will change—sometimes dramatically and permanently—over time and space. If we accept that the earth is one interconnected system, then changes in one subsystem or one place will cause changes, not always predictable or expected, in others. There are global consequences to local actions. In addition, not all biogeochemical systems are equally resilient; each system differs in its ability to recover from disturbances—human or natural—and its resilience or lack thereof will have an effect on other systems.

The interconnected nature of its subject matter also creates problems for conducting environmental science. Western science favors reductionism; the scientific method demands that problems be framed in such a way that variables can be identified, isolated, and controlled, allowing experimental results to be reproduced and verified by others. The inherent complexity and interdependent nature of the environment, to say nothing of its sheer magnitude, resists this kind of reduction, analysis, and manipulation and thus creates unique problems for a science of the environment.

This sense of the interconnectedness of the earth's systems is not new, but it is an increasingly dominant theme in the natural sciences, land management, and global politics. Vernadsky's biosphere, Clements's superorganism, Thomas's "organized, self-contained . . . live creature," and Lovelock's Gaia are all efforts to articulate or model this intuition of connectedness. Tansley coined the term *ecosystem* in an attempt to capture his sense of community, and Annie Dillard reflects on the remarkable fact that hemoglobin and chlorophyll—the bearers of life for the animal and plant kingdoms—differ by one simple atom.

The great importance of interconnectedness as a theme for the study of environmental science is reflected in the fact that most of the readings in this anthology have some bearing on it: Vernadsky, Clements, Tansley, Leopold, Boulding, Commoner, Thomas, Dillard, and Lovelock.

IV. Human Alterations

Like all other living organisms, humans alter the natural systems in which they live. The impact of the human species on the planet is not new; we have been altering local environments to suit our needs and desires for millions of years. What is new is the extent of our abilities to alter and manipulate nature. Technology has enabled us to increase the rate and scale of our alterations. Observation, however, has taught us that these actions have unexpected and unforeseen consequences in far-flung places.

Population growth is also a form of alteration. The more members a species has, the more impact that species will have on the environment. This is as true of white-tailed deer and wolves as it is of humans. But environmental alteration is not just an effect of numbers. It is also an effect of patterns of consumption and land use. Thus, we must consider not only how many members a species has, but also the different ways these members have of sustaining themselves.

We cannot expect to live without altering natural systems: every living creature does so. It is not then a question of whether we should alter systems or not. Rather, it is a question of how much and what types of alteration we can inflict upon ecological systems and at what point the systems will fail to recover. At what point does irreversible entropy ensue?

Altered landscapes prompt discussions of ethics, aesthetics, justice, knowledge, and limits. George Perkins Marsh sounds an early warning on the potentially devastating impact of human alterations. Leopold accepts that alterations are inevitable, and even desirable in some instances, but urges "intelligent tinkering" in which all parts are saved. Kenneth Boulding, Garrett Hardin, and Barry Commoner grapple with the economic and social causes and consequences that are inextricably linked to human alterations of the environment.

Almost all of the writers in this anthology are concerned either centrally or peripherally with the theme of humans altering natural systems: Thoreau, Marsh, Leopold, Boulding, Hardin, Commoner, McKibben, Snyder, Williams, Grumbine, Grover, and Miller.

V. Environmental Problems: Social and Cultural Context

Environmental science is concerned with not only the natural environment, but also the social and cultural environment. Indeed, it is impossible to understand the natural environment without understanding, to some degree, the evolving social and cultural practices that have shaped that environment over the millennia. Thus, environmental science does not attempt to treat environmental issues outside of the cultural context in which those problems develop and persist.

If environmental problems have a social and cultural context, environmental solutions also have a social and cultural context. Recognizing that different peoples and cultures have different understandings of both the problems *and* the solutions is critical to developing strategies for solving environmental problems.

While environmental science remains essentially based in the natural sciences, it nonetheless recognizes that human knowledge, perceptions, and values are key components in identifying issues and developing solutions. That recognition is demonstrated in environmental science's mission to educate citizens so that they can make informed, knowledgeable decisions about environmental issues.

There are ethical, economic, technological, philosophical, and political dimensions to environmental problems. Leopold argues that we must develop not only our ecological knowledge, but also an ecological conscience. Boulding and Commoner investigate the assumptions buried in our economic frameworks—assumptions that determine our perceptions of our well-being, our productive technologies, and our patterns of consumption.

Bill McKibben, R. Edward Grumbine, and Gordon Miller are more interested in how culturally determined patterns of thought affect our attitudes
toward and perceptions of nature. In a more literary vein, Gary Snyder rumi-
nates on the power of language to literally create the world; his discursive
etymology of the terms *nature, wild,* and *wilderness* reveals the long history of
our paradoxical and ambiguous relationship with the environment.

**In this anthology, Thoreau, Leopold, Boulding, Hardin, Commoner,
McKibben, Snyder, Williams, Grumbine, Grover, and Miller are particularly concerned with the cultural and social context of environmental
problems.**

VI. Survival and Sustainability

Environmental science, unlike most other sciences, contains a unique
prescriptive component: hidden within the statement that human survival
depends upon developing new sustainable practices is the premise that
human actions are currently not sustainable and our survival is at risk. This
claim is by no means universally accepted. One task of environmental science
is to collect the evidence that demonstrates the validity of this premise. Conversely, one might say that this assertion is the result of decades of research
into the environmental changes effected by human existence. Regardless of
which comes first—the knowledge or the claim—environmental science is
not disinterested: it is problem based and solution oriented.

To that end, gathering and analyzing data enables environmental scientists to formulate theories of what a sustainable system might look like and
what sorts of practices we might undertake to achieve it. This task is not easy
and there is no one correct answer. In fact, we quickly encounter the limits
of science, since what science tells us may be necessary or desirable from an
environmental perspective may not be acceptable from a political, social, or
moral perspective.

Environmental science can help us identify problems, develop solutions, and assess the potential consequences of certain actions. The ultimate
determination of which solution to implement is not, however, a scientific
one, but a philosophical, political, and moral one. Environmental scientists
are concerned then with social justice as well as environmental justice.

Almost all of the authors in this anthology are advocates, as well as
scientists, philosophers, and writers. They make no pretense to being value

neutral, though each brings objective information to bear in the service of his or her cause. Almost invariably that cause is the care of the environment and the betterment of humankind. Leopold's land ethic is not only about conserving nature; it is about enriching the material and ethical life of humans in unconventional ways. Hardin's argument to maintain population and resource consumption at optimal rather than maximal levels is about improving the quality of life for the many rather than the few, and for those in this generation as well as those in generations to come. McKibben's efforts to reinvest nature with a sense of the sacred is not only a way to save nature, but also a way to save ourselves.

It has been almost 140 years since Marsh wrote that "the earth is fast becoming an unfit home for its noblest inhabitant, and another era of equal human crime and human improvidence . . . would reduce it to such a condition of impoverished productiveness, of shattered surface, of climatic excess, as to threaten the depravation, barbarism, and perhaps even extinction of the species." It remains to be seen whether this era will be one of human crime and human improvidence by which we bring about our own destruction, or one of human grace and providence by which we sustain both ourselves and the environment upon which we depend.

In this anthology, Marsh, Leopold, Boulding, Hardin, Commoner, McKibben, and Grumbine address the theme of human survival as related to sustainable systems.

Thematic Table

This table provides an overview of the major themes and subject areas addressed by each of the selections in this anthology.

Theme	I. Natural Science	II. Social Science	III. Philosophy and Literature
1. SCIENCE AS A PROCESS			
Descartes			Descartes
Clements	Clements		
Tansley	Tansley		
Leopold	Leopold		Leopold
Lovelock	Lovelock		
Miller	Miller		Miller
2. ENERGY CONVERSION			
Vernadsky	Vernadsky		
Leopold	Leopold		Leopold
Boulding		Boulding	
Commoner	Commoner	Commoner	
Thomas	Thomas		Thomas
Dillard	Dillard		Dillard
Lovelock	Lovelock		
3. EARTH'S INTERCONNECTEDNESS			
Vernadsky	Vernadsky		
Clements	Clements		
Tansley	Tansley		
Leopold	Leopold		Leopold
Boulding		Boulding	
Commoner		Commoner	
Thomas	Thomas		Thomas
Dillard	Dillard		Dillard
Lovelock	Lovelock		
4. HUMAN ALTERATIONS			
Thoreau			Thoreau
Marsh	Marsh	Marsh	
Leopold	Leopold	Leopold	Leopold
Boulding		Boulding	

Theme	I. Natural Science	II. Social Science	III. Philosophy and Literature
4. HUMAN ALTERATIONS (continued)			
Hardin		Hardin	Hardin
Commoner	Commoner	Commoner	
McKibben			McKibben
Snyder			Snyder
Williams	Williams		Williams
Grumbine	Grumbine	Grumbine	Grumbine
Grover			Grover
Miller	Miller		Miller
5. ENVIRONMENTAL PROBLEMS: SOCIAL AND CULTURAL CONTEXT			
Thoreau			Thoreau
Leopold	Leopold	Leopold	Leopold
Boulding		Boulding	
Hardin		Hardin	Hardin
Commoner	Commoner	Commoner	
McKibben			McKibben
Snyder			Snyder
Williams	Williams		Williams
Grumbine	Grumbine	Grumbine	Grumbine
Grover	Grover	Grover	Grover
Miller	Miller		Miller
6. SURVIVAL AND SUSTAINABILITY			
Marsh	Marsh	Marsh	
Leopold	Leopold	Leopold	Leopold
Boulding		Boulding	
Hardin		Hardin	Hardin
Commoner	Commoner	Commoner	
McKibben			McKibben
Grumbine	Grumbine	Grumbine	Grumbine

About Shared Inquiry

Shared Inquiry is the effort to achieve a more thorough understanding of a text by discussing questions, responses, and insights with others. For both the leader and the participants, careful listening is essential. The leader guides the discussion by asking questions about specific ideas and problems of meaning in the text, but does not seek to impose his or her own interpretation on the group.

During a Shared Inquiry discussion, group members consider a number of possible ideas and weigh the evidence for each. Ideas that are entertained and then refined or abandoned are not thought of as mistakes, but as valuable parts of the thinking process. Group members gain experience in communicating complex ideas and in supporting, testing, and expanding their thoughts. Everyone in the group contributes to the discussion, and while participants may disagree with each other, they treat each other's ideas respectfully.

This process of communal discovery is vital to developing an understanding of important texts and ideas, rather than merely cataloging knowledge about them. By reading and thinking together about important works, you and the other members of your group are joining a great conversation that extends across the centuries.

Guidelines for Leading and Participating in Discussion

Over the past fifty years, the Great Books Foundation has developed guidelines that distill the experience of many discussion groups, with participants of all ages. We have found that when groups follow the procedures outlined below, discussions are most focused and fruitful:

1. **Read the selection before participating in the discussion.** This ensures that all participants are equally prepared to talk about the ideas in the work and helps prevent talk that would distract the group from its purpose.

2. **Support your ideas with evidence from the text.** This keeps the discussion focused on understanding the selection and enables the group to weigh textual support for different answers and to choose intelligently among them.

3. **Discuss the ideas in the selection, and try to understand them fully before exploring issues that go beyond the selection.** Reflecting on a range of ideas and the evidence to support them makes the exploration of related issues more productive.

4. **Listen to others and respond to them directly.** Shared Inquiry is about the give-and-take of ideas, a willingness to listen to others and to talk to them respectfully. Directing your comments and questions to other group members, not always to the leader, will make the discussion livelier and more dynamic.

5. **Expect the leader to ask questions, rather than answer them.** The leader is a kind of chief learner, whose role is to keep discussion effective and interesting by listening and asking questions. The leader's goal is to help the participants develop their own ideas, with everyone (the leader included) gaining a new understanding in the process. When participants hang back and wait for the leader to suggest answers, discussion falters.

How to Make Discussions More Effective

- **Ask questions when something is unclear.** Simply asking someone to explain what he or she means by a particular word, or to repeat a comment, can give everyone in the group time to think about the idea in depth.

- **Ask for evidence.** Asking "What in the text gave you that idea?" helps everyone better understand the reasoning behind an answer, and it allows the group to consider which ideas have the best support.

- **Ask for agreement and disagreement.** "Does your idea agree with hers, or is it different?" Questions of this kind help the group understand how ideas are related or distinct.

- **Reflect on discussion afterward.** Sharing comments about how the discussion went and ideas for improvement can make each discussion better than the last.

Room Arrangement and Group Size

Ideally, everyone in a discussion should be able to see and hear everyone else. When it isn't possible to arrange the seating in a circle or horseshoe, encourage group members to look at the person talking, acknowledging one another and not just the leader.

In general, Shared Inquiry discussion is most effective in groups of ten to twenty participants. If a group is much bigger than twenty, it is important to ensure that everyone has a chance to speak. This can be accomplished either by dividing the group in half for discussion or by setting aside time at the end of discussion to go around the room and give each person a chance to make a brief final comment.

Using the Questions for Each Reading

Content Questions

These questions will help you grasp more fully the scientific information in each selection. You will be able to answer content questions on the basis of the selections themselves; no additional sources are needed.

Application Questions

Going beyond the material covered in the reading is the distinguishing factor of these questions. They require you to bring in and apply information from other sources, and they may entail some research. Application questions will enable you to work more concretely with the ideas expressed in the readings.

Discussion Questions

These questions may be reasonably answered in many different ways because they ask you to express your own ideas about the issues raised in the selections. Discussion questions offer you the opportunity to weigh evidence, consider your own convictions, connect your study of environmental science to other subjects, and respond to scientific thinkers with your own reasoned judgment.

René Descartes

René Descartes (1596–1650) was a physicist, physiologist, mathematician, and philosopher. He was well known during his lifetime for his work in physics and the natural sciences, but he is most often remembered today for his groundbreaking work in mathematics and philosophy.

Descartes was born in a village near Tours, France. He was educated in the Scholastic and Aristotelian traditions at a Jesuit college, took a degree in law from Poitiers, and served for a time in the military. After a decade of study and travel, he retired to Holland, where he lived in seclusion for more than twenty years. A year before his death in 1650, he moved to Stockholm to tutor Queen Christina of Sweden at her request.

Descartes's procedure for investigation—analytic, reductionist, skeptical, ordered, and systematic—is generally considered the source of our current scientific method. In his search for a firm foundation for philosophical and scientific knowledge, he rejected the tradition of knowledge based on church or Scholastic authority, just as he distrusted knowledge derived solely from speculation or sensory data. Starting from the recognition that the only clear, certain, and distinct idea was his own doubt, Descartes proposed to reconstruct human knowledge of the rest of existence through inferential reasoning.

In *Rules for the Direction of the Mind* (begun in 1619), from which the following selection is taken, Descartes proposes what he believes to be the proper method for pursuing both scientific and philosophical knowledge. Our understanding of this method, and its reductionist consequences, has had a profound impact on Western approaches to knowing nature and the environment.

Immiſſione Refractoria compoſita.

Daniel
Widman
Sculps

Rules for the Direction
of the Mind

(selection)

Rule V

Method consists entirely in the order and disposition of the objects toward which our mental vision must be directed if we would find out any truth. We shall comply with it exactly if we reduce involved and obscure propositions step by step to those that are simpler, and then starting with the intuitive apprehension of all those that are absolutely simple, attempt to ascend to the knowledge of all others by precisely similar steps.

In this alone lies the sum of all human endeavor, and he who would approach the investigation of truth must hold to this rule as closely as he who enters the labyrinth must follow the thread which guided Theseus. But many people either do not reflect on the precept at all, or ignore it altogether, or presume not to need it. Consequently, they often investigate the most difficult questions with so little regard to order, that, to my mind, they act like a man who should attempt to leap with one bound from the base to the summit of a house, either making no account of the ladders provided for his ascent or not noticing them. It is thus that all astrologers behave, who, though in ignorance of the nature of the heavens, and even without having made proper observations of the movements of the heavenly bodies, expect to be able to indicate their effects. This is also what many do who study mechanics apart from physics, and rashly set about devising new instruments for producing motion. Along with them go also those philosophers who, neglecting experience, imagine that truth will spring from their brain like Pallas from the head of Zeus.

Now it is obvious that all such people violate the present rule. But since the order here required is often so obscure and intricate that not everyone can make it out, they can scarcely avoid error unless they diligently observe what is laid down in the following proposition.

Rule VI

In order to separate out what is quite simple from what is complex, and to arrange these matters methodically, we ought, in the case of every series in which we have deduced certain facts the one from the other, to notice which fact is simple, and to mark the interval, greater, less, or equal, which separates all the others from this.

Although this proposition seems to teach nothing very new, it contains, nevertheless, the chief secret of method, and none in the whole of this treatise is of greater utility. For it tells us that all facts can be arranged in certain series, not indeed in the sense of being referred to some ontological genus such as the categories employed by philosophers in their classification, but insofar as certain truths can be known from others; and thus, whenever a difficulty occurs we are able at once to perceive whether it will be profitable to examine certain others first, and which, and in what order.

Further, in order to do that correctly, we must note first that for the purpose of our procedure, which does not regard things as isolated realities, but compares them with one another in order to discover the dependence in knowledge of one upon the other, all things can be said to be either absolute or relative.

I call that absolute which contains within itself the pure and simple essence of which we are in quest. Thus the term will be applicable to whatever is considered as being independent, or a cause, or simple, universal, one, equal, like, straight, and so forth; and the absolute I call the simplest and the easiest of all, so that we can make use of it in the solution of questions.

But the relative is that which, while participating in the same nature, or at least sharing in it to some degree which enables us to relate it to the absolute and to deduce it from that by a chain of operations, involves in addition something else in its concept which I call relativity. Examples of this are found in whatever is said to be dependent, or an effect, composite, particular, many, unequal, unlike, oblique, etc. These relatives are the further removed from the absolute, in proportion as they contain more elements of relativity subordinate the one to the other. We state in this rule that these should all be distinguished and their correlative connection and natural order so observed, that we may be able by traversing all the intermediate steps to proceed from the most remote to that which is in the highest degree absolute.

Herein lies the secret of this whole method, that in all things we should diligently mark that which is most absolute. For some things are from one point of view more absolute than others, but from a different standpoint are more relative. Thus, though the universal is more absolute than the particular because its essence is simpler, yet it can be held to be more relative than the latter, because it depends upon individuals for its existence, and so on. Certain things likewise are truly more absolute than others, but yet are not the most absolute of all. Thus, relatively to individuals, species is something absolute, but contrasted with genus it is relative. So too, among things that can be measured, extension is something absolute, but among the various aspects of extension it is length that is absolute, and so on. Finally also, in order to bring out more clearly that we are considering here not the nature of each thing taken in isolation, but the series involved in knowing them, we have purposely enumerated cause and equality among our absolutes, though the nature of these terms is really relative. For though philosophers make cause and effect correlative, we find that here even, if we ask what the effect is, we must first know the cause and not conversely. Equals too mutually imply one another, but we can know unequals only by comparing them with equals and not per contra.

Secondly, we must note that there are but few pure and simple essences, which either our experiences or some sort of light innate in us enable us to behold as primary and existing per se, not as depending on any others. These we say should be carefully noticed, for they are just those facts which we have called the simplest in any single series. All the others can only be perceived as deductions from these, either immediate and proximate, or not to be attained save by two or three or more acts of inference. The number of these acts should be noted in order that we may perceive whether the facts are separated from the primary and simplest proposition by a greater or smaller number of steps. And so pronounced is everywhere the interconnection of ground and consequence, which gives rise, in the objects to be examined, to those series to which every inquiry must be reduced, that it can be investigated by a sure method. But because it is not easy to make a review of them all, and besides, since they have not so much to be kept in the memory as to be detected by a sort of mental penetration, we must seek for something which will so mold our intelligence as to let it perceive these connected sequences immediately whenever it needs to do so. For this purpose I have found nothing so effectual as to accustom ourselves to turn our attention with a sort of penetrative insight on the very minutest of the facts which we have already discovered.

Finally, we must in the third place note that our inquiry ought not to start with the investigation of difficult matters. Rather, before setting out to attack any definite problem, it behooves us first, without making any selection, to assemble those truths that are obvious as they present themselves to us, and afterward, proceeding step by step, to inquire whether any others can be deduced from these, and again any others from these conclusions and so on, in order. This done, we should attentively think over the truths we have discovered and mark with diligence the reasons why we have been able to detect some more easily than others, and which these are. Thus, when we come to attack some definite problem we shall be able to judge what previous questions it were best to settle first.

Rule IX

We ought to give the whole of our attention to the most insignificant and most easily mastered facts, and remain a long time in contemplation of them until we are accustomed to behold the truth clearly and distinctly.

We have now indicated the two operations of our understanding, intuition and deduction, on which alone we have said we must rely in the acquisition of knowledge. Let us therefore in this and in the following proposition proceed to explain how we can render ourselves more skillful in employing them, and at the same time cultivate the two principal faculties of the mind, to wit perspicacity, by viewing single objects distinctly, and sagacity, by the skillful deduction of certain facts from others.

Truly we shall learn how to employ our mental intuition from comparing it with the way in which we employ our eyes. For he who attempts to view a multitude of objects with one and the same glance, sees none of them distinctly; and similarly the man who is wont to attend to many things at the same time by means of a single act of thought is confused in mind. But just as workmen, who are employed in very fine and delicate operations and are accustomed to direct their eyesight attentively to separate points, by practice have acquired a capacity for distinguishing objects of extreme minuteness and subtlety; so likewise people, who do not allow their thought to be distracted by various objects at the same time, but always concentrate it in attending to the simplest and easiest particulars, are clearheaded.

But it is a common failing of mortals to deem the more difficult the fairer; and they often think that they have learned nothing when they see a very clear and simple cause for a fact, while at the same time they are lost in admiration of certain sublime and profound philosophical explanations, even though these for the most part are based upon foundations which no one had adequately surveyed—a mental disorder which prizes the darkness higher than the light. But it is notable that those who have real knowledge discern the truth with equal facility whether they evolve it from matter that is simple or that is obscure; they grasp each fact by an act of thought that is similar, single, and distinct, after they have once arrived at the point in question. The whole of the difference between the apprehension of the simple and of the obscure lies in the route taken, which certainly ought to be longer if it conducts us from our initial and most absolute principles to a truth that is somewhat remote.

Everyone ought therefore to accustom himself to grasp in his thought at the same time facts that are at once so few and so simple, that he shall never believe that he has knowledge of anything which he does not mentally behold with a distinctness equal to that of the objects which he knows most distinctly of all. It is true that some men are born with a much greater aptitude for such discernment than others, but the mind can be made much more expert at such work by art and exercise. But there is one fact which I should here emphasize above all others; and that is that everyone should firmly persuade himself that none of the sciences, however abstruse, is to be deduced from lofty and obscure matters, but that they all proceed only from what is easy and more readily understood.

Content Questions

1. What is an "intuitive apprehension" of an "absolutely simple" proposition? (27)

2. What is the "chief secret of method"? (28)

3. What does Descartes mean when he says that "all facts can be arranged in certain series, not indeed in the sense of being referred to some ontological genus such as the categories . . . but insofar as certain truths can be known from others"? (28)

4. Why is it the case that "all things can be said to be either absolute or relative"? In what sense are all things either absolute or relative? (28)

5. What does Descartes mean when he says that he is not considering "the nature of each thing taken in isolation, but the series involved in knowing them"? (29)

6. What are the "two principal faculties of the mind" and how do we cultivate them? (30)

7. What does Descartes mean when he says that "it is notable that those who have real knowledge discern the truth with equal facility whether they evolve it from matter that is simple or that is obscure. . . . The whole of the difference between the apprehension of the simple and of the obscure lies in the route taken"? (31)

8. How does one get from a firm and certain grasp of simple, "insignificant" facts to knowledge of the more "lofty and obscure matters"? (30–31)

Application Question

How might one go about understanding "lofty and obscure matters" like global warming, species extinction, urban air pollution, or sustainable development using Descartes's method? Identify, and then order, the basic facts and propositions that are relevant to your investigation.

Discussion Questions

1. According to Descartes, is order found in nature or is it imposed upon nature by the human mind in search of knowledge?

2. What is the role of experience and the mind (e.g., intuition, inference, deduction) in acquiring true knowledge?

3. Why, according to Descartes, do we need an order in searching for true knowledge?

4. Can one adhere to the Cartesian method and still successfully practice environmental science?

5. What degree of uncertainty is acceptable in making decisions about complex environmental issues? Is it possible (or necessary) to know with absolute clarity and certainty all relevant aspects of an issue?

6. Does certain knowledge of "absolutely simple" parts necessarily lead to true knowledge of wholes? (27)

Henry David Thoreau

Henry David Thoreau (1817–1862) met Ralph Waldo Emerson in 1837 and with
him formed the transcendentalist group, an association of writers and philosophers
that included the social reformer and feminist Margaret Fuller and the educator
Bronson Alcott. As set forth in Emerson's essay "Nature" (1836), the transcendental
mindset was one of idealism and optimism; transcendentalists argued that it is
necessary to transcend the empirical and scientific through intuition to arrive
at an ideal spiritual reality where truth is revealed. But Thoreau's distrust
of like-minded communities and his propensity for detailed observation—that is,
empirical methods—eventually led him away from the group and forced him
to reject some of Emerson's tenets.

In 1845, Thoreau built a cabin on Emerson's property at Walden Pond, near
Concord, Massachusetts, the town where he was born. There Thoreau set out to test
his transcendental convictions, going to the woods to "live deliberately, to front
only the essential facts of life," and to exercise self-reliance. His observations
and meditations at Walden from 1845 to 1847 convinced him that nature is less
benevolent than Emerson believed, but still sublime—even awesome—in its
profound indifference. *Walden,* finally published in 1854, with its surveys
of the pond and the surrounding terrain, brought Thoreau recognition as one
of America's early naturalists.

As a protest against slavery and war with Mexico, Thoreau refused to pay his
poll tax and spent a night in jail in 1846. He explained his actions in "Resistance
to Civil Government" (1849), later published as "Civil Disobedience." Throughout
the 1850s, Thoreau worked as a surveyor and became deeply involved in the
abolitionist movement, sheltering escaped slaves on their way to Canada. His political
activism, his support of abolition, and the popularity of *Walden* make Thoreau
a forerunner of the civil rights and ecology movements.

"Katahdin" was first published in 1848. "Death of a Pine" was Thoreau's
journal entry for December 30, 1851.

Katahdin

(selection)

Setting out on our return to the river, still at an early hour in the day, we decided to follow the course of the torrent, which we supposed to be Murch Brook, as long as it would not lead us too far out of our way. We thus traveled about four miles in the very torrent itself, continually crossing and recrossing it, leaping from rock to rock, and jumping with the stream down falls of seven or eight feet, or sometimes sliding down on our backs in a thin sheet of water. This ravine had been the scene of an extraordinary freshet in the spring, apparently accompanied by a slide from the mountain. It must have been filled with a stream of stones and water, at least twenty feet above the present level of the torrent. For a rod or two on either side of its channel, the trees were barked and splintered up to their tops, the birches bent over, twisted, and sometimes finely split like a stable broom; some a foot in diameter snapped off, and whole clumps of trees bent over with the weight of rocks piled on them. In one place we noticed a rock two or three feet in diameter, lodged nearly twenty feet high in the crotch of a tree. For the whole four miles, we saw but one rill emptying in, and the volume of water did not seem to be increased from the first. We traveled thus very rapidly with a downward impetus, and grew remarkably expert at leaping from rock to rock, for leap we must, and leap we did, whether there was any rock at the right distance or not. It was a pleasant picture when the foremost turned about and

looked up the winding ravine, walled in with rocks and the green forest, to
see at intervals of a rod or two, a red-shirted or green-jacketed mountaineer
against the white torrent, leaping down the channel with his pack on his
back, or pausing upon a convenient rock in the midst of the torrent to
mend a rent in his clothes, or unstrap the dipper at his belt to take a draft
of the water. At one place we were startled by seeing, on a little sandy shelf
by the side of the stream, the fresh print of a man's foot, and for a moment
realized how Robinson Crusoe felt in a similar case; but at last we remembered that we had struck this stream on our way up, though we could not
have told where, and one had descended into the ravine for a drink. The
cool air above, and the continual bathing of our bodies in mountain water,
alternate foot, sitz, douche, and plunge baths, made this walk exceedingly
refreshing, and we had traveled only a mile or two after leaving the torrent
before every thread of our clothes was as dry as usual, owing perhaps to a
peculiar quality in the atmosphere.

After leaving the torrent, being in doubt about our course, Tom threw
down his pack at the foot of the loftiest spruce tree at hand and shinned up
the bare trunk some twenty feet, and then climbed through the green tower,
lost to our sight, until he held the topmost spray in his hand. . . . To Tom
we cried, where away does the summit bear? Where the burnt lands? The
last he could only conjecture; he descried, however, a little meadow and
pond, lying probably in our course, which we concluded to steer for. On
reaching this secluded meadow, we found fresh tracks of moose on the
shore of the pond, and the water was still unsettled as if they had fled before
us. A little further, in a dense thicket, we seemed to be still on their trail. It
was a small meadow, of a few acres, on the mountainside, concealed by the
forest, and perhaps never seen by a white man before, where one would
think that the moose might browse and bathe, and rest in peace. Pursuing
this course, we soon reached the open land, which went sloping down
some miles toward the Penobscot.

Perhaps I most fully realized that this was primeval, untamed, and
forever untamable *Nature*, or whatever else men call it, while coming down
this part of the mountain. We were passing over "Burnt Lands," burnt by
lightning, perchance, though they showed no recent marks of fire, hardly so
much as a charred stump, but looked rather like a natural pasture for the
moose and deer, exceedingly wild and desolate, with occasional strips of
timber crossing them, and low poplars springing up, and patches of blue-

berries here and there. I found myself traversing them familiarly, like some pasture run to waste, or partially reclaimed by man; but when I reflected what man, what brother or sister or kinsman of our race made it and claimed it, I expected the proprietor to rise up and dispute my passage. It is difficult to conceive of a region uninhabited by man. We habitually presume his presence and influence everywhere. And yet we have not seen pure Nature, unless we have seen her thus vast, and drear, and inhuman, though in the midst of cities. Nature was here something savage and awful, though beautiful. I looked with awe at the ground I trod on, to see what the Powers had made there, the form and fashion and material of their work. This was that Earth of which we have heard, made out of Chaos and Old Night. Here was no man's garden, but the unhandseled globe. It was not lawn, nor pasture, nor mead, nor woodland, nor lea, nor arable, nor waste-land. It was the fresh and natural surface of the planet Earth, as it was made forever and ever—to be the dwelling of man, we say—so Nature made it, and many may use it if he can. Man was not to be associated with it. It was Matter, vast, terrific—not his Mother Earth that we have heard of, not for him to tread on, or be buried in—no, it were being too familiar even to let his bones lie there—the home this of Necessity and Fate. There was there felt the presence of a force not bound to be kind to man. It was a place for heathenism and superstitious rites—to be inhabited by men nearer of kin to the rocks and to wild animals than we. We walked over it with a certain awe, stopping from time to time to pick the blueberries which grew there and had a smart and spicy taste. Perchance where *our* wild pines stand, and leaves lie on their forest floor in Concord, there were once reapers, and husbandmen planted grain; but here not even the surface had been scarred by man, but it was a specimen of what God saw fit to make this world. What is it to be admitted to a museum, to see a myriad of particular things, compared with being shown some star's surface, some hard matter in its home! I stand in awe of my body, this matter to which I am bound has become so strange to me. I fear not spirits, ghosts, of which I am one—*that* my body might—but I fear bodies, I tremble to meet them. What is this Titan that has possession of me? Talk of mysteries! Think of our life in nature—daily to be shown matter, to come in contact with it—rocks, trees, wind on our cheeks! The *solid* earth! The *actual* world! The *common sense!* *Contact! Contact! Who* are we? *Where* are we?

Content Questions

1. What do Thoreau's observations while hiking down Murch Brook reveal about the terrain? (37–38)

2. What does Thoreau mean when he speaks of "passing over 'Burnt Lands,' . . . though they showed no recent marks of fire"? (38)

3. According to Thoreau, why is it "difficult to conceive of a region uninhabited by man"? What must we see or experience to see "pure Nature"? (39)

Application Question

Choose a familiar place—your backyard, a city or state park—and, following Thoreau's example, pay careful attention to what surrounds you. What new information does this familiar place reveal through careful observation?

Discussion Questions

1. What does Thoreau mean by the word *Nature?* Why does he assert that the terrain of Katahdin is "primeval, untamed, and forever untamable"? (38)

2. What is it that Thoreau sees on Katahdin that makes him look upon it "with awe"? (39)

3. If, as Thoreau says, we believe the earth "was made forever . . . to be the dwelling of man," then why does Thoreau observe of Katahdin, "Man was not to be associated with it"? (39)

4. How does Thoreau's experience on Katahdin contradict the common image of "Mother Earth"? (39)

5. Why is Thoreau suddenly at odds with his own body, saying that "this matter to which I am bound has become so strange to me"? Why does he "fear bodies" and "tremble to meet them"? (39)

6. Why does coming in contact with other matter create so many mysteries and questions in Thoreau's mind?

Death of a Pine

This afternoon, being on Fair Haven Hill, I heard the sound of a saw, and soon after from the cliff saw two men sawing down a noble pine beneath, about forty rods off. I resolved to watch it till it fell, the last of a dozen or more which were left when the forest was cut and for fifteen years have waved in solitary majesty over the sproutland. I saw them like beavers or insects gnawing at the trunk of this noble tree, the diminutive manikins with their crosscut saw which could scarcely span it. It towered up a hundred feet as I afterward found by measurement, one of the tallest probably in the township and straight as an arrow, but slanting a little toward the hillside, its top seen against the frozen river and the hills of Conantum. I watch closely to see when it begins to move. Now the sawers stop, and with an ax open it a little on the side toward which it leans, that it may break the faster. And now their saw goes again. Now surely it is going; it is inclined one quarter of the quadrant, and, breathless, I expect its crashing fall. But no, I was mistaken; it has not moved an inch; it stands at the same angle as at first. It is fifteen minutes yet to its fall. Still its branches wave in the wind, as if it were destined to stand for a century, and the wind soughs through its needles as of yore; it is still a forest tree, the most majestic tree that waves over Musketaquid. The silvery sheen of the sunlight is reflected from its needles; it still affords an inaccessible crotch for the squirrel's nest; not a lichen has forsaken its mastlike stem, its raking mast—the hill is the hulk. Now, now's the moment! The manikins at its base are flee-ing from their crime. They have dropped the guilty saw and ax. How slowly and majestically it starts! As if it were only swayed by a summer breeze, and would return without a sigh to its location in the air. And now it fans the hillside with its fall, and it lies down to its bed in the valley, from which it is never to rise, as softly as a feather, folding its green mantle about it like a warrior, as if, tired of standing, it embraced the earth with silent joy, return-ing its elements to the dust again. But hark! There you only saw, but did not hear. There now comes up a deafening crash to these rocks, advertising you that even trees do not die without a groan. It rushes to embrace the earth, and mingle its elements with the dust. And now all is still once more and forever, both to eye and ear.

I went down and measured it. It was about four feet in diameter where it was sawed, about one hundred feet long. Before I had reached it the axmen had already half divested it of its branches. Its gracefully spreading top was a perfect wreck on the hillside as if it had been made of glass, and the tender cones of one year's growth upon its summit appealed in vain and too late to the mercy of the chopper. Already he has measured it with his ax, and marked off the mill logs it will make. And the space it occupied in upper air is vacant for the next two centuries. It is lumber. He has laid waste the air. When the fish hawk in the spring revisits the banks of the Musketaquid, he will circle in vain to find his accustomed perch, and the hen hawk will mourn for the pines lofty enough to protect her brood. A plant which it has taken two centuries to perfect, rising by slow stages into the heavens, has this afternoon ceased to exist. Its sapling top had expanded to this January thaw as the forerunner of summers to come. Why does not the village bell sound a knell? I hear no knell tolled. I see no procession of mourners in the streets, or the woodland aisles. The squirrel has leaped to another tree; the hawk has circled further off, and has now settled upon a new eyrie, but the woodman is preparing [to] lay his ax at the root of that also.

Application Question

How is death related to the perpetuation of life? Find and describe an example of this relation in your immediate surroundings.

Discussion Questions

1. What is Thoreau's attitude toward the two men sawing down the tree?

2. What does the tree represent for Thoreau?

3. Why does Thoreau make a point of saying he "was mistaken" in his first observation of the tree's angle and its readiness to fall? (41)

4. What is the effect of first seeing the tree fall and then hearing it?

5. What does Thoreau mean when he says, "It is lumber. He has laid waste the air"? (42)

6. What difference does Thoreau suggest between his own expectations after the fall and the behavior of the squirrel and the hawk? What is Thoreau observing in suggesting this difference?

7. How does Thoreau's reaction to the terrain of Katahdin differ from his reaction to the felling of the pine? What are the implications of his different reactions?

George Perkins Marsh

A lifelong spokesman for the preservation and care of natural resources, George Perkins Marsh (1801–1882) was a linguist, lawyer, diplomat, and member of the U.S. Congress. He studied silviculture and soil conservation, and his speech in 1847 to the Agricultural Society of Rutland County, Vermont, warned of the human capacity for environmental destruction. He also argued for less profligate use of resources and land restoration—unorthodox ideas in his day.

Marsh graduated from Dartmouth College in 1820, having mastered several languages. He then taught for several years before starting what would soon be a successful law practice in Burlington, Vermont. Using his law experience as a platform, Marsh entered politics and was elected to the House of Representatives in 1842. He published a history of the English language and continued to expand his knowledge of languages, including Icelandic.

In 1861, Abraham Lincoln made Marsh the first U.S. minister to Italy, a position he held until his death. It was in Italy that Marsh wrote and published *Man and Nature* (1864), from which the following selection is taken. Ignored at the time of its publication, *Man and Nature* found an audience during the environmental crisis of the 1930s. Given its argument that humans have disturbed nature's equilibrium and must therefore work with nature to restore the "damaged fabric," it is now recognized as an early masterwork of the conservation movement.

Man and Nature

(selection)

Stability of Nature

Nature, left undisturbed, so fashions her territory as to give it almost unchanging permanence of form, outline, and proportion, except when shattered by geologic convulsions; and in these comparatively rare cases of derangement, she sets herself at once to repair the superficial damage, and to restore, as nearly as practicable, the former aspect of her dominion. In new countries, the natural inclination of the ground, the self-formed slopes and levels, are generally such as best secure the stability of the soil. They have been graded and lowered or elevated by frost and chemical forces and gravitation and the flow of water and vegetable deposit and the action of the winds, until, by a general compensation of conflicting forces, a condition of equilibrium has been reached which, without the action of man, would remain, with little fluctuation, for countless ages.

We need not go far back to reach a period when, in all that portion of the North American continent which has been occupied by British colonization, the geographical elements very nearly balanced and compensated each other. At the commencement of the seventeenth century, the soil, with insignificant exceptions, was covered with forests; and whenever the Indian, in consequence of war or the exhaustion of the beasts of the chase, abandoned

This selection is taken from chapter 1, "Introductory."

the narrow fields he had planted and the woods he had burned over, they speedily returned, by a succession of herbaceous, arborescent, and arboreal growths, to their original state. Even a single generation sufficed to restore them almost to their primitive luxuriance of forest vegetation. The unbroken forests had attained to their maximum density and strength of growth, and, as the older trees decayed and fell, they were succeeded by new shoots or seedlings, so that from century to century no perceptible change seems to have occurred in the wood, except the slow, spontaneous succession of crops. This succession involved no interruption of growth, and but little break in the "boundless contiguity of shade;" for, in the husbandry of nature, there are no fallows. Trees fall singly, not by square roods, and the tall pine is hardly prostrate before the light and heat, admitted to the ground by the removal of the dense crown of foliage which had shut them out, stimulate the germination of the seeds of broad-leaved trees that had lain, waiting this kindly influence, perhaps for centuries. Two natural causes, destructive in character, were, indeed, in operation in the primitive American forests, though, in the northern colonies, at least, there were sufficient compensations; for we do not discover that any considerable permanent change was produced by them. I refer to the action of beavers and of fallen trees in producing bogs, and of smaller animals, insects, and birds, in destroying the woods. Bogs are less numerous and extensive in the northern states of the American Union, because the natural inclination of the surface favors drainage; but they are more frequent, and cover more ground, in the southern states, for the opposite reason. They generally originate in the checking of watercourses by the falling of timber, or of earth and rocks, across their channels. If the impediment thus created is sufficient to retain a permanent accumulation of water behind it, the trees whose roots are overflowed soon perish, and then by their fall increase the obstruction, and, of course, occasion a still wider spread of the stagnating stream. This process goes on until the water finds a new outlet, at a higher level, not liable to similar interruption. The fallen trees not completely covered by water are soon overgrown with mosses; aquatic and semiaquatic plants propagate themselves, and spread until they more or less completely fill up the space occupied by the water, and the surface is gradually converted from a pond to a quaking morass. The morass is slowly solidified by vegetable production and deposit, then very often restored to the forest condition by the growth of black ashes, cedars, or, in southern latitudes, cypresses, and other trees suited to such a soil, and thus the interrupted harmony of nature is at last reestablished.

I am disposed to think that more bogs in the northern states owe their origin to beavers than to accidental obstructions of rivulets by wind-fallen or naturally decayed trees; for there are few swamps in those states, at the outlets of which we may not, by careful search, find the remains of a beaver dam. The beaver sometimes inhabits natural lakelets, but he prefers to owe his pond to his own ingenuity and toil. The reservoir once constructed, its inhabitants rapidly multiply, and as its harvests of pond lilies, and other aquatic plants on which this quadruped feeds in winter, become too small for the growing population, the beaver metropolis sends out expeditions of discovery and colonization. The pond gradually fills up, by the operation of the same causes as when it owes its existence to an accidental obstruction, and when, at last, the original settlement is converted into a bog by the usual processes of vegetable life, the remaining inhabitants abandon it and build on some virgin brooklet a new city of the waters.

In countries somewhat further advanced in civilization than those occupied by the North American Indians, as in medieval Ireland, the forma-tion of bogs may be commenced by the neglect of man to remove, from the natural channels of superficial drainage, the tops and branches of trees felled for the various purposes to which wood is applicable in his rude industry; and, when the flow of the water is thus checked, nature goes on with the processes I have already described. In such half-civilized regions, too, windfalls are more frequent than in those where the forest is unbroken, because, when openings have been made in it, for agricultural or other purposes, the entrance thus afforded to the wind occasions the sudden overthrow of hundreds of trees which might otherwise have stood for generations, and thus have fallen to the ground, only one by one, as natu-ral decay brought them down. Besides this, the flocks bred by man in the pastoral state keep down the incipient growth of trees on the half-dried bogs, and prevent them from recovering their primitive condition.

Young trees in the native forest are sometimes girdled and killed by the smaller rodent quadrupeds, and their growth is checked by birds which feed on the terminal bud; but these animals, as we shall see, are generally found on the skirts of the wood only, not in its deeper recesses, and hence the mischief they do is not extensive. The insects which damage primitive forests by feeding upon products of trees essential to their growth are not numerous, nor is their appearance in destructive numbers frequent; and those which perforate the stems and branches, to deposit and hatch their eggs, more commonly select dead trees for that purpose, though, unhappily, there are important exceptions to this latter remark. I do not know that we have any evidence of the destruction or serious injury of American forests by insects, before or even soon after the period of colonization; but since the white man has laid bare a vast proportion of the earth's surface, and thereby produced changes favorable, perhaps, to the multiplication of these pests, they have greatly increased in numbers, and, apparently, in voracity also. Not many years ago, the pines on thousands of acres of land in North Carolina were destroyed by insects not known to have ever done serious injury to that tree before. In such cases as this and others of the like sort, there is good reason to believe that man is the indirect cause of an evil for which he pays so heavy a penalty. Insects increase whenever the birds which feed upon them disappear. Hence, in the wanton destruction of the robin and other insectivorous birds, the *bipes implumis,* the featherless biped, man, is not only exchanging the vocal orchestra which greets the rising sun for the drowsy beetle's evening drone, and depriving his groves and his fields of their fairest ornament, but he is waging a treacherous warfare on his natural allies.

In fine, in countries untrodden by man, the proportions and relative positions of land and water, the atmospheric precipitation and evaporation, the thermometric mean, and the distribution of vegetable and animal life, are subject to change only from geological influences so slow in their operation that the geographical conditions may be regarded as constant and immutable. These arrangements of nature it is, in most cases, highly desirable substantially to maintain, when such regions become the seat of organized commonwealths. It is, therefore, a matter of the first importance, that, in commencing the process of fitting them for permanent civilized occupation, the transforming operations should be so conducted as not unnecessarily to derange and destroy what, in too many cases, it is beyond the power of man to rectify or restore.

Restoration of Disturbed Harmonies

In reclaiming and reoccupying lands laid waste by human improvidence or malice, and abandoned by man, or occupied only by a nomad or thinly scattered population, the task of the pioneer settler is of a very different character. He is to become a coworker with nature in the reconstruction of the damaged fabric which the negligence or the wantonness of former lodgers has rendered untenantable. He must aid her in reclothing the mountain slopes with forests and vegetable mold, thereby restoring the fountains which she provided to water them; in checking the devastating fury of torrents, and bringing back the surface drainage to its primitive narrow channels; and in drying deadly morasses by opening the natural sluices which have been choked up, and cutting new canals for drawing off their stagnant waters. He must thus, on the one hand, create new reservoirs, and, on the other, remove mischievous accumulations of moisture, thereby equalizing and regulating the sources of atmospheric humidity and of flowing water, both which are so essential to all vegetable growth, and, of course, to human and lower animal life.

Destructiveness of Man

Man has too long forgotten that the earth was given to him for usufruct alone, not for consumption, still less for profligate waste. Nature has provided against the absolute destruction of any of her elementary matter, the raw material of her works; the thunderbolt and the tornado, the most convulsive throes of even the volcano and the earthquake, being only phenomena of decomposition and recomposition. But she has left it within the power of man irreparably to derange the combinations of inorganic matter and of organic life, which through the night of eons she had been proportioning and balancing, to prepare the earth for his habitation, when, in the fullness of time, his creator should call him forth to enter into its possession.

Apart from the hostile influence of man, the organic and the inorganic world are, as I have remarked, bound together by such mutual relations and adaptations as secure, if not the absolute permanence and equilibrium of both, a long continuance of the established conditions of each at any given time and place, or at least a very slow and gradual succession of changes in those conditions. But man is everywhere a disturbing agent. Wherever he plants his foot, the harmonies of nature are turned to discords. The proportions and accommodations which insured the stability of existing arrangements are overthrown. Indigenous vegetable and animal species are extirpated, and supplanted by others of foreign origin, spontaneous

51

production is forbidden or restricted, and the face of the earth is either laid bare or covered with a new and reluctant growth of vegetable forms, and with alien tribes of animal life. These intentional changes and substitutions constitute, indeed, great revolutions; but vast as is their magnitude and importance, they are, as we shall see, insignificant in comparison with the contingent and unsought results which have flowed from them.

The fact that, of all organic beings, man alone is to be regarded as essentially a destructive power, and that he wields energies to resist which, nature—that nature whom all material life and all inorganic substance obey—is wholly impotent, tends to prove that, though living in physical nature, he is not of her, that he is of more exalted parentage, and belongs to a higher order of existences than those born of her womb and submissive to her dictates.

There are, indeed, brute destroyers, beasts and birds and insects of prey—all animal life feeds upon, and, of course, destroys other life—but this destruction is balanced by compensations. It is, in fact, the very means by which the existence of one tribe of animals or of vegetables is secured against being smothered by the encroachments of another; and the reproductive powers of species, which serve as the food of others, are always proportioned to the demand they are destined to supply. Man pursues his victims with reckless destructiveness; and, while the sacrifice of life by the lower animals is limited by the cravings of appetite, he unsparingly persecutes, even to extirpation, thousands of organic forms which he cannot consume.

The earth was not, in its natural condition, completely adapted to the use of man, but only to the sustenance of wild animals and wild vegetation. These live, multiply their kind in just proportion, and attain their perfect measure of strength and beauty, without producing or requiring any change in the natural arrangements of surface, or in each other's spontaneous tendencies, except such mutual repression of excessive increase as may prevent the extirpation of one species by the encroachments of another. In short, without man, lower animal and spontaneous vegetable life would have been constant in type, distribution, and proportion, and the physical geography of the earth would have remained undisturbed for indefinite periods, and been subject to revolution only from possible, unknown cosmical causes, or from geological action.

But man, the domestic animals that serve him, the field and garden plants the products of which supply him with food and clothing, cannot subsist and rise to the full development of their higher properties, unless brute and unconscious nature be effectually combated, and, in a great degree, vanquished by human art. Hence, a certain measure of transformation of terrestrial surface, of suppression of natural, and stimulation of artificially modified productivity becomes necessary. This measure man has unfortunately exceeded. He has felled the forests whose network of fibrous roots bound the mold to the rocky skeleton of the earth; but had he allowed here and there a belt of woodland to reproduce itself by spontaneous propagation, most of the mischiefs which his reckless destruction of the natural protection of the soil has occasioned would have been averted. He has broken up the mountain reservoirs, the percolation of whose waters through unseen channels supplied the fountains that refreshed his cattle and fertilized his fields; but he has neglected to maintain the cisterns and the canals of irrigation which a wise antiquity had constructed to neutralize the consequences of its own imprudence. While he has torn the thin glebe which confined the light earth of extensive plains, and has destroyed the fringe of semiaquatic plants which skirted the coast and checked the drifting of the sea sand, he has failed to prevent the spreading of the dunes by clothing them with artificially propagated vegetation. He has ruthlessly warred on all the tribes of animated nature whose spoil he could convert to his own uses, and he has not protected the birds which prey on the insects most destructive to his own harvests.

Purely untutored humanity, it is true, interferes comparatively little with the arrangements of nature, and the destructive agency of man becomes more and more energetic and unsparing as he advances in civilization, until the impoverishment, with which his exhaustion of the natural resources of the soil is threatening him, at last awakens him to the necessity of preserving what is left, if not of restoring what has been wantonly wasted. The wandering savage grows no cultivated vegetable, fells no forest, and extirpates no useful plant, no noxious weed. If his skill in the chase enables him to entrap numbers of the animals on which he feeds, he compensates this loss by destroying also the lion, the tiger, the wolf, the otter, the seal, and the eagle, thus indirectly protecting the feebler quadrupeds and fish and fowls, which would otherwise become the booty of beasts and birds of prey. But with stationary life, or rather with the pastoral state, man at once commences an almost indiscriminate warfare upon all the forms of animal and vegetable existence around him, and as he advances in civilization, he gradually eradicates or transforms every spontaneous product of the soil he occupies.

Human and Brute Action Compared

It has been maintained by authorities as high as any known to modern science, that the action of man upon nature, though greater in *degree*, does not differ in *kind*, from that of wild animals. It appears to me to differ in essential character, because, though it is often followed by unforeseen and undesired results, yet it is nevertheless guided by a self-conscious and intelligent will aiming as often at secondary and remote as at immediate objects. The wild animal, on the other hand, acts instinctively, and, so far as we are able to perceive, always with a view to single and direct purposes. The backwoodsman and the beaver alike fell trees; the man that he may convert the forest into an olive grove that will mature its fruit only for a succeeding generation, the beaver that he may feed upon their bark or use them in the construction of his habitation. Human differs from brute action, too, in its influence upon the material world, because it is not controlled by natural compensations and balances. Natural arrangements, once disturbed by man, are not restored until he retires from the field, and leaves free scope to spontaneous recuperative energies; the wounds he inflicts upon the material creation are not healed until he withdraws the arm that gave the blow. On the other hand, I am not aware of any evidence that wild animals have ever destroyed the smallest forest, extirpated any organic species, or modified its natural character, occasioned any permanent change of terrestrial surface, or produced any disturbance of physical conditions which nature has not, of herself, repaired without the expulsion of the animal that had caused it.

The form of geographical surface and very probably the climate of a given country depend much on the character of the vegetable life belonging to it. Man has, by domestication, greatly changed the habits and properties of the plants he rears; he has, by voluntary selection, immensely modified the forms and qualities of the animated creatures that serve him; and he has, at the same time, completely rooted out many forms of both vegetable and animal being. What is there, in the influence of brute life, that corresponds to this? We have no reason to believe that in that portion of the American continent which, though peopled by many tribes of quadruped and fowl, remained uninhabited by man, or only thinly occupied by purely savage tribes, any sensible geographical change had occurred within twenty centuries before the epoch of discovery and colonization while, during the same period, man had changed millions of square miles, in the fairest and most fertile regions of the Old World, into the barrenest deserts.

The ravages committed by man subvert the relations and destroy the balance which nature had established between her organized and her inorganic creations; and she avenges herself upon the intruder, by letting loose upon her defaced provinces destructive energies hitherto kept in check by organic forces destined to be his best auxiliaries, but which he has unwisely dispersed and driven from the field of action. When the forest is gone, the great reservoir of moisture stored up in its vegetable mold is evaporated, and returns only in deluges of rain to wash away the parched dust into which that mold has been converted. The well-wooded and humid hills are turned to ridges of dry rock, which encumbers the low grounds and chokes the watercourses with its debris, and—except in countries favored with an equable distribution of rain through the seasons, and a moderate and regular inclination of surface—the whole earth, unless rescued by human art from the physical degradation to which it tends, becomes an assemblage of bald mountains, of barren, turfless hills, and of swampy and malarious plains. There are parts of Asia Minor, of North Africa, of Greece, and even of Alpine Europe, where the operation of causes set in action by man has brought the face of the earth to a desolation almost as complete as that of the moon; and though, within that brief space of time which we call "the historical period," they are known to have been covered with luxuriant woods, verdant pastures, and fertile meadows, they are now too far deteriorated to be reclaimable by man, nor can they become again fitted for human use, except through great geological changes, or other mysterious influences or agencies of which we have no present knowledge, and over which we have no prospective control. The earth is fast becoming an unfit home for its noblest inhabitant, and another era of equal human crime and human improvidence, and of like duration with that through which traces of that crime and that improvidence extend, would reduce it to such a condition of impoverished productiveness, of shattered surface, of climatic excess, as to threaten the depravation, barbarism, and perhaps even extinction of the species.

Content Questions

1. According to Marsh, how and for what purposes does nature achieve a "condition of equilibrium"? (47)

2. How do "natural causes" contribute to the destruction of North American forests? (48–49)

3. What effect has human colonization had on the population of insects in North American forests? Why is the proper equilibrium of insects important? (50)

4. Why does Marsh think of human beings as "essentially a destructive power"? (51–53)

5. According to Marsh, why is "purely untutored humanity" or the "wandering savage" less destructive to nature than man "as he advances in civilization"? (53–54)

Application Questions

1. Find a vacant lot or abandoned field in your area. What knowledge (e.g., of native plants and animals, food webs, chemical and nutrient cycles, past human uses of the land) do you need to carry out a restoration? What materials (e.g., seeds, fertilizers, hay bales, seedlings, tools) will you need? Research the types of plant and animal communities historically common in your region, and decide how you will restore your field or lot. What kinds of constraints will limit your ability to restore it to any one particular condition? For example, reintroducing some species of wildlife that were present at different times in history would be unfeasible.

2. The winding Kissimmee River in Florida was *channelized,* or turned into a straight ditch, in the 1960s. In the 1990s, work began on a ten-mile stretch to restore the river to its "original" meandering course. Do some research into the ecology of the Kissimmee River before, during, and after channelization. Why was it channelized? What were the advantages and disadvantages of channelization? What are some of the things that scientists and others must consider when restoring the river to its "original" course?

Discussion Questions

1. What does Marsh mean by saying that the earth is "for usufruct alone, not for consumption, still less for profligate waste"? (51)

2. Why does Marsh say that although man lives in nature, "in physical nature, he is not of her"? (52) What are the implications of this statement?

3. What is Marsh's purpose in saying that man is "of more exalted parentage, and belongs to a higher order of existences than those born of [nature's] womb and submissive to her dictates," while also observing that "man pursues his victims with reckless destructiveness," persecuting "even to extirpation, thousands of organic forms which he cannot consume"? (52)

4. Why do human beings believe that "brute and unconscious nature [must] be effectually combated"? (53)

5. Why is the "self-conscious and intelligent will" of human beings important when comparing the influence and result of human and "brute action" on nature? (54)

6. In Marsh's view, how does nature respond to the "ravages committed by man"? (55) What are the implications of this view?

Vladimir I. Vernadsky

Although Vladimir I. Vernadsky (1863–1945) is recognized in his native Russia as one of the most important scientists of the early twentieth century, the significance of his work has become known to the rest of the world only in recent years. Born in St. Petersburg just after the immense social changes brought about by the emancipation of several million Russian serfs, he experienced the great historical disruptions of World War I, the Russian Revolution, Soviet Stalinism, and World War II.

After graduating with a degree in physics from St. Petersburg University in 1885, Vernadsky taught mineralogy and crystallography at Moscow University from 1890 to 1911. From 1912 until his death, he conducted numerous research projects in geochemistry as a member of the Russian Academy of Sciences. He was one of the first scientists to recognize the possibility of using radioactive elements to generate energy, sending an expedition to find uranium deposits in Russia and central Asia. In 1922, Vernadsky founded and became director of the Radium Institute in St. Petersburg. His opening speech at the institute prophetically warned of the dangers of misusing atomic power.

Early in his study of the chemical composition of minerals, Vernadsky developed a lifelong interest in the distribution of individual chemical elements in the earth's crust, the hydrosphere, and the atmosphere, including their incidence in the tissues of plants and animals. Taking into account how these elements have migrated in time and place throughout the regions where life occurs, Vernadsky developed the theory of the *biosphere,* the open system that supports life, which he claimed has existed since the beginning of the earth's history, persisting through long and complex evolutionary changes. In 1926, Vernadsky published *The Biosphere,* from which the following selection is taken. In his last years, he developed a more comprehensive world model called the *noosphere,* a system that takes into account the rational and spiritual evolution of human beings.

The Biosphere

(selection)

The Biosphere in the Cosmic Medium

The face of the earth viewed from celestial space presents a unique appearance, different from all other heavenly bodies. The surface that separates the planet from the cosmic medium is the *biosphere*, visible principally because of light from the sun, although it also receives an infinite number of other radiations from space, of which only a small fraction are visible to us. We hardly realize the variety and importance of these rays, which cover a huge range of wavelengths.

A new character is imparted to the planet by this powerful cosmic force. The radiations that pour upon the earth cause the biosphere to take on properties unknown to lifeless planetary surfaces, and thus transform the face of the earth. Activated by radiation, the matter of the biosphere collects and redistributes solar energy, and converts it ultimately into free energy capable of doing work on earth.

The outer layer of the earth must, therefore, not be considered as a region of matter alone, but also as a region of energy and a source of transformation of the planet. To a great extent, exogenous cosmic forces shape the face of the earth, and as a result, the biosphere differs historically from other parts of the planet. This biosphere plays an extraordinary planetary role.

61

The biosphere is at least as much a *creation of the sun* as a result of terrestrial processes. Ancient religious intuitions that considered terrestrial creatures, especially man, to be *children of the sun* were far nearer the truth than is thought by those who see earthly beings simply as ephemeral creations arising from blind and accidental interplay of matter and forces. Creatures on earth are the fruit of extended, complex processes, and are an essential part of a harmonious cosmic mechanism, in which it is known that fixed laws apply and chance does not exist.

The Biosphere as a Region of Transformation of Cosmic Energy

The biosphere may be regarded as a region of transformers that convert cosmic radiations into active energy in electrical, chemical, mechanical, thermal, and other forms. Radiations from all stars enter the biosphere, but we catch and perceive only an insignificant part of the total; this comes almost exclusively from the sun. . . .

The action of solar radiation on earth processes provides a precise basis for viewing the biosphere as both a terrestrial and a cosmic mechanism. The sun has completely transformed the face of the earth by penetrating the biosphere, which has changed the history and destiny of our planet by converting rays from the sun into new and varied forms of energy. At the same time, the biosphere is largely the product of this radiation.

The biosphere's essential sources of energy do not lie in the ultraviolet and infrared spectral regions, which have only an indirect action on its chemical processes. It is *living matter*—the earth's sum total of living organisms—that transforms the radiant energy of the sun into the active chemical energy of the biosphere.

Living matter creates innumerable new chemical compounds by photosynthesis, and extends the biosphere at incredible speed as a thick layer of new molecular systems. These compounds are rich in free energy in the thermodynamic field of the biosphere. Many of the compounds, however, are unstable, and are continuously converted to more stable forms. . . .

Living organisms are distinct from all other atomic, ionic, or molecular systems in the earth's crust, both within and outside the biosphere. The structures of living organisms are analogous to those of inert matter, only more complex. Due to the changes that living organisms effect on the chemical processes of the biosphere, however, living structures must not be considered simply as agglomerations of inert stuff. Their energetic character, as manifested in multiplication, cannot be compared geochemically with the static chemistry of the molecular structures of which inert (and *once*-living) matter are composed.

Living Matter in the Biosphere

Life exists only in the biosphere; organisms are found only in the thin outer layer of the earth's crust, and are always separated from the surrounding inert matter by a clear and firm boundary. Living organisms have never been produced by inert matter. In its life, its death, and its decomposition an organism circulates its atoms through the biosphere over and over again, but living matter is always generated from life itself.

A considerable portion of the atoms in the earth's surface are united in life, and these are in perpetual motion. Millions of diverse compounds are constantly being created, in a process that has been continuing, essentially unchanged, since the early Archean, four billion years ago.

Because no chemical force on earth is more constant than living organisms taken in aggregate, none is more powerful in the long run. The more we learn, the more convinced we become that biospheric chemical phenomena never occur independent of life.

It is evident that if life were to cease, the great chemical processes connected with it would disappear, both from the biosphere and probably also from the crust. All minerals in the upper crust—the free alumino-siliceous acids (clays), the carbonates (limestones and dolomites), the hydrated oxides of iron and aluminum (limonites and bauxites), as well as hundreds of others, are continuously created by the influence of life. In the absence of life, the elements in these minerals would immediately form new chemical groups corresponding to the new conditions. Their previous mineral forms would disappear permanently, and there would be no energy in the earth's crust capable of continuous generation of new chemical compounds.

A stable equilibrium, a chemical calm, would be permanently established, troubled from time to time only by the appearance of matter from the depths of the earth at certain points (e.g., emanations of gas, thermal springs, and volcanic eruptions). But this freshly appearing matter would, relatively quickly, adopt and maintain the stable molecular forms consistent with the lifeless conditions of the earth's crust.

Although there are thousands of outlets for matter that arise from the depths of the earth, they are lost in the immensity of the earth's surface; and even recurrent processes such as volcanic eruptions are imperceptible, in the infinity of terrestrial time.

After the disappearance of life, changes in terrestrial tectonics would slowly occur on the earth's surface. The time scale would be quite different from the years and centuries we experience. Change would be perceptible only in the scale of cosmic time, like radioactive alterations of atomic systems.

The incessant forces in the biosphere—the sun's heat and the chemical action of water—would scarcely alter the picture, because the extinction of life would result in the disappearance of free oxygen, and a marked reduction of carbonic acid. The chief agents in the alteration of the surface, which under present conditions are constantly absorbed by the inert matter of the biosphere and replaced in equal quantity by living matter, would therefore disappear.

Life is, thus, potently and continuously the disturbing chemical inertia on the surface of our planet. It creates the colors and forms of nature, the associations of animals and plants, and the creative labor of civilized humanity, and also becomes a part of the diverse chemical processes of the earth's crust. There is no substantial chemical equilibrium on the crust in which the influence of life is not evident, and in which chemistry does not display life's work.

Life is, therefore, not an external or accidental phenomenon of the earth's crust. It is closely bound to the structure of the crust, forms part of its mechanism, and fulfills functions of prime importance to the existence of this mechanism. Without life, the crustal mechanism of the earth would not exist.

All living matter can be regarded as a single entity in the mechanism of the biosphere, but only one part of life, *green vegetation*, the carrier of chlorophyll, makes direct use of solar radiation. Through photosynthesis, chlorophyll produces chemical compounds that, following the death of the organism of which they are part, are unstable in the biosphere's thermodynamic field.

The whole living world is connected to this green part of life by a direct and unbreakable link. The matter of animals and plants that do not contain chlorophyll has developed from the chemical compounds produced by green life. One possible exception might be autotrophic bacteria, but even these bacteria are in some way connected to green plants by a genetic link in their past. We can therefore consider this part of living nature as a development that came after the transformation of solar energy into active planetary forces. Animals and fungi accumulate nitrogen-rich substances which, as centers of chemical free energy, become even more powerful agents of change. Their energy is also released through decomposition when, after death, they leave the thermodynamic field in which they were stable, and enter the thermodynamic field of the biosphere.

Living matter as a whole—the totality of living organisms—is therefore a unique system, which accumulates chemical free energy in the biosphere by the transformation of solar radiation.

The Multiplication of Organisms and Geochemical Energy in Living Matter

The diffusion of living matter *by multiplication*, a characteristic of all living matter, is the most important manifestation of life in the biosphere and is the essential feature by which we distinguish life from death. It is a means by which the energy of life unifies the biosphere. It becomes apparent through the *ubiquity of life*, which occupies all free space if no insurmountable obstacles are met. The whole surface of the planet is the domain of life, and if any part should become barren, it would soon be reoccupied by living things. In each geological period (representing only a brief interval in the planet's history), organisms have developed and adapted to conditions which were initially fatal to them. Thus, the limits of life seem to expand with geological time. In any event, during the entirety of geological history, life has tended to take possession of, and utilize, all possible space.

This tendency of life is clearly inherent; it is not an indication of an external force, such as is seen, for example, in the dispersal of a heap of sand or a glacier by the force of gravity.

The diffusion of life is a sign of internal energy—of the chemical work life performs—and is analogous to the diffusion of a gas. It is caused, not by gravity, but by the separate energetic movements of its component parti-cles. The diffusion of living matter on the planet's surface is an inevitable movement caused by new organisms, which derive from multiplication and occupy new places in the biosphere; this diffusion is the autonomous energy of life in the biosphere, and becomes known through the transfor-mation of chemical elements and the creation of new matter from them. We shall call this energy *the geochemical energy of life in the biosphere*.

The uninterrupted movement resulting from the multiplication of living organisms is executed with an inexorable and astonishing mathematical regularity, and is the most characteristic and essential trait of the biosphere. It occurs on the land surfaces, penetrates all of the hydrosphere, and can be observed in each level of the troposphere. It even penetrates the interior of living matter, itself, in the form of parasites. Throughout myriads of years, it accomplishes a colossal geochemical labor, and provides a means for both the penetration and distribution of solar energy on our planet.

It thus not only transports matter, but also transmits energy. The trans-port of matter by multiplication thus becomes a process *sui generis*. It is not an ordinary, mechanical displacement of the earth's surface matter, inde-pendent of the environment in which the movement occurs. The environ-ment resists this movement, causing a friction analogous to that which arises in the motion of matter caused by forces of electrostatic attraction. But movement of life is connected with the environment in a deeper sense, since it can occur only through a gaseous exchange between the moving matter and the medium in which it moves. The more intense the exchange of gases, the more rapid the movement, and when the exchange of gases stops, the movement also stops. This exchange is the *breathing* of organisms; and, as we shall see, it exerts a strong, controlling influence on multiplica-tion. Movement due to multiplication is therefore of great geochemical importance in the mechanisms of the biosphere and, like respiration, is a manifestation of solar radiation.

Although this movement is continually taking place around us, we hardly notice it, grasping only the general result that nature offers us—the beauty and diversity of form, color, and movement. We view the fields and forests with their flora and fauna, and the lakes, seas, and soil with their abun-dance of life, as though the movement did not exist. We see the static result of the dynamic equilibrium of these movements, but only rarely can we observe them directly.

Let us dwell then for a moment on some examples of this movement, the creator of living nature, which plays such an essential yet invisible role. From time to time, we observe the disappearance of higher plant life from locally restricted areas. Forest fires, burning steppes, plowed or abandoned fields, newly formed islands, solidified lava flows, land covered by volcanic dust or created by glaciers and fluvial basins, and new soil formed by lichens and mosses on rocks are all examples of phenomena that, for a time, create an absence of grass and trees in particular places. But this vacancy does not last; life quickly regains its rights, as green grasses, and then arboreal vegetation, reinhabit the area. The new vegetation enters partially from the outside, through seeds carried by the wind or by mobile organisms; but it also comes from the store of seeds lying latent in the soil, sometimes for centuries.

The development of vegetation in a disturbed environment clearly requires seeds, but even more critical is the geochemical energy of multiplication. The speed at which equilibrium is reestablished is a function of the transmission of geochemical energy of higher green plants.

The careful observer can witness this movement of life, and even sense its pressure, when defending his fields and open spaces against it. In the impact of a forest on the steppe, or in a mass of lichens moving up from the tundra to stifle a forest, we see the actual movement of solar energy being transformed into the chemical energy of our planet.

Organisms cannot exist without exchange of gases—*respiration*—and the intensity of life can be judged by the rate of gaseous exchange.

On a global scale, we must look at the general result of respiration, rather than at the breathing of a single organism. The respiration of all living organisms must be recognized as part of the mechanism of the biosphere. There are some long-standing empirical generalizations in this area, which have not yet been sufficiently considered by scientists.

The first of these is that *the gases of the biosphere are identical to those created by the gaseous exchange of living organisms.* Only the following gases are found in noticeable quantities in the biosphere, namely oxygen, nitrogen, carbon dioxide, water, hydrogen, methane, and ammonia. This cannot be an accident. . . . Such a close correspondence between terrestrial gases and life strongly suggests that the breathing of organisms has primary importance in the gaseous system of the biosphere; in other words, *it must be a planetary phenomenon.*

Breathing clearly controls the whole process of multiplication on the earth's surface. It establishes mutual connections between the numbers of organisms of differing fecundity, and determines, in a manner analogous to temperature, the value of Δ [generations per day] that an organism of given dimensions can attain. Limitations to the ability to respire are the primary impediment to the attainment of maximum population density.

Within the biosphere, there is a desperate struggle among biospheric organisms, not only for food, but also for air; and the struggle for the latter is the more essential, for it controls multiplication. Thus respiration (or breathing) controls maximal possible geochemical energy transfer per hectare surface area.

Some Remarks on Living Matter in the Mechanism of the Biosphere

The study of life phenomena on the scale of the biosphere shows that the functions fulfilled by living matter, in its ordered and complex mechanism, are profoundly reflected in the properties and structures of living things.

In this connection, the exchange of gases must be placed in the first rank. There is a close link between breathing and the gaseous exchange of the planet.

J. B. Dumas and J. Boussingault showed, at a remarkable conference in Paris in 1844, that living matter can be taken as an *appendage of the atmosphere.* Living matter builds bodies of organisms out of atmospheric gases such as oxygen, carbon dioxide, and water, together with compounds of nitrogen and sulfur, converting these gases into liquid and solid combustibles that collect the cosmic energy of the sun. After death, it restores these same gaseous elements to the atmosphere by means of life's processes.

This idea accords well with the facts. The firm, generative connection between life and the gases of the biosphere is more profound than it seems at first sight. The gases of the biosphere are generatively linked with living matter which, in turn, determines the essential chemical composition of the atmosphere. We dealt earlier with this phenomenon, in speaking of gaseous exchange in relation to the creation and control of multiplication and the geochemical energy of organisms.

The gases of the entire atmosphere are in an equilibrium state of dynamic and perpetual exchange with living matter. Gases freed by living matter promptly return to it. They enter into and depart from organisms almost instantaneously. The gaseous current of the biosphere is thus closely connected with photosynthesis, the cosmic energy factor.

After destruction of an organism, most of its atoms return immediately to living matter, but a small amount leave the vital process for a long time. This is not accidental. The small percentage is probably constant and unchangeable for each element, and returns to living matter by another path, thousands or millions of years afterward. During this interval, the compounds set free by living matter play an important role in the history of the biosphere, and even of the entire crust, because a significant fraction of their atoms *leave the biosphere* for extended periods.

We now have a new process to consider: *the slow penetration into the earth of radiant energy from the sun.* By this process, living matter transforms the biosphere and the crust. It constantly secretes part of the elements that pass through it, creating an enormous mass of minerals unique to life; it also penetrates inert matter of the biosphere with the fine powder of its own debris. Living matter uses its cosmic energy to produce modifications in abiogenic compounds. Radiant energy, penetrating ever more deeply due to the action of living matter on the interior of the planet, has altered the earth's crust throughout the whole depth accessible to observation. Biogenic minerals converted into phreatic molecular systems have been the instruments of this penetration.

The inert matter of the biosphere is largely the creation of life.

In short, a considerable amount of matter in the biosphere has been accumulated and united by living organisms, and transformed by the energy of the sun. The weight of the biosphere should amount to some 10^{24} grams. Of this, activated living matter that absorbs cosmic energy accounts for, at most, one percent, and probably only a fraction of one percent. In some places, however, this activated living matter predominates, constituting 25 percent of thin beds such as soil.

The appearance and formation of living matter on our planet is clearly a phenomenon of cosmic character. It is also very clear that living matter becomes manifest without abiogenesis. In other words, living organisms have always sprung from living organisms during the whole of geological history; they are all genetically connected; and nowhere can solar radiation be converted into chemical energy independent of a prior, living organism.

We do not know how the extraordinary mechanism of the earth's crust could have been formed. This mechanism is, and always has been, saturated with life. Although we do not understand the origin of the matter of the biosphere, it is clear that it has been functioning in the same way for billions of years. It is a mystery, just as life itself is a mystery, and constitutes a gap in the framework of our knowledge.

The Biosphere: An Envelope of the Earth

Living organisms bring solar energy into the physico-chemical processes of the crust, but they are essentially different from all other independent variables of the biosphere, because they are independent of the secondary systems of equilibria within the primary thermodynamic field. The autonomy of living organisms is shown by the fact that the parameters of their own thermodynamic fields are absolutely different from those observed elsewhere in the biosphere. For example, some organisms maintain their own individual temperatures (independent of the temperature of the surrounding medium) and have their own internal pressure. They are isolated in the biosphere. Although the thermodynamic field of the latter determines the regions in which their autonomous systems can exist, it does not determine their internal field.

Their autonomy is also shown by their chemical compounds, most of which cannot be formed outside themselves in the inert milieu of the biosphere. Unstable in this medium, these compounds decompose, passing into other bodies where they disturb the equilibrium and thereby become a source of free energy in the biosphere.

The conditions under which these chemical compounds are formed, in living beings, are often very different from those in the biosphere. In the biosphere, we never observe the decomposition of carbon dioxide and water, for example, although this is a fundamental biochemical process. In our planet this process only takes place in the deep regions of the magmasphere apart from the biosphere, and can be reproduced in the laboratory only at temperatures much higher than those in the biosphere. It is a fundamental observation that living organisms, carriers of the solar energy that created them, may be empirically described as particular thermodynamic fields foreign to, and isolated within, the biosphere, of which they constitute a comparatively insignificant fraction. The sizes of organisms range from 10^{-12} to 10^8 centimeters. Whatever explanation may be given for their existence and formation, it is a fact that all chemical equilibria in the medium of the biosphere are changed by their presence, while the general laws of equilibria of course remain unchangeable. The activity of the sum total of living creatures, or in other words, living matter, is fully analogous to the activity of other independent variables. Living matter may be regarded as a special kind of independent variable in the energetic budget of the planet.

Living Matter of the First and Second Orders in the Biosphere

While the boundaries of the biosphere are primarily determined by the *field of vital existence*, there is no doubt that a *field of vital stability* extends beyond its boundaries. We do not know how far beyond the confines of the biosphere it can go because of uncertainties about adaptation, which is obviously a function of time, and manifests itself in the biosphere in strict relation to how many millions of years an organism has existed. Since we do not have such lengths of time at our disposal and are currently unable to compensate for them in our experiments, we cannot accurately assess the adaptive power of organisms.

All experiments on living organisms have been made on bodies which have adapted to surrounding conditions during the course of immeasurable time and have developed the matter and structure necessary for life. Their matter is modified as it passes through geologic time, but we do not know the extent of the changes and cannot deduce them from their chemical characteristics.

In spite of the fact that the study of nature shows unambiguous evidence of the adaptation of life and the development of different forms of organisms, modified to ensure their continued existence throughout centuries, it can be deduced from preceding remarks that life in the crust occupies a smaller part of the envelopes than is potentially for it to expand into.

The synthesis of the age-old study of nature—the unconscious empirical generalization upon which our knowledge and scientific labor rests—could not be formulated better than by saying that life has encompassed the biosphere by slow and gradual adaptation, and that this process has not yet attained its zenith. The pressure of life is felt as an expansion of the field of vital existence beyond the field of vital stability.

The field of vital stability therefore is the product of adaptation throughout time. It is neither permanent nor unchangeable, and its present limits cannot clearly predict its potential limits.

The study of paleontology and ecology shows that this field has gradually increased during the existence of the planet.

The Limits of Life in the Biosphere

The terrestrial envelope occupied by living matter, which can be regarded as the entire field of existence of life, is a continuous envelope, and should be differentiated from discontinuous envelopes such as the hydrosphere.

The field of vital stability is, of course, far from completely occupied by living matter; we can see that a slow penetration of life into new regions has occurred during geological time.

Two regions of the field of vital stability must be distinguished: (1) the region of temporary penetration, where organisms are not subject to sudden annihilation, and (2) the region of stable existence of life, where multiplication can occur.

The extreme limits of life in the biosphere probably represent absolute conditions for all organisms. These limits are reached when any one of these conditions, which can be expressed as independent variables of equilibrium, becomes insurmountable for living matter; it might be temperature, chemical composition, ionization of the medium, or the wavelength of radiations.

Definitions of this kind are not absolute, since adaptation gives organisms immense ability to protect themselves against harmful environmental conditions. The limits of adaptation are unknown, but are increasing with time on a planetary scale.

Establishing such limits on the basis of known adaptations of life requires guesswork, always a hazardous and uncertain undertaking. Man, in particular, being endowed with understanding and the ability to direct his will, can reach places that are inaccessible to any other living organisms.

Given the indissoluble unity of all living beings, an insight flashes upon us. When we view life as a planetary phenomenon, this capacity of *Homo sapiens* cannot be regarded as accidental. It follows that the question of unchanging limits of life in the biosphere must be treated with caution.

The boundaries of life, based upon the range of existence of contemporary organisms and their powers of adaptation, clearly show that the biosphere is a terrestrial *envelope*. For the conditions that make life impossible occur simultaneously over the whole planet. It is therefore sufficient to determine only the upper and lower limits of the vital field.

The upper limit is determined by the radiant energy which eliminates life. The lower limit is formed by temperatures so high that life becomes impossible.

By all appearances the natural forms of life cannot pass beyond the upper stratosphere. . . . Ultraviolet radiation is a very active chemical agent, which in the 160–180 nanometer range destroys all life, even spores that are stable in dry media or a vacuum. It seems certain that this radiation penetrates the upper stratosphere.

This radiation reaches no further down because of its complete absorption *by ozone,* which is continually formed in relatively large quantities from free oxygen (and perhaps water) by the action of this same ultraviolet radiation. . . .

The ozone is recreated as fast as it is destroyed, because the ultraviolet radiation meets an abundance of oxygen atoms lower in the stratosphere. Life is thus protected by an *ozone screen* five millimeters thick, which marks the natural upper limit of the biosphere.

The free oxygen necessary for the creation of ozone is formed in the biosphere solely through biochemical processes, and would disappear if life were to stop. *Life creates both the free oxygen in the earth's crust, and also the ozone that protects the biosphere from the harmful short-wavelength radiation of celestial bodies.*

Obviously, life's latest manifestation—civilized man—can protect himself in other ways, and thus penetrate beyond the ozone screen with impunity.

The Relationship Between the Living Films and Concentrations of the Hydrosphere and Those of Land

It follows from the preceding that life presents an indivisible and indissoluble whole, in which all parts are interconnected both among themselves and with the inert medium of the biosphere. In the future, this picture will no doubt rest upon a precise and quantitative basis. At the moment, we are only able to follow certain general outlines, but the foundations of this approach seem solid.

The principal fact is that the biosphere *has existed throughout all geological periods*, from the most ancient indications of the Archean.

In its essential traits, the biosphere has always been constituted in the same way. One and the same chemical apparatus, created and kept active by living matter, has been functioning continuously in the biosphere throughout geologic times, driven by the uninterrupted current of radiant solar energy. This apparatus is composed of definite vital concentrations which occupy the same places in the terrestrial envelopes of the biosphere, while constantly being transformed. These vital films and concentrations form definite secondary subdivisions of the terrestrial envelopes. They maintain a generally concentric character, though never covering the whole planet in an uninterrupted layer. They are the planet's active chemical regions and contain the diverse, stable, dynamic equilibrium systems of the terrestrial chemical elements.

These are the regions where the radiant energy of the sun is transformed into free, terrestrial chemical energy. These regions depend, on the one hand, upon the energy they receive from the sun; and on the other hand, upon the properties of living matter, the accumulator and transformer of energy. The transformation occurs in different degrees for different elements, and the properties and the distribution of the elements themselves play an important role.

All the living concentrations are closely related to one another, and cannot exist independently. The link between the living films and concentrations, and their unchanging character throughout time, is an eternal characteristic of the mechanism of the earth's crust.

As no geological period has existed independently of continental areas, so no period has existed when there was only land. Only abstract scientific fantasy could conceive our planet in the form of a spheroid washed by an ocean, in the form of the "Panthalassa" of E. Suess, or in the form of a lifeless and arid peneplain, as imagined long ago by I. Kant and more recently by P. Lowell.

The land and the ocean have coexisted since the most remote geological times. This coexistence is basically linked with the geochemical history of the biosphere, and is a fundamental characteristic of its mechanism. From this point of view, discussions on the marine origin of continental life seem vain and fantastic. Subaerial life must be just as ancient as marine life, within the limits of geological times; its forms evolve and change, but the change always takes place on the earth's surface and not in the ocean. If it were otherwise, a sudden revolutionary change would have had to occur in the mechanism of the biosphere, and the study of geochemical processes would have revealed this. But from Archean times until the present day, the mechanism of the planet and its biosphere has remained unchanged in its essential characteristics.

Recent discoveries in paleobotany seem to be changing current opinions in the ways indicated above. The earliest plants, of basal Paleozoic age, have an unexpected complexity which indicates a drawn-out history of subaerial evolution.

Life remains unalterable in its essential traits throughout all geological times, and changes only in form. All the vital films (plankton, bottom, and soil) and all the vital concentrations (littoral, sargassic, and fresh water) have always existed. Their mutual relationships, and the quantities of matter connected with them, have changed from time to time; but these modifications could not have been large, because the energy input from the sun has been constant, or nearly so, throughout geological time, and because the distribution of this energy in the vital films and concentrations can only have been determined by living matter—the fundamental part, and the only variable part, of the thermodynamic field of the biosphere.

But living matter is not an accidental creation. Solar energy is reflected in it, as in all its terrestrial concentrations.

We could push this analysis further, and examine in greater depth the complex mechanism of the living films and concentrations, and the mutual chemical relationships which link them together. We hope to return at a later time to problems of homogenous living matter and to the structure of living nature in the biosphere.

Content Questions

1. When Vernadsky refers to the biosphere as a region, does he mean a geographical place? (62)

2. In what ways is the biosphere both a cosmic and a terrestrial mechanism? (62)

3. What does Vernadsky mean when he says that "if life were to cease, the great chemical processes connected with it would disappear"? (63)

4. Why does Vernadsky claim that "the uninterrupted movement resulting from the multiplication of living organisms . . . is the most characteristic and essential trait of the biosphere"? (66)

5. What is the importance of respiration and the exchange of gases in the biosphere? (68–69)

6. How are living organisms different from all other independent variables of the biosphere? (70–71)

7. What is the difference between the "field of vital existence" and the "field of vital stability"? (71–73)

8. Why does Vernadsky claim that *"the biosphere has always been constituted in the same way"* even though it *"has existed throughout all geological periods"?* (74)

Application Questions

1. Consider any landscape of the earth's crust with respect to its geological formations: for example, hills, rocks, soil, shoreline. Vernadsky claims that life "is closely bound to the structure of the crust, forms part of its mechanism, and fulfills functions of prime importance to the existence of this mechanism." (64) He also claims that "the inert matter of the biosphere is largely the creation of life." (69) Using the basic principles, theory, and language of geology, explain the features and morphology of the landscape. Then give an alternative description of the geological features and explanation of the morphology that emphasizes the "prime importance" of living matter.

2. Vernadsky says, "The more we learn, the more convinced we become that biospheric chemical phenomena never occur independent of life." (63) What knowledge and information can you assemble that would begin to make a case for this assertion?

Discussion Questions

1. For Vernadsky, what is the difference between inert and living matter?

2. What is the relation of the powers of adaptation of living organisms—including human beings—to the boundaries of the biosphere?

3. Is the concept of the biosphere incompatible with the belief that living matter is the result of chance and accidental creation?

4. Is Vernadsky saying that because the biosphere *"has existed throughout all geological periods,"* there has never been a time when life has not existed on earth?

5. Is there anything in the concept of life as an "indivisible and indissoluble whole, in which all parts are interconnected both among themselves and with the inert medium of the biosphere" that implies how change and alteration—including that induced by humans—should happen?

Frederic E. Clements

Frederic E. Clements (1874–1945) was one of a group of botanists who took a keen interest in the ecology of the prairie, believing that the grasslands of North America were threatened by spreading farms and cultivation. He attended the University of Nebraska in Lincoln, which in the early twentieth century was a center for study of the grasslands of the United States.

Clements and his colleagues devised a painstaking method of marking off measured areas, usually one meter square, and then documenting by species and quantity every plant growing within the area. This method of investigation is now the standard procedure for all applied field sciences.

Clements sometimes cleared an area of vegetation and then watched the way species returned to it. He observed a series of stages in this process and called the final stage a *climax,* which refers to the type of vegetation that will emerge when large areas are free from interference. The following selection details his observations.

Clements eventually developed a holistic philosophy of ecology, adopting the view that the plant community was a superorganism and that its natural climax was superior to anything influenced by human activity. Ecologists have since determined that the climax community is only an ideal state—one never achieved in nature because time and change never stop. Despite later refutation, Clements's idea of climax influenced resource management for decades.

The Climax Concept

The idea of a climax in the development of vegetation was first suggested by Hult in 1885[1] and then was advanced more or less independently by several investigators during the next decade or so (cf. Clements, 1916[2]; Phillips, 1935[3]). It was applied to a more or less permanent and final stage of a particular succession and hence one characteristic of a restricted area. The concept of the climax as a complex organism inseparably connected with its climate and often continental in extent was introduced by Clements (1916). According to this view, the climax constitutes the major unit of vegetation and as such forms the basis for the natural classification of plant communities. The relation between climate and climax is considered to be the paramount one, while the intimate bond between the two is emphasized by the derivation of the terms from the same Greek root. In consequence, under this concept climax is invariably employed with reference to the climatic community alone, namely, the formation or its major divisions.

At the outset it was recognized that animals must also be considered members of the climax, and the word *biome* was proposed for the purpose of laying stress upon the mutual roles of plants and animals (Clements, 1916[4]; Clements and Shelford, 1936[5]). With this went the realization that the primary relations to the habitat, or ece, were necessarily different by virtue of the fact that plants are producents and animals consuments. On land, moreover, plants constitute the fixed matrix of the biome in direct connection with the climate, while the animals bear a dual relation, to plants as well as to climate. The outstanding effect of the one is displayed in reaction upon the ece, of the other in coaction upon plants, which constitutes the primary bond of the biotic community.

Because of its emphasis upon the climatic relation, the term *climax* has come more and more to replace the word *formation*, which is regarded as an exact synonym, and this process may have been favored by a tendency to avoid confusion with the geological use. The designation "climatic formation" has now and then been employed but this is merely to accentuate its nature and to distinguish it from less definite usages. Furthermore, climax and biome are complete synonyms when the biotic community is to be indicated, though climax will necessarily continue to be employed for the matrix when plants alone are considered.

The inherent unity of the climax rests upon the fact that it is not merely the response to a particular climate, but is at the same time the expression and the indicator of it. Because of extent, variation in space and time, and the usually gradual transition into adjacent climates, to say nothing of the human equation, neither physical nor human measures of a climate are adequately satisfactory. By contrast, the visibility, continuity, and sessile nature of the plant community are peculiarly helpful in indicating the fluctuating limits of a climate, while its direct response in terms of food making, growth, and life form provides the fullest possible integration of physical factors. Naturally, both physical and human values have a part in analyzing and in interpreting the climate as outlined by the climax, but these can only supplement and not replace the biotic indicators.

It may seem logical to infer that the unity of both climax and climate should be matched by a similar uniformity, but reflection will make clear that such is not the case. This is due in the first place to the gradual but marked shift in rainfall or temperature from one boundary to the other, probably best illustrated by the climate of the prairie. In terms of precipitation, the latter may range along the parallel of 40° from nearly 40 inches at the eastern edge of the true prairie to approximately 10 inches at the western border of the mixed grassland, or even to 6 inches in the desert plains and the Great Valley of California. Such a change is roughly 1 inch for 50 miles and is regionally all but imperceptible. The temperature change along the 100th meridian from the mixed prairie in Texas to that of Manitoba and Saskatchewan is even more striking, since only one association is concerned. At the south the average period without killing frost is about nine months, but at the north it is less than three, while the mean annual temperatures are 70°F and 33°F, respectively. The variation of the two major factors at the extremes of the climatic cycle is likewise great, the maximum rainfall not infrequently amounting to three to four times that of the minimum.

The visible unity of the climax is due primarily to the life form of the dominants, which is the concrete expression of the climate. In prairie and steppe, this is the grass form, with which must be reckoned the sedges, especially in the tundra. The shrub characterizes the three scrub climaxes of North America, namely, desert, sagebrush, and chaparral, while the tree appears in three subforms, coniferous, deciduous, and broad-leaved evergreen, to typify the corresponding boreal, temperate, and tropical climaxes. The life form is naturally reflected in the genus, though not without exceptions, since two or more forms or subforms, herb or shrub, deciduous or evergreen, annual or perennial, may occur in the same genus. Hence, the essential unity of a climax is to be sought in its dominant species, since these embody not only the life form and the genus, but also denote in themselves a definite relation to the climate. Their reactions and coactions are the most controlling both in kind and amount, and thus they determine the conditions under which all the remaining species are associated with them. This is true to a lesser degree of the animal influents, though their coactions may often be more significant than those of plants.

Under the growing tendency to abandon static concepts, it is comprehensible that the pendulum should swing too far and change be overstressed. This consequence is fostered by the fact that most ecological studies are carried out in settled regions where disturbance is the ruling process. As a result, the climax is badly fragmented or even absent over wide areas and subseres are legion. In all such instances it is exceedingly difficult or entirely impossible to strike a balance between stability and change, and it becomes imperative to turn to regions much less disturbed by man, where climatic control is still paramount. It is likewise essential to employ a conceivable measure of time, such as can be expressed in human terms of millennia rather than in eons. No student of past vegetation entertains a doubt that climaxes have evolved, migrated, and disappeared under the compulsion of great climatic changes from the Paleozoic onward, but he is also insistent that they persist through millions of years in the absence of such changes and of destructive disturbances by man. There is good and even conclusive evidence within the limitations of fossil materials that the prairie climax has been in existence for several millions of years at least and with most of the dominant species of today. This is even more certainly true of forests on the Pacific coast, owing to the wealth of fossil evidence (Chaney, 1925, 1935[6]), while the generic dominants of the deciduous forests of the Dakota Cretaceous and of today are strikingly similar.

It can still be confidently affirmed that stabilization is the universal tendency of all vegetation under the ruling climate, and that climaxes are characterized by a high degree of stability when reckoned in thousands or even millions of years. No one realizes more clearly than the devotee of succession that change is constantly and universally at work, but in the absence of civilized man this is within the fabric of the climax and not destructive of it. Even in country as intensively developed as the Midwest, the prairie relicts exhibit almost complete stability of dominants and subdominants in spite of being surrounded by cultivation (cf. Weaver and Flory, 1934[7]). It is obvious that climaxes display superficial changes with the season, year, or cycle, as in aspection and annuation, but these modify the matrix itself little or not at all. The annuals of the desert may be present in millions one year and absent the next, or one dominant grass may seem prevailing one season and a different one the following year, but these changes are merely recurrent or indeed only apparent. While the modifications represented by bare areas and by seres in every stage are more striking, these are all in the irresistible process of being stabilized as rapidly as the controlling climate and the interference of man permit.

In brief, the changes due to aspection, annuation, or natural coaction are superficial, fleeting, or periodic and leave no permanent impress, while those of succession are an intrinsic part of the stabilizing process. Man alone can destroy the stability of the climax during the long period of control by its climate, and he accomplishes this by fragments in consequence of a destruction that is selective, partial, or complete, and continually renewed.

Notes

1. Hult, R. "Blekinges vegetation. Ett bidrag till växformationernas utvecklingshistorie." *Medd. Soc. Faun. Flor. Fenn.* 12: 161 (1885). *Bot. Zbl.* 27: 192 (1888).

2. Clements, F. E. *Plant Succession,* Washington, 1916.

3. Phillips, J. "Succession, development, the climax and the complex organism: an analysis of concepts. Parts II and III." *The Journ. of Ecology.* 23: 210–46, 488–508 (1935).

4. Clements, F. E. "Development and structure of the biome." *Ecol. Soc. Abs.* 1916.

5. Clements, F. E., and V. E. Shelford. *Bio-ecology,* 1936.

6. Chaney, R. W. "A comparative study of the Bridge Creek flora and the modern redwood forest." *Publ. Carneg. Instn,* no. 349, 1925.

7. Weaver, J. E., and E. L. Flory. "Stability of climax prairie and some environmental changes resulting from breaking." *Ecology* 15: 333–47 (1934).

Content Questions

1. How does Clements define *climax?* (81–82)

2. What role do animals play as "members of the climax"? Why did Clements find it necessary to introduce the word *biome?* (81)

3. What constitutes the "visible unity of the climax"? (83)

4. How does Clements organize the "dominants" of vegetation in the various climaxes of North America? (83)

Application Questions

1. Using Clements's definition, identify a "climax community." What criteria did you use to determine your community—biological diversity, biomass, nutrient cycling, chemical storage? Trace the successional stages that lead up to this community, thinking in terms of not only ecological time but also geological time. What has changed over the decades? The centuries? The millennia? What is changing now? How does your notion of a climax community change as the time frame expands? Is the idea of a climax community useful or deceptive?

2. Under Clements's definition, why is an old-growth forest considered a climax community? By modern standards, why is it no longer considered so? Give your answer in terms of biomass, net primary productivity, biodiversity, chemical storage, and nutrient cycling. Discuss the advantages and disadvantages of Clements's idea of a climax and the notion of successional stages.

Discussion Questions

1. Why is the "inherent unity of the climax" both a "response to a particular climate" and "at the same time the expression and the indicator of it"? What does Clements mean by "expression"? (82)

2. In examining a climax, why is it "exceedingly difficult or entirely impossible to strike a balance between stability and change"? (83)

3. Why is stabilization "the universal tendency of all vegetation under the ruling climate"? (84)

4. Why and how is it that only humans can "destroy the stability of the climax"? (84) What consequences should we consider when cultivating or developing a climax such as the Midwestern prairie?

5. Given Clements's definition of the term *climax*, can there be a climax community in nature? What are the potential gains or losses of adhering to this idea?

A. G. Tansley

A. G. Tansley (1871–1955) was a prominent conservationist who held faculty positions at the Universities of Cambridge and Oxford. Building on Britain's new and growing interest in plant geography and botanical surveys, Tansley argued for ecology as the larger framework for botanical study. While Tansley agreed that one of the keys to understanding natural communities was the close examination of vegetation, he also emphasized the relationships among different plants species and between plants and animals.

By 1935, Tansley's concept of natural communities had expanded, eventually including all the physical and chemical factors—such as climate and soil—of an environment or habitat. To speak effectively of this broader concept, Tansley coined the term *ecosystem,* now a central idea in the understanding of ecology and an idea of such magnitude that ecosystems ecology is a field of study in itself.

Tansley argued that ecology and the exploitation of natural environments are not necessarily in opposition. He believed that human beings are part of nature, rather than apart from it, and that despite the human tendency to disrupt existing ecosystems, new and quite different ecosystems can form as a result. In this way, human activity is part of the natural order.

The Ecosystem

Clements's earlier term *biome* for the whole complex of organisms inhabiting a given region is unobjectionable, and for some purposes convenient. But the more fundamental conception is, as it seems to me, the whole *system* (in the sense of physics), including not only the organism-complex, but also the whole complex of physical factors forming what we call the environment of the biome—the habitat factors in the widest sense. Though the organisms may claim our primary interest, when we are trying to think fundamentally we cannot separate them from their special environment, with which they form one physical system.

It is the systems so formed which, from the point of view of the ecologist, are the basic units of nature on the face of the earth. Our natural human prejudices force us to consider the organisms (in the sense of the biologist) as the most important parts of these systems, but certainly the inorganic "factors" are also parts—there could be no systems without them, and there is constant interchange of the most various kinds within each system, not only between the organisms but between the organic and the inorganic. These *ecosystems*, as we may call them, are of the most various kinds and sizes. They form one category of the multitudinous physical systems of the universe, which range from the universe as a whole down to the atom. The whole method of science, as H. Levy[1] has most convincingly

91

pointed out, is to isolate systems mentally for the purposes of study, so that the series of *isolates* we make become the actual objects of our study, whether the isolate be a solar system, a planet, a climatic region, a plant or animal community, an individual organism, an organic molecule, or an atom. Actually the systems we isolate mentally are not only included as parts of larger ones, but they also overlap, interlock, and interact with one another. The isolation is partly artificial, but is the only possible way in which we can proceed.

Some of the systems are more isolated in nature, more autonomous, than others. They all show organization, which is the inevitable result of the interactions and consequent mutual adjustment of their components. If organization of the possible elements of a system does not result, no system forms or an incipient system breaks up. There is in fact a kind of natural selection of incipient systems, and those which can attain the most stable equilibrium survive the longest. It is in this way that the dynamic equilibrium, of which Professor Phillips writes, is attained.[2] The universal tendency to the evolution of dynamic equilibria has long been recognized. A corresponding idea was fully worked out by Hume and even stated by Lucretius. The more relatively separate and autonomous the system, the more highly integrated it is, and the greater the stability of its dynamic equilibrium.

Some systems develop gradually, steadily becoming more highly integrated and more delicately adjusted in equilibrium. The ecosystems are of this kind, and the normal autogenic succession is a progress toward greater integration and stability. The *climax* represents the highest stage of integration and the nearest approach to perfect dynamic equilibrium that can be attained in a system developed under the given conditions and with the available components.

The great regional climatic complexes of the world are important determinants of the primary terrestrial ecosystems, and they contribute *parts* (components) to the systems, just as do the soils and the organisms. In any fundamental consideration of the ecosystem it is arbitrary and misleading to abstract the climatic factors, though for purposes of separation and classification of systems it is a legitimate procedure. In fact, the climatic complex has more effect on the organisms and on the soil of an ecosystem than these have on the climatic complex, but the reciprocal action is not wholly absent. Climate acts on the ecosystem rather like an acid or an alkaline "buffer" on a chemical soil complex.

Next comes the soil complex which is created and developed partly by the subjacent rock, partly by climate, and partly by the biome. Relative maturity of the soil complex, conditioned alike by climate, by subsoil, by physiography, and by the vegetation, may be reached at a different time from that at which the vegetation attains its climax. Owing to the much greater local variation of subsoil and physiography than of climate, and to the fact that some of the existing variants prevent the climatic factors from playing the full part of which they are capable, the developing soil complex, jointly with climate, may determine variants of the biome. Phillips's contention that soil never does this is too flatly contrary to the experience of too many ecologists to be admitted. Hence we must recognize ecosystems differentiated by soil complexes, subordinate to those primarily determined by climate, but nonetheless real.

Finally comes the organism-complex or biome, in which the vegetation is of primary importance, except in certain cases, for example many marine ecosystems. The primary importance of vegetation is what we should expect when we consider the complete dependence, direct or indirect, of animals upon plants. This fact cannot be altered or gainsaid, however loud the trumpets of the "biotic community" are blown. This is not to say that animals may not have important effects on the vegetation and thus on the whole organism-complex. They may even alter the primary structure of the climax vegetation, but usually they certainly do not. By all means let animal and plant ecologists study the composition, structure, and behavior of the biome together. Until they have done so we shall not be in possession of the facts which alone will enable us to get a true and complete picture of the life of the biome, for both animals and plants are components. But is it really necessary to formulate the unnatural conception of biotic *community* to get such cooperative work carried out? I think not. What we have to deal with is a *system*, of which plants and animals are components, though not the only components. The biome is determined by climate and soil and in its turn reacts, sometimes and to some extent on climate, always on soil.

Clements's *prisere*[3] is the gradual development of an ecosystem as we may see it taking place before us today. The gradual attainment of more complete dynamic equilibrium (which Phillips quite rightly stresses) is the fundamental characteristic of this development. It is a particular case of the universal process of the evolution of systems in dynamic equilibrium. The equilibrium attained is however never quite perfect: its degree of perfection

93

is measured by its stability. The atoms of the chemical elements of low atomic number are examples of exceptionally stable systems—they have existed for many millions of millennia: those of the radioactive elements are decidedly less stable. But the order of stability of all the chemical elements is of course immensely higher than that of an ecosystem, which consists of components that are themselves more or less unstable—climate, soil, and organisms. Relatively to the more stable systems the ecosystems are extremely vulnerable, both on account of their own unstable components and because they are very liable to invasion by the components of other systems. Nevertheless some of the fully developed systems—the climaxes—have actually maintained themselves for thousands of years. In others, there are elements whose slow change will ultimately bring about the disintegration of the system.

This relative instability of the ecosystem, due to the imperfections of its equilibrium, is of all degrees of magnitude, and our means of appreciating and measuring it are still very rudimentary. Many systems (represented by vegetation climaxes) which appear to be stable during the period for which they have been under accurate observation may in reality have been slowly changing all the time, because the changes effected have been too slight to be noted by observers. Many ecologists hold that *all* vegetation is *always* changing. It may be so: we do not know enough either to affirm or to deny so sweeping a statement. But there may clearly be minor changes within a system which do not bring about the destruction of the system as such.

Owing to the position of the climate-complexes as primary determinants of the major ecosystems, a marked change of climate must bring about destruction of the ecosystem of any given geographical region, and its replacement by another. This is the *clisere* of Clements.[4] If a continental ice sheet slowly and continuously advances or recedes over a considerable period of time, all the zoned climaxes which are subjected to the decreasing or increasing temperature will, according to Clements's conception, move across the continent "as if they were strung on a string," much as the plant communities zoned round a lake will move toward its center as the lake fills up. If on the other hand a whole continent desiccates or freezes, many of the ecosystems which formerly occupied it will be destroyed altogether. Thus whereas the prisere is the development of a single ecosystem in situ, the clisere involves their destruction or bodily shifting.

When we consider long periods of geological time we must naturally also take into account the progressive evolution and rise to dominance of new types of organism and the decline and disappearance of older types. From the earlier Paleozoic, where we get the first glimpses of the constitution of the organic world, through the later Paleozoic where we can form some fairly comprehensive picture of what it was like, through the Mesozoic where we witness the decline and dying out of the dominant Paleozoic groups and the rise to prominence of others, the Tertiary with its overwhelming dominance of angiosperms, and finally the Pleistocene Ice Age with its disastrous results for much of the life of the Northern Hemisphere, the shifting panorama of the organic world presents us with an infinitely complex history of the formation and destruction of ecosystems, conditioned not only by radical changes of land surface and climate but by the supply of constantly fresh organic components. We can never hope to achieve more than a fragmentary view of this history, though doubtless our knowledge will be very greatly extended in the future, as it has been already notably extended during the last thirty years. In detail the initiation and development of the ecosystems in past times must have been governed by the same principles that we can recognize today. But we gain nothing by trying to envisage in the same concepts such very different processes as are involved in the shifting or destruction of ecosystems on the one hand and the development of individual systems on the other. It is true, as Cooper insists,[5] that the changes of vegetation on the earth's surface form a continuous story: they form in fact only a part of the story of the changes of the surface of this planet. But to analyze them effectively we must split up the story and try to focus its phases according to the various kinds of process involved.

ຽ ຽ ຽ

Professor Phillips makes a point of separating the effect of grazing herbivorous animals *naturally* belonging to the "biotic community," e.g., the bison of the North American prairie or the antelopes, etc., of the South African veld, from the effect of grazing animals introduced by man. The former are said to have cooperated in the production of the short grass vegetation of the Great Plains, which has even been called the *Bison-Bouteloa* climax, and to have kept back the forest from invading the edges of the grassland formation. The latter are supposed to be merely destructive in their effects, and to play no part in any successional or developmental process. This is perhaps

95

legitimate as a description of the ecosystems of the world before the advent of man, or rather with the activities of man deliberately ignored. It is obvious that modern civilized man upsets the "natural" ecosystems or "biotic communities" on a very large scale. But it would be difficult, not to say impossible, to draw a natural line between the activities of the human tribes which presumably fitted into and formed parts of "biotic communities" and the destructive human activities of the modern world. Is man part of "nature" or not? Can his existence be harmonized with the conception of the "complex organism"? Regarded as an exceptionally powerful biotic factor which increasingly upsets the equilibrium of preexisting ecosystems and eventually destroys them, at the same time forming new ones of very different nature, human activity finds its proper place in ecology.

As an ecological factor acting on vegetation, the effect of grazing heavy enough to prevent the development of woody plants is essentially the same effect wherever it occurs. If such grazing exists, the grazing animals are an important factor in the biome actually present, whether they came by themselves or were introduced by man. The dynamic equilibrium maintained is primarily an equilibrium between the grazing animals and the grasses and other hemicryptophytes which can exist and flourish although they are continually eaten back.

Forest may be converted into grassland by grazing animals. The substitution of the one type of vegetation for the other involves destruction of course, but not merely destruction: it also involves the appearance and gradual establishment of new vegetation. It is a successional process culminating in a climax under the influence of the actual combination of factors present, and since this climax is a well-defined entity it is also the development of that entity. It is true of course that when man introduces sheep and cattle he protects them by destroying carnivores and thus artificially maintains the ecosystem whose essential feature is the equilibrium between the grassland and the grazing animals. He may also alter the position of equilibrium by feeding his animals not only on the pasture but also partly away from it, so that their dung represents food for the grassland brought from outside, and the floristic composition of the grassland is thereby altered. In such ways *anthropogenic ecosystems* differ from those developed independently of man. But the essential formative processes of the vegetation are the same, however the factors initiating them are directed.

We must have a system of ecological concepts which will allow of the inclusion of *all* forms of vegetational expression and activity. We cannot confine ourselves to the so-called "natural" entities and ignore the processes and expressions of vegetation now so abundantly provided us by the activities of man. Such a course is not scientifically sound, because scientific analysis must penetrate beneath the forms of the "natural" entities, and it is not practically useful because ecology must be applied to conditions brought about by human activity. The "natural" entities and the anthropogenic derivates alike must be analyzed in terms of the most appropriate concepts we can find. Plant community, succession, development, climax, used in their wider and not in specialized senses, represent such concepts. They certainly involve an abstraction of the vegetation as such from the whole complex of components of the ecosystem, the remaining components being regarded as factors. This abstraction is a convenient isolate which has served and is continuing to serve us well. It has in fact many, though by no means all, of the qualities of an organism. The biome is a less convenient isolate for most purposes, though it has some uses, and it is not in the least improved by being called a "biotic community" or a "complex organism," terms which are illegitimately derived and which introduce misleading implications.

~ ~ ~

There can be no doubt that the firm establishment of the concept of succession has led directly to the creation of what is now often called dynamic ecology and that this in its turn has greatly increased our insight into the nature and behavior of vegetation. The simplest possible scheme involves a succession of vegetational stages (the prisere of Clements) on an initially "bare" area, culminating in a stage (the climax) beyond which no further advance is possible under the given conditions of habitat (in the widest sense) and in the presence of the available colonizing species. If we recognize that the climax with its whole environment represents a system in relatively stable dynamic equilibrium while the preceding stages are not, we have already the *essential framework* into which we can fit our detailed investigations of particular successions. Unless we use this framework, unless we recognize the universal tendency of the system in which vegetation is the most conspicuous component to attain dynamic equilibrium by the most complete adjustment possible of all the complexes involved, we have no key to correct interpretation of the observed phenomena, which are open to every kind of misinterpretation. From the results of detailed investigations of successions, which incidentally throw a great deal of new light on existing vegetation whose nature and status were previously obscure, we may deduce certain general laws and formulate a number of useful subsidiary concepts. So far, the concept of succession has proved itself of prime methodological value.

Succession is a continuous process of change in vegetation which can be separated into a series of phases. When the dominating factors of change depend directly on the activities of the plants themselves (autogenic factors) the succession is *autogenic:* when the dominating factors are external to the plants (allogenic factors) it is *allogenic.* The successions (priseres) which lead from bare substrata to the highest types of vegetation actually present in a climatic region (progressive) are primarily autogenic. Those which lead away from these higher forms of vegetation (retrogressive) are largely allogenic, though both types of factor enter into all successions.

A *climax* is a relatively stable phase reached by successional change. Change may still be proceeding within a climax, but if it is too slow to appreciate or too small to affect the general nature of the vegetation, the apparently stable phase must still be called a climax. The highest types of vegetation characteristic of a climatic region and limited only by climate form the *climatic climax.* Other climaxes may be determined by other factors such as certain soil types, grazing animals, fire and the like.

The term *development* may be applied, as in ordinary speech, to the appearance of any well-defined vegetational entity; but the term is more strictly applied to the autogenic successions leading to climaxes, which have several features in common with the development of organisms. Such climaxes may be considered as *quasi-organisms.*

The concept of the "biotic community" is unnatural because animals and plants are too different in nature to be considered as members of the same community. The whole complex of organisms present in an ecological unit may be called the *biome.*

The concept of the "complex organism" as applied to the biome is objectionable both because the term is already in common use for an individual higher animal or plant, and because the biome is not an organism except in the sense in which inorganic systems are organisms.

The fundamental concept appropriate to the biome considered

together with all the effective inorganic factors of its environment is the *ecosystem*, which is a particular category among the physical systems that make up the universe. In an ecosystem, the organisms and the inorganic factors alike are *components* which are in relatively stable dynamic equilibrium. Succession and development are instances of the universal processes tending toward the creation of such equilibrated systems.

From the standpoint of vegetation, biotic factors, in the sense of decisive influences of animal action, are a legitimate and useful conception. Of these biotic factors, heavy and continuous grazing which changes and stabilizes the vegetation is an outstanding example.

The supposed methodological value of the ideas of the biotic community and the complex organism is illusory, unlike the values of plant community, succession, development, climax, and ecosystem, the concepts of which form the essential framework into which detailed studies of successional processes must be fitted.

Notes

1. Levy, H. 1932. *The Universe of Science*. London.

2. Phillips, John. 1931. The biotic community. *Jour. Ecol.* 19: 1–24.
———. 1934. Succession, development, the climax and the complex organism: an analysis of concepts. I. *Jour. Ecol.* 22: 554–571.
———. 1935. Idem II, III. Ibid. 23: 210–246, 488–508.

3. Clements, F. E. 1916. Plant Succession. *Carnegie Inst. Wash. Publ.* 242.

4. Ibid.

5. Cooper, W. S. 1926. Fundamentals of vegetational change. *Ecology* 7: 391–413.

Content Questions

1. What is Tansley referring to when he speaks of the "whole *system*"? (91)

2. According to Tansley, why is it important to "isolate systems mentally for the purposes of study"? Why is this process "partly artificial"? (92)

3. Why are organization and equilibrium important to any ecosystem? (92)

4. According to Tansley, what correlation is there between the speed of a system's development and the degree of its integration and equilibrium? (92)

5. What does Tansley mean by saying that equilibrium's "degree of perfection is measured by its stability"? (93–94)

6. According to Tansley, how can human activity find "its proper place in ecology"? (96)

7. What stage does "climax" describe in successional change? What is the correlation between "climax" and equilibrium? (97)

8. In relation to the process of succession in vegetation, what is the difference between "autogenic" and "allogenic" factors? (98)

Application Question

Define an ecosystem—for example, the gastrointestinal tract of a moose, the island of Hawaii, a hot spring, a watershed, the Pacific Ocean. What criteria did you use (e.g., structure, function, energy flow, a keystone species, chemical cycling, predator-prey relationship) to define your ecosystem? Give an account of the major biotic and abiotic relationships, structures, and functions of your ecosystem, including tracing energy flow and chemical cycling, and explaining the food web, food chains, and trophic levels.

Discussion Questions

1. What does Tansley mean when he says that our "natural human prejudices force us to consider the organisms . . . as the most important parts" of ecosystems? (91)

2. What is the relationship between "climatic complexes" and "terrestrial ecosystems"? (92)

3. Why did some scientists believe that soil played no part in determining the "variants of the biome"? (93)

4. Tansley asks the question "Is man part of 'nature' or not?" (96) Does he answer this question? What is the importance of this question?

5. Why does Tansley argue that climax is an "essential framework" for studying and understanding succession? (97)

6. Why does Tansley reject the term *biotic community?* Why does he prefer the terms *biome* and *ecosystem?*

Aldo Leopold

In 1935, Aldo Leopold (1887–1948) bought the depleted farmland in Wisconsin that would become the focus of his renowned book, *A Sand County Almanac* (1949), from which these selections are taken. At the time, he was already an internationally respected and widely published scientist.

Born in Iowa, Leopold spent his childhood exploring the natural world along the Mississippi River. His formal education culminated with a master's degree from Yale University in forestry, then a relatively new field. In 1909, he joined the newly formed U.S. Forest Service. Leopold worked for the forest service for nineteen years, accumulating extensive experience in resource management in Arizona. During this time, he developed a strong sense of the land as a living organism and the complexity of ecological communities. In 1933, he invented the field of wildlife management with his textbook, *Game Management,* and was appointed to a new chair in that field at the University of Wisconsin. Wildlife management, as Leopold conceived it, prefigures the cross-disciplinary characteristic of environmental science, combining forestry, agriculture, biology, zoology, ecology, education, economics, and communications. Leopold eventually created a new Department of Wildlife Management at the university and served on the faculty until his death in 1948.

Leopold and his family nurtured their worn-out Wisconsin farmland, using it as a living laboratory for his theories about conservation and ecology. Like Thoreau's Walden Pond, it has assumed almost mythic stature through the widespread influence of *A Sand County Almanac*. This book placed Leopold among the first contemporary thinkers in conservation theory and practice. His keen observations of nature, along with his philosophical consideration of conservation's ethical dimension, have made the *Almanac* a cornerstone of environmental science literature.

The Land Ethic

hen godlike Odysseus returned from the wars in Troy, he hanged all on one rope a dozen slave girls of his household whom he suspected of misbehavior during his absence.

This hanging involved no question of propriety. The girls were property. The disposal of property was then, as now, a matter of expediency, not of right and wrong.

Concepts of right and wrong were not lacking from Odysseus's Greece: witness the fidelity of his wife through the long years before at last his black-prowed galleys clove the wine-dark seas for home. The ethical structure of that day covered wives, but had not yet been extended to human chattels. During the three thousand years which have since elapsed, ethical criteria have been extended to many fields of conduct, with corresponding shrinkages in those judged by expediency only.

The Ethical Sequence

This extension of ethics, so far studied only by philosophers, is actually a process in ecological evolution. Its sequences may be described in ecological as well as in philosophical terms. An ethic, ecologically, is a limitation on freedom of action in the struggle for existence. An ethic, philosophically,

is a differentiation of social from antisocial conduct. These are two definitions of one thing. The thing has its origin in the tendency of interdependent individuals or groups to evolve modes of cooperation. The ecologist
calls these symbioses. Politics and economics are advanced symbioses in
which the original free-for-all competition has been replaced, in part, by
cooperative mechanisms with an ethical content.

The complexity of cooperative mechanisms has increased with population density, and with the efficiency of tools. It was simpler, for example, to
define the antisocial uses of sticks and stones in the days of the mastodons
than of bullets and billboards in the age of motors.

The first ethics dealt with the relation between individuals; the Mosaic
Decalogue is an example. Later accretions dealt with the relation between
the individual and society. The golden rule tries to integrate the individual
to society; democracy to integrate social organization to the individual.

There is as yet no ethic dealing with man's relation to land and to the
animals and plants which grow upon it. Land, like Odysseus's slave girls, is
still property. The land relation is still strictly economic, entailing privileges
but not obligations.

The extension of ethics to this third element in human environment is,
if I read the evidence correctly, an evolutionary possibility and an ecological necessity. It is the third step in a sequence. The first two have already
been taken. Individual thinkers since the days of Ezekiel and Isaiah have
asserted that the despoliation of land is not only inexpedient but wrong.
Society, however, has not yet affirmed their belief. I regard the present
conservation movement as the embryo of such an affirmation.

An ethic may be regarded as a mode of guidance for meeting ecological
situations so new or intricate, or involving such deferred reactions, that the
path of social expediency is not discernible to the average individual.
Animal instincts are modes of guidance for the individual in meeting such
situations. Ethics are possibly a kind of community instinct in the making.

The Community Concept

All ethics so far evolved rest upon a single premise: that the individual is a
member of a community of interdependent parts. His instincts prompt him
to compete for his place in the community, but his ethics prompt him also
to cooperate (perhaps in order that there may be a place to compete for).

The land ethic simply enlarges the boundaries of the community to include soils, waters, plants, and animals, or collectively: the land.

This sounds simple: do we not already sing our love for and obligation to the land of the free and the home of the brave? Yes, but just what and whom do we love? Certainly not the soil, which we are sending helter-skelter downriver. Certainly not the waters, which we assume have no function except to turn turbines, float barges, and carry off sewage. Certainly not the plants, of which we exterminate whole communities without batting an eye. Certainly not the animals, of which we have already extirpated many of the largest and most beautiful species. A land ethic of course cannot prevent the alteration, management, and use of these "resources," but it does affirm their right to continued existence and, at least in spots, their continued existence in a natural state.

In short, a land ethic changes the role of *Homo sapiens* from conqueror of the land community to plain member and citizen of it. It implies respect for his fellow members, and also respect for the community as such.

In human history, we have learned (I hope) that the conqueror role is eventually self-defeating. Why? Because it is implicit in such a role that the conqueror knows, ex cathedra, just what makes the community clock tick, and just what and who is valuable, and what and who is worthless, in community life. It always turns out that he knows neither, and this is why his conquests eventually defeat themselves.

In the biotic community, a parallel situation exists. Abraham knew exactly what the land was for: it was to drip milk and honey into Abraham's mouth. At the present moment, the assurance with which we regard this assumption is inverse to the degree of our education.

The ordinary citizen today assumes that science knows what makes the community clock tick; the scientist is equally sure that he does not. He knows that the biotic mechanism is so complex that its workings may never be fully understood.

That man is, in fact, only a member of a biotic team is shown by an ecological interpretation of history. Many historical events, hitherto explained solely in terms of human enterprise, were actually biotic interactions between people and land. The characteristics of the land determined the facts quite as potently as the characteristics of the men who lived on it.

Consider, for example, the settlement of the Mississippi valley. In the years following the Revolution, three groups were contending for its control: the native Indian, the French and English traders, and the American settlers. Historians wonder what would have happened if the English at Detroit had thrown a little more weight into the Indian side of those tipsy scales which decided the outcome of the colonial migration into the cane lands of Kentucky. It is time now to ponder the fact that the cane lands, when subjected to the particular mixture of forces represented by the cow, plow, fire, and ax of the pioneer, became bluegrass. What if the plant succession inherent in this dark and bloody ground had, under the impact of these forces, given us some worthless sedge, shrub, or weed? Would Boone and Kenton have held out? Would there have been any overflow into Ohio, Indiana, Illinois, and Missouri? Any Louisiana Purchase? Any transcontinental union of new states? Any Civil War?

Kentucky was one sentence in the drama of history. We are commonly told what the human actors in this drama tried to do, but we are seldom told that their success, or the lack of it, hung in large degree on the reaction of particular soils to the impact of the particular forces exerted by their occupancy. In the case of Kentucky, we do not even know where the bluegrass came from—whether it is a native species, or a stowaway from Europe.

Contrast the cane lands with what hindsight tells us about the Southwest, where the pioneers were equally brave, resourceful, and persevering. The impact of occupancy here brought no bluegrass, or other plant fitted to withstand the bumps and buffetings of hard use. This region, when grazed by livestock, reverted through a series of more and more worthless grasses, shrubs, and weeds to a condition of unstable equilibrium. Each recession of plant types bred erosion; each increment to erosion bred a further recession of plants. The result today is a progressive and mutual deterioration, not only of plants and soils, but of the animal community subsisting thereon. The early settlers did not expect this: on the *ciénegas* of New Mexico some even cut ditches to hasten it. So subtle has been its progress that few residents of the region are aware of it. It is quite invisible to the tourist who finds this wrecked landscape colorful and charming (as indeed it is, but it bears scant resemblance to what it was in 1848).

This same landscape was "developed" once before, but with quite different results. The Pueblo Indians settled the Southwest in pre-Columbian times, but they happened *not* to be equipped with range livestock. Their civilization expired, but not because their land expired.

In India, regions devoid of any sod-forming grass have been settled, apparently without wrecking the land, by the simple expedient of carrying the grass to the cow, rather than vice versa. (Was this the result of some deep wisdom, or was it just good luck? I do not know.)

In short, the plant succession steered the course of history; the pioneer simply demonstrated, for good or ill, what successions inhered in the land. Is history taught in this spirit? It will be, once the concept of land as a community really penetrates our intellectual life.

The Ecological Conscience

Conservation is a state of harmony between men and land. Despite nearly a century of propaganda, conservation still proceeds at a snail's pace; progress still consists largely of letterhead pieties and convention oratory. On the back forty we still slip two steps backward for each forward stride.

The usual answer to this dilemma is "more conservation education." No one will debate this, but is it certain that only the *volume* of education needs stepping up? Is something lacking in the *content* as well?

It is difficult to give a fair summary of its content in brief form, but, as I understand it, the content is substantially this: obey the law, vote right, join some organizations, and practice what conservation is profitable on your own land; the government will do the rest.

Is not this formula too easy to accomplish anything worthwhile? It defines no right or wrong, assigns no obligation, calls for no sacrifice, implies no change in the current philosophy of values. In respect of land use, it urges only enlightened self-interest. Just how far will such education take us? An example will perhaps yield a partial answer.

By 1930, it had become clear to all except the ecologically blind that southwestern Wisconsin's topsoil was slipping seaward. In 1933, the farmers were told that if they would adopt certain remedial practices for five years, the public would donate CCC [Civilian Conservation Corps] labor to install them, plus the necessary machinery and materials. The offer was widely accepted, but the practices were widely forgotten when the five-year contract period was up. The farmers continued only those practices that yielded an immediate and visible economic gain for themselves.

This led to the idea that maybe farmers would learn more quickly if they themselves wrote the rules. Accordingly, the Wisconsin legislature in

1937 passed the Soil Conservation District Law. This said to farmers, in effect: *We, the public, will furnish you free technical service and loan you specialized machinery, if you will write your own rules for land use. Each county may write its own rules, and these will have the force of* law. Nearly all the counties promptly organized to accept the proffered help, but after a decade of operation, *no county has yet written a single rule.* There has been visible progress in such practices as strip-cropping, pasture renovation, and soil liming, but none in fencing woodlots against grazing, and none in excluding plow and cow from steep slopes. The farmers, in short, have selected those remedial practices which were profitable anyhow, and ignored those which were profitable to the community, but not clearly profitable to themselves.

When one asks why no rules have been written, one is told that the community is not yet ready to support them; education must precede rules. But the education actually in progress makes no mention of obligations to land over and above those dictated by self-interest. The net result is that we have more education but less soil, fewer healthy woods, and as many floods as in 1937.

The puzzling aspect of such situations is that the existence of obligations over and above self-interest is taken for granted in such rural community enterprises as the betterment of roads, schools, churches, and baseball teams. Their existence is not taken for granted, nor as yet seriously discussed, in bettering the behavior of the water that falls on the land, or in the preserving of the beauty or diversity of the farm landscape. Land-use ethics are still governed wholly by economic self-interest, just as social ethics were a century ago.

To sum up: we asked the farmer to do what he conveniently could to save his soil, and he has done just that, and only that. The farmer who clears the woods off a 75 percent slope, turns his cows into the clearing, and dumps its rainfall, rocks, and soil into the community creek, is still (if otherwise decent) a respected member of society. If he puts lime on his fields and plants his crops on contour, he is still entitled to all the privileges and emoluments of his Soil Conservation District. The District is a beautiful piece of social machinery, but it is coughing along on two cylinders because we have been too timid, and too anxious for quick success, to tell the farmer the true magnitude of his obligations. Obligations have no meaning without conscience, and the problem we face is the extension of the social conscience from people to land.

No important change in ethics was ever accomplished without an internal change in our intellectual emphasis, loyalties, affections, and convictions. The proof that conservation has not yet touched these foundations of conduct lies in the fact that philosophy and religion have not yet heard of it. In our attempt to make conservation easy, we have made it trivial.

Substitutes for a Land Ethic

When the logic of history hungers for bread and we hand out a stone, we are at pains to explain how much the stone resembles bread. I now describe some of the stones which serve in lieu of a land ethic.

One basic weakness in a conservation system based wholly on economic motives is that most members of the land community have no economic value. Wildflowers and songbirds are examples. Of the 22,000 higher plants and animals native to Wisconsin, it is doubtful whether more than 5 percent can be sold, fed, eaten, or otherwise put to economic use. Yet these creatures are members of the biotic community, and if (as I believe) its stability depends on its integrity, they are entitled to continuance.

When one of these noneconomic categories is threatened, and if we happen to love it, we invent subterfuges to give it economic importance. At the beginning of the century songbirds were supposed to be disappearing. Ornithologists jumped to the rescue with some distinctly shaky evidence to the effect that insects would eat us up if birds failed to control them. The evidence had to be economic in order to be valid.

It is painful to read these circumlocutions today. We have no land ethic yet, but we have at least drawn nearer the point of admitting that birds should continue as a matter of biotic right, regardless of the presence or absence of economic advantage to us.

A parallel situation exists in respect of predatory mammals, raptorial birds, and fish-eating birds. Time was when biologists somewhat overworked the evidence that these creatures preserve the health of game by killing weaklings, or that they control rodents for the farmer, or that they prey only on "worthless" species. Here again, the evidence had to be economic in order to be valid. It is only in recent years that we hear the more honest argument that predators are members of the community, and that no special interest has the right to exterminate them for the sake of a benefit, real or fancied, to itself. Unfortunately, this enlightened view is still in the talk stage. In the field the extermination of predators goes merrily on: witness the impending erasure of the timber wolf by fiat of Congress, the conservation bureaus, and many state legislatures.

Some species of trees have been "read out of the party" by economics-minded foresters because they grow too slowly, or have too low a sale value to pay as timber crops: white cedar, tamarack, cypress, beech, and hemlock are examples. In Europe, where forestry is ecologically more advanced, the noncommercial tree species are recognized as members of the native forest community, to be preserved as such, within reason. Moreover some (like beech) have been found to have a valuable function in building up soil fertility. The interdependence of the forest and its constituent tree species, ground flora, and fauna is taken for granted.

Lack of economic value is sometimes a character not only of species or groups, but of entire biotic communities: marshes, bogs, dunes, and "deserts" are examples. Our formula in such cases is to relegate their conservation to government as refuges, monuments, or parks. The difficulty is that these communities are usually interspersed with more valuable private lands; the government cannot possibly own or control such scattered parcels. The net effect is that we have relegated some of them to ultimate extinction over large areas. If the private owner were ecologically minded, he would be proud to be the custodian of a reasonable proportion of such areas, which add diversity and beauty to his farm and to his community.

In some instances, the assumed lack of profit in these "waste" areas has proved to be wrong, but only after most of them had been done away with. The present scramble to reflood muskrat marshes is a case in point.

There is a clear tendency in American conservation to relegate to government all necessary jobs that private landowners fail to perform. Government ownership, operation, subsidy, or regulation is now widely prevalent in forestry, range management, soil and watershed management, park and wilderness conservation, fisheries management, and migratory bird management, with more to come. Most of this growth in governmental conservation is proper and logical; some of it is inevitable. That I imply no disapproval of it is implicit in the fact that I have spent most of my life working for it. Nevertheless the question arises: What is the ultimate magnitude of the enterprise? Will the tax base carry its eventual ramifications? At what point will governmental conservation, like the mastodon, become handicapped by its own dimensions? The answer, if there is any, seems to be in a land ethic, or some other force which assigns more obligation to the private landowner.

Industrial landowners and users, especially lumbermen and stockmen, are inclined to wail long and loudly about the extension of government ownership and regulation to land, but (with notable exceptions) they show little disposition to develop the only visible alternative: the voluntary practice of conservation on their own lands.

When the private landowner is asked to perform some unprofitable act for the good of the community, he today assents only with outstretched palm. If the act costs him cash this is fair and proper, but when it costs only forethought, open-mindedness, or time, the issue is at least debatable. The overwhelming growth of land-use subsidies in recent years must be ascribed, in large part, to the government's own agencies for conservation education: the land bureaus, the agricultural colleges, and the extension services. As far as I can detect, no ethical obligation toward land is taught in these institutions.

To sum up: a system of conservation based solely on economic self-interest is hopelessly lopsided. It tends to ignore, and thus eventually to eliminate, many elements in the land community that lack commercial value, but that are (as far as we know) essential to its healthy functioning. It assumes, falsely, I think, that the economic parts of the biotic clock will function without the uneconomic parts. It tends to relegate to government many functions eventually too large, too complex, or too widely dispersed to be performed by government.

An ethical obligation on the part of the private owner is the only visible remedy for these situations.

The Land Pyramid

An ethic to supplement and guide the economic relation to land presupposes the existence of some mental image of land as a biotic mechanism. We can be ethical only in relation to something we can see, feel, understand, love, or otherwise have faith in.

The image commonly employed in conservation education is "the balance of nature." For reasons too lengthy to detail here, this figure of speech fails to describe accurately what little we know about the land mechanism. A much truer image is the one employed in ecology: the biotic pyramid.

113

I shall first sketch the pyramid as a symbol of land, and later develop some of its implications in terms of land use.

Plants absorb energy from the sun. This energy flows through a circuit called the biota, which may be represented by a pyramid consisting of layers. The bottom layer is the soil. A plant layer rests on the soil, an insect layer on the plants, a bird and rodent layer on the insects, and so on up through various animal groups to the apex layer, which consists of the larger carnivores.

The species of a layer are alike not in where they came from, or in what they look like, but rather in what they eat. Each successive layer depends on those below it for food and often for other services, and each in turn furnishes food and services to those above. Proceeding upward, each successive layer decreases in numerical abundance. Thus, for every carnivore there are hundreds of its prey, thousands of their prey, millions of insects, uncountable plants. The pyramidal form of the system reflects this numerical progression from apex to base. Man shares an intermediate layer with the bears, raccoons, and squirrels, which eat both meat and vegetables.

The lines of dependency for food and other services are called food chains. Thus soil-oak-deer-Indian is a chain that has now been largely converted to soil-corn-cow-farmer. Each species, including ourselves, is a link in many chains. The deer eats a hundred plants other than oak, and the cow a hundred plants other than corn. Both, then, are links in a hundred chains. The pyramid is a tangle of chains so complex as to seem disorderly, yet the stability of the system proves it to be a highly organized structure. Its functioning depends on the cooperation and competition of its diverse parts.

In the beginning, the pyramid of life was low and squat; the food chains short and simple. Evolution has added layer after layer, link after link. Man is one of thousands of accretions to the height and complexity of the pyramid. Science has given us many doubts, but it has given us at least one certainty: the trend of evolution is to elaborate and diversify the biota.

Land, then, is not merely soil; it is a fountain of energy flowing through a circuit of soils, plants, and animals. Food chains are the living channels which conduct energy upward; death and decay return it to the soil. The circuit is not closed; some energy is dissipated in decay, some is added by absorption from the air, some is stored in soils, peats, and long-lived forests; but it is a sustained circuit, like a slowly augmented revolving fund of life. There is always a net loss by downhill wash, but this is normally small and offset by the decay of rocks. It is deposited in the ocean and, in the course of geological time, raised to form new lands and new pyramids.

The velocity and character of the upward flow of energy depend on the complex structure of the plant and animal community, much as the upward flow of sap in a tree depends on its complex cellular organization. Without this complexity, normal circulation would presumably not occur. *Structure* means the characteristic numbers, as well as the characteristic kinds and functions, of the component species. This interdependence between the complex structure of the land and its smooth functioning as an energy unit is one of its basic attributes.

When a change occurs in one part of the circuit, many other parts must adjust themselves to it. Change does not necessarily obstruct or divert the flow of energy; evolution is a long series of self-induced changes, the net result of which has been to elaborate the flow mechanism and to lengthen the circuit. Evolutionary changes, however, are usually slow and local. Man's invention of tools has enabled him to make changes of unprecedented violence, rapidity, and scope.

One change is in the composition of floras and faunas. The larger predators are lopped off the apex of the pyramid; food chains, for the first time in history, become shorter rather than longer. Domesticated species from other lands are substituted for wild ones, and wild ones are moved to new habitats. In this worldwide pooling of faunas and floras, some species get out of bounds as pests and diseases; others are extinguished. Such effects are seldom intended or foreseen; they represent unpredicted and often untraceable readjustments in the structure. Agricultural science is largely a race between the emergence of new pests and the emergence of new techniques for their control.

Another change touches the flow of energy through plants and animals and its return to the soil. Fertility is the ability of soil to receive, store, and release energy. Agriculture, by overdrafts on the soil, or by too radical a substitution of domestic for native species in the superstructure, may derange the channels of flow or deplete storage. Soils depleted of their storage, or of the organic matter which anchors it, wash away faster than they form. This is erosion.

Waters, like soil, are part of the energy circuit. Industry, by polluting waters or obstructing them with dams, may exclude the plants and animals necessary to keep energy in circulation.

Transportation brings about another basic change: the plants or animals grown in one region are now consumed and returned to the soil in another. Transportation taps the energy stored in rocks, and in the air, and uses it elsewhere; thus we fertilize the garden with nitrogen gleaned by the guano birds from the fishes of seas on the other side of the equator. Thus the formerly localized and self-contained circuits are pooled on a worldwide scale.

The process of altering the pyramid for human occupation releases stored energy, and this often gives rise, during the pioneering period, to a deceptive exuberance of plant and animal life, both wild and tame. These releases of biotic capital tend to becloud or postpone the penalties of violence.

〜 〜 〜

This thumbnail sketch of land as an energy circuit conveys three basic ideas:

1. That land is not merely soil.
2. That the native plants and animals kept the energy circuit open; others may or may not.
3. That man-made changes are of a different order than evolutionary changes, and have effects more comprehensive than is intended or foreseen.

These ideas, collectively, raise two basic issues: Can the land adjust itself to the new order? Can the desired alterations be accomplished with less violence?

Biotas seem to differ in their capacity to sustain violent conversion. Western Europe, for example, carries a far different pyramid than Caesar found there. Some large animals are lost; swampy forests have become meadows or plow land; many new plants and animals are introduced, some of which escape as pests; the remaining natives are greatly changed in distribution and abundance. Yet the soil is still there and, with the help of imported nutrients, still fertile; the waters flow normally; the new structure seems to function and to persist. There is no visible stoppage or derangement of the circuit.

Western Europe, then, has a resistant biota. Its inner processes are tough, elastic, resistant to strain. No matter how violent the alterations, the pyramid, so far, has developed some new modus vivendi which preserves its habitability for man, and for most of the other natives.

Japan seems to present another instance of radical conversion without disorganization.

Most other civilized regions, and some as yet barely touched by civilization, display various stages of disorganization, varying from initial symptoms to advanced wastage. In Asia Minor and North Africa, diagnosis is confused by climatic changes, which may have been either the cause or the effect of advanced wastage. In the United States, the degree of disorganization varies locally; it is worst in the Southwest, the Ozarks, and parts of the South, and least in New England and the Northwest. Better land uses may still arrest it in the less advanced regions. In parts of Mexico, South America, South Africa, and Australia, a violent and accelerating wastage is in progress, but I cannot assess the prospects.

This almost worldwide display of disorganization in the land seems to be similar to disease in an animal, except that it never culminates in complete disorganization or death. The land recovers, but at some reduced level of complexity, and with a reduced carrying capacity for people, plants, and animals. Many biotas currently regarded as "lands of opportunity" are in fact already subsisting on exploitative agriculture, that is, they have already exceeded their sustained carrying capacity. Most of South America is overpopulated in this sense.

In arid regions, we attempt to offset the process of wastage by reclamation, but it is only too evident that the prospective longevity of reclamation projects is often short. In our own West, the best of them may not last a century.

The combined evidence of history and ecology seems to support one general deduction: the less violent the man-made changes, the greater the probability of successful readjustment in the pyramid. Violence, in turn, varies with human population density; a dense population requires a more violent conversion. In this respect, North America has a better chance for permanence than Europe, if she can contrive to limit her density.

This deduction runs counter to our current philosophy, which assumes that because a small increase in density enriched human life, that an indefinite increase will enrich it indefinitely. Ecology knows of no density relationship that holds for indefinitely wide limits. All gains from density are subject to a law of diminishing returns.

Whatever may be the equation for men and land, it is improbable that we as yet know all its terms. Recent discoveries in mineral and vitamin nutrition reveal unsuspected dependencies in the up circuit: incredibly minute quantities of certain substances determine the value of soils to plants, of plants to animals. What of the down circuit? What of the vanishing species, the preservation of which we now regard as an aesthetic luxury? They helped build the soil; in what unsuspected ways may they be essential to its maintenance? Professor Weaver proposes that we use prairie flowers to reflocculate the wasting soils of the dust bowl; who knows for what purpose cranes and condors, otters and grizzlies may someday be used?

Land Health and the A-B Cleavage

A land ethic, then, reflects the existence of an ecological conscience, and this in turn reflects a conviction of individual responsibility for the health of the land. Health is the capacity of the land for self-renewal. Conservation is our effort to understand and preserve this capacity.

Conservationists are notorious for their dissensions. Superficially, these seem to add up to mere confusion, but a more careful scrutiny reveals a single plane of cleavage common to many specialized fields. In each field one group (A) regards the land as soil, and its function as commodity production; another group (B) regards the land as a biota, and its function as something broader. How much broader is admittedly in a state of doubt and confusion.

In my own field, forestry, group A is quite content to grow trees like cabbages, with cellulose as the basic forest commodity. It feels no inhibition against violence; its ideology is agronomic. Group B, on the other hand, sees forestry as fundamentally different from agronomy because it employs natural species, and manages a natural environment rather than creating an artificial one. Group B prefers natural reproduction on principle. It worries on biotic as well as economic grounds about the loss of species like chestnut, and the threatened loss of the white pines. It worries about a whole series of secondary forest functions: wildlife, recreation, watersheds, wilderness areas. To my mind, Group B feels the stirrings of an ecological conscience.

In the wildlife field, a parallel cleavage exists. For Group A, the basic commodities are sport and meat; the yardsticks of production are ciphers of take in pheasants and trout. Artificial propagation is acceptable as a permanent as well as a temporary recourse—if its unit costs permit. Group B, on the other hand, worries about a whole series of biotic side issues. What is the cost in predators of producing a game crop? Should we have further recourse to exotics? How can management restore the shrinking species, like prairie grouse, already hopeless as shootable game? How can management restore the threatened ratites, like trumpeter swan and whooping crane? Can management principles be extended to wildflowers? Here again it is clear to me that we have the same A-B cleavage as in forestry.

In the larger field of agriculture, I am less competent to speak, but there seem to be somewhat parallel cleavages. Scientific agriculture was actively developing before ecology was born, hence a slower penetration of ecological concepts might be expected. Moreover the farmer, by the very nature of his techniques, must modify the biota more radically than the forester or the wildlife manager. Nevertheless, there are many discontents in agriculture which seem to add up to a new vision of "biotic farming."

Perhaps the most important of these is the new evidence that poundage or tonnage is no measure of the food value of farm crops; the products of fertile soil may be qualitatively as well as quantitatively superior. We can bolster poundage from depleted soils by pouring on imported fertility, but we are not necessarily bolstering food value. The possible ultimate ramifications of this idea are so immense that I must leave their exposition to abler pens.

The discontent that labels itself "organic farming," while bearing some of the earmarks of a cult, is nevertheless biotic in its direction, particularly in its insistence on the importance of soil flora and fauna.

The ecological fundamentals of agriculture are just as poorly known to the public as in other fields of land use. For example, few educated people realize that the marvelous advances in technique made during recent decades are improvements in the pump, rather than the well. Acre for acre, they have barely sufficed to offset the sinking level of fertility.

In all of these cleavages, we see repeated the same basic paradoxes: man the conqueror versus man the biotic citizen; science the sharpener of his sword versus science the searchlight on his universe; land the slave and servant versus land the collective organism. Robinson's injunction to Tristram may well be applied, at this juncture, to *Homo sapiens* as a species in geological time:

> Whether you will or not
> You are a King, Tristram, for you are one
> Of the time-tested few that leave the world,
> When they are gone, not the same place it was.
> Mark what you leave.

The Outlook

It is inconceivable to me that an ethical relation to land can exist without love, respect, and admiration for land, and a high regard for its value. By value, I of course mean something far broader than mere economic value; I mean value in the philosophical sense.

Perhaps the most serious obstacle impeding the evolution of a land ethic is the fact that our educational and economic system is headed away from, rather than toward, an intense consciousness of land. Your true modern is separated from the land by many middlemen, and by innumerable physical gadgets. He has no vital relation to it; to him it is the space between cities on which crops grow. Turn him loose for a day on the land, and if the spot does not happen to be a golf links or a "scenic" area, he is bored stiff. If crops could be raised by hydroponics instead of farming, it would suit him very well. Synthetic substitutes for wood, leather, wool, and other natural land products suit him better than the originals. In short, land is something he has "outgrown."

Almost equally serious as an obstacle to a land ethic is the attitude of the farmer for whom the land is still an adversary, or a taskmaster that keeps him in slavery. Theoretically, the mechanization of farming ought to cut the farmer's chains, but whether it really does is debatable.

One of the requisites for an ecological comprehension of land is an understanding of ecology, and this is by no means coextensive with "education"; in fact, much higher education seems deliberately to avoid ecological concepts. An understanding of ecology does not necessarily originate in courses bearing ecological labels; it is quite as likely to be labeled geography, botany, agronomy, history, or economics. This is as it should be, but whatever the label, ecological training is scarce.

The case for a land ethic would appear hopeless but for the minority which is in obvious revolt against these "modern" trends.

The "key log" which must be moved to release the evolutionary process for an ethic is simply this: quit thinking about decent land use as solely an economic problem. Examine each question in terms of what is ethically and aesthetically right, as well as what is economically expedient. A thing is right when it tends to preserve the integrity, stability, and beauty of the biotic community. It is wrong when it tends otherwise.

It of course goes without saying that economic feasibility limits the tether of what can or cannot be done for land. It always has and it always will. The fallacy the economic determinists have tied around our collective neck, and which we now need to cast off, is the belief that economics determines *all* land use. This is simply not true. An innumerable host of actions and attitudes, comprising perhaps the bulk of all land relations, is determined by the land user's tastes and predilections, rather than by his purse. The bulk of all land relations hinges on investments of time, forethought, skill, and faith rather than on investments of cash. As a land user thinketh, so is he.

I have purposely presented the land ethic as a product of social evolution because nothing so important as an ethic is ever "written." Only the most superficial student of history supposes that Moses "wrote" the Decalogue; it evolved in the minds of a thinking community, and Moses wrote a tentative summary of it for a "seminar." I say tentative because evolution never stops.

The evolution of a land ethic is an intellectual as well as emotional process. Conservation is paved with good intentions which prove to be futile, or even dangerous, because they are devoid of critical understanding either of the land, or of economic land use. I think it is a truism that as the ethical frontier advances from the individual to the community, its intellectual content increases.

The mechanism of operation is the same for any ethic: social approbation for right actions; social disapproval for wrong actions.

By and large, our present problem is one of attitudes and implements. We are remodeling the Alhambra with a steam shovel, and we are proud of our yardage. We shall hardly relinquish the shovel, which after all has many good points, but we are in need of gentler and more objective criteria for its successful use.

Content Questions

1. What is the land ethic?

2. According to Leopold, why is the extension of ethics to the land the "third step in a sequence"? (106) What does Leopold mean by "land"? (114–115)

3. How does Leopold show that historical events "were actually biotic interactions between people and land"? (107) What does Leopold claim about the relation of human activity to soils and plants in explaining these events?

4. In the case of the Wisconsin Soil Conservation District Law of 1937, why did farmers fail to formulate and adopt a full range of remedial conservation practices? (110)

5. What reasons does Leopold give for the "clear tendency in American conservation to relegate to government all necessary jobs that private landowners fail to perform"? (112)

6. In Leopold's sketch of the biotic pyramid, what is the relation between the complex structure of the land and its functioning as an "energy unit"? In what sense does he mean us to understand "unit"? (115)

7. What happens when the introduction of nonindigenous flora and fauna disrupts the biotic pyramid? (115)

8. What is meant by a "resistant biota"? (116) How is this related to the "degree of disorganization" of a region? (117)

Application Questions

1. Leopold uses the word *community* repeatedly in "The Land Ethic." What is the precise meaning of this word in ecological terms? In social terms? How do these meanings complement, overlap, or contradict each other?

2. What is the distinction between *conservation* and *preservation?* In what ways can both be part of the land ethic?

3. In what ways can members of a biotic community be said to have no economic value?

4. Are there nonconsumptive uses of the land that could produce economic value and be compatible with the land ethic?

Discussion Questions

1. Why is "enlightened self-interest" or scientific knowledge inadequate, in Leopold's view, for establishing guidelines for our relation to land? (109)

2. What does Leopold mean by claiming that "the evolution of a land ethic is an intellectual as well as emotional process"? Does the intellectual part of this process presuppose some specific kind of knowledge? What does Leopold mean when he says that the good intentions of conservation are futile because they are "devoid of critical understanding either of the land, or of economic land use"? (121)

3. Is the economic view of land use compatible with Leopold's concept of the land ethic? Can one accommodate the other, or are they fundamentally opposed?

4. Does Leopold believe that the extension of ethics to land is an inevitable evolutionary movement, or does he see it as the outcome of a reasoned assessment of needs and values that may or may not take place?

5. Can education produce an ecological conscience?

6. Since human beings must use natural resources in order to live, what limitations does the land ethic impose on us in relation to the survival of individual members of a species? In relation to a species itself?

7. In a conflict over the inherent value of a natural resource and its potential to be of use to humans, what kind of resolution would the land ethic offer?

8. Leopold states that "a thing is right when it tends to preserve the integrity, stability, and beauty of the biotic community." (120) Does this view subordinate the value of the individual, whether plant or animal, to the greater value of the community? If so, how can we judge whether this subordination is a good thing?

9. Since "beauty" is often thought to be in the eye of the beholder, how can Leopold's aesthetic criterion enter into the science of resource management? (120)

Odyssey

X had marked time in the limestone ledge since the Paleozoic seas covered the land. Time, to an atom locked in a rock, does not pass.

The break came when a bur-oak root nosed down a crack and began prying and sucking. In the flash of a century the rock decayed, and X was pulled out and up into the world of living things. He helped build a flower, which became an acorn, which fattened a deer, which fed an Indian, all in a single year.

From his berth in the Indian's bones, X joined again in chase and flight, feast and famine, hope and fear. He felt these things as changes in the little chemical pushes and pulls that tug timelessly at every atom. When the Indian took his leave of the prairie, X moldered briefly underground, only to embark on a second trip through the bloodstream of the land.

This time it was a rootlet of bluestem that sucked him up and lodged him in a leaf that rode the green billows of the prairie June, sharing the common task of hoarding sunlight. To this leaf also fell an uncommon task: flicking shadows across a plover's eggs. The ecstatic plover, hovering overhead, poured praises on something perfect: perhaps the eggs, perhaps the shadows, or perhaps the haze of pink phlox that lay on the prairie.

When the departing plovers set wing for the Argentine, all the bluestems waved farewell with tall new tassels. When the first geese came out of the north and all the bluestems glowed wine red, a forehanded deer mouse cut the leaf in which X lay, and buried it in an underground nest, as if to hide a bit of Indian summer from the thieving frosts. But a fox detained the mouse, molds and fungi took the nest apart, and X lay in the soil again, footloose and fancy-free.

Next, he entered a tuft of side-oats grama, a buffalo, a buffalo chip, and again the soil. Next a spiderwort, a rabbit, and an owl. Thence a tuft of *Sporobolus.*

All routines come to an end. This one ended with a prairie fire, which reduced the prairie plants to smoke, gas, and ashes. Phosphorus and potash atoms stayed in the ash, but the nitrogen atoms were gone with the wind. A spectator might, at this point, have predicted an early end of the biotic drama, for with fires exhausting the nitrogen, the soil might well have lost its plants and blown away.

But the prairie had two strings to its bow. Fires thinned its grasses, but they thickened its stand of leguminous herbs: prairie clover, bush clover, wild bean, vetch, leadplant, trefoil, and *Baptisia,* each carrying its own bacteria housed in nodules on its rootlets. Each nodule pumped nitrogen out of the air into the plant, and then ultimately into the soil. Thus, the prairie savings bank took in more nitrogen from its legumes than it paid out to its fires. That the prairie is rich is known to the humblest deer mouse; why the prairie is rich is a question seldom asked in all the still lapse of ages.

Between each of his excursions through the biota, X lay in the soil and was carried by the rains, inch by inch, downhill. Living plants retarded the wash by impounding atoms; dead plants by locking them to their decayed tissues. Animals ate the plants and carried them briefly uphill or downhill, depending on whether they died or defecated higher or lower than they fed. No animal was aware that the altitude of his death was more important than his manner of dying. Thus a fox caught a gopher in a meadow, carrying X uphill to his bed on the brow of a ledge, where an eagle laid him low. The dying fox sensed the end of his chapter in foxdom, but not the new beginning in the odyssey of an atom.

An Indian eventually inherited the eagle's plumes, and with them propitiated the Fates, whom he assumed had a special interest in Indians. It did not occur to him that they might be busy casting dice against gravity; that mice and men, soils and songs, might be merely ways to retard the march of atoms to the sea.

One year, while X lay in a cottonwood by the river, he was eaten by a beaver, an animal that always feeds higher than he dies. The beaver starved when his pond dried up during a bitter frost. X rode the carcass down the spring freshet, losing more altitude each hour than heretofore in a century. He ended up in the silt of a backwater bayou, where he fed a crayfish, a coon, and then an Indian, who laid him down to his last sleep in a mound on the riverbank. One spring an oxbow caved the bank, and, after one short week of freshet, X lay again in his ancient prison, the sea.

An atom at large in the biota is too free to know freedom; an atom back in the sea has forgotten it. For every atom lost to the sea, the prairie pulls another out of the decaying rocks. The only certain truth is that its creatures must suck hard, live fast, and die often, lest its losses exceed its gains.

Content Questions

1. What is Leopold referring to when he says that X embarked "on a second trip through the bloodstream of the land"? (124)

2. What is "the common task of hoarding sunlight"? (124)

3. What "routine" comes to an end with the prairie fire? (125)

4. Why does Leopold say after the prairie fire that "a spectator might, at this point, have predicted an early end of the biotic drama"? (125)

5. What are the two bowstrings of the prairie? (125)

6. What is the process that makes the prairie rich? (125)

7. What is the significance of the altitude of an animal's death? (125)

Application Questions

1. Leopold describes the odyssey through the biota without specifying the chemical element of atom X. Assume that the element is nitrogen, then choose one of the episodes in the odyssey and specify the biochemical processes in which the nitrogen atom plays a part.

2. Describe the events—natural or induced by humans—that might take place in the prairie so that its losses would exceed its gains. Do so using atom X as a marker in this kind of biotic history.

Discussion Questions

1. What changes for X when it passes from the Paleozoic limestone ledge "into the world of living things"? (124)

2. What does Leopold mean when he says that X experienced the Indian's life "in the little chemical pushes and pulls that tug timelessly at every atom"? (124)

3. Why is shading the plover's eggs "an uncommon task"? (124)

4. Why does Leopold say that a fox "detained" the mouse? (125)

5. Why is the question of the prairie's richness seldom asked?

6. In his story, why does Leopold place X in the Indian's eagle plumes?

7. Does "casting dice against gravity" mean that retarding the "march of atoms to the sea" is a matter of chance? (125)

8. Why is the sea said to be a prison for X?

9. How is it possible for X to be free and not know freedom?

Kenneth E. Boulding

Kenneth E. Boulding (1910–1993) sometimes referred to himself as an "impure" econo-mist. Throughout his long teaching and prolific writing career, he reached beyond the boundaries of the discipline of economics to make important contributions to political science, sociology, philosophy, and social psychology.

Born into a working class family in Liverpool, England, Boulding attended Oxford University before embarking on an itinerant academic career that took him to Harvard University, the University of Chicago, Iowa State University, the University of Edinburgh, and finally the University of Colorado. While at Colorado, Boulding—a Quaker and committed pacifist—organized the first anti–Vietnam War teach-in, in 1965.

Boulding's analysis of economic behavior repeatedly returned to the problem of how the consumption of assets—including natural resources—can be balanced against maximizing the enjoyment of those assets. To emphasize the broadest environmental aspects of this problem, Boulding invoked the image of the earth as a spaceship, a closed system, because he believed that the images human beings have of the world determine their behavior within it. "Earth has become a spaceship," he said, "not only in our imagination but also in the hard realities of the social, biological, and physical system in which man is enmeshed. . . . He must live in the whole system, in which he must recycle his wastes. . . . In a spaceship there are no sewers."

The Economics of the Coming Spaceship Earth

(selection)

We are now in the middle of a long process of transition in the nature of the image which man has of himself and his environment. Primitive men, and to a large extent also men of the early civilizations, imagined themselves to be living on a virtually illimitable plane. There was almost always somewhere beyond the known limits of human habitation, and over a very large part of the time that man has been on earth, there has been something like a frontier. That is, there was always someplace else to go when things got too difficult, either by reason of the deterioration of the natural environment or a deterioration of the social structure in places where people happened to live. The image of the frontier is probably one of the oldest images of mankind, and it is not surprising that we find it hard to get rid of.

Gradually, however, man has been accustoming himself to the notion of the spherical earth and a closed sphere of human activity. A few unusual spirits among the ancient Greeks perceived that the earth was a sphere. It was only with the circumnavigations and the geographical explorations of the fifteenth and sixteenth centuries, however, that the fact that the earth was a sphere became at all widely known and accepted. Even in the nineteenth century, the commonest map was Mercator's projection, which visualizes the earth as an illimitable cylinder, essentially a plane wrapped around the globe, and it was not until the Second World War and the

131

development of the air age that the global nature of the planet really entered the popular imagination. Even now we are very far from having made the moral, political, and psychological adjustments which are implied in this transition from the illimitable plane to the closed sphere.

Economists in particular, for the most part, have failed to come to grips with the ultimate consequences of the transition from the open to the closed earth. One hesitates to use the terms *open* and *closed* in this connection, as they have been used with so many different shades of meaning. Nevertheless, it is hard to find equivalents. The open system, . . . implies that some kind of structure is maintained in the midst of a throughput from inputs to outputs. In a closed system, the outputs of all parts of the system are linked to the inputs of other parts. There are no inputs from outside and no outputs to the outside; indeed, there is no outside at all. Closed systems, in fact, are very rare in human experience, in fact almost by definition unknowable, for if there are genuinely closed systems around us, we have no way of getting information into them or out of them; and hence if they are really closed, we would be quite unaware of their existence. We can only find out about a closed system if we participate in it. Some isolated primitive societies may have approximated to this, but even these had to take inputs from the environment and give outputs to it. All living organisms, including man himself, are open systems. They have to receive inputs in the shape of air, food, water, and give off outputs in the form of effluvia and excrement. Deprivation of input of air, even for a few minutes, is fatal. Deprivation of the ability to obtain any input or to dispose of any output is fatal in a relatively short time. All human societies have likewise been open systems. They receive inputs from the earth, the atmosphere, and the waters, and they give outputs into these reservoirs; they also produce inputs internally in the shape of babies and outputs in the shape of corpses. Given a capacity to draw upon inputs and to get rid of outputs, an open system of this kind can persist indefinitely.

Systems may be open or closed in respect to a number of classes of inputs and outputs. Three important classes are matter, energy, and information. The present world economy is open in regard to all three. We can think of the world economy or *econosphere* as a subset of the *world set*, which is the set of all objects of possible discourse in the world. We then think of the state of the econosphere at any one moment as being the total capital stock, that is, the set of all objects, people, organizations, and so on, which are interesting from the point of view of the system of exchange. This total stock of capital is clearly an open system in the sense that it has inputs and outputs, inputs being production which adds to the capital stock, outputs being consumption which subtracts from it. From a material point of view, we see objects passing from the noneconomic into the economic set in the process of production, and we similarly see products passing out of the economic set as their value becomes zero. Thus, we see the econosphere as a material process involving the discovery and mining of fossil fuels, ores, etc., and at the other end a process by which the effluents of the system are passed out into noneconomic reservoirs—for instance, the atmosphere and the oceans—which are not appropriated and do not enter into the exchange system.

From the point of view of the energy system, the econosphere involves inputs of available energy in the form, say, of water power, fossil fuels, or sunlight, which are necessary in order to create the material throughput and to move matter from the noneconomic set into the economic set or even out of it again; and energy itself is given off by the system in a less available form, mostly in the form of heat. These inputs of available energy must come either from the sun (the energy supplied by other stars being assumed to be negligible) or it may come from the earth itself, either through its internal heat or through its energy of rotation or other motions, which generate, for instance, the energy of the tides. Agriculture, a few solar machines, and water power use the current available energy income. In advanced societies this is supplemented very extensively by the use of fossil fuels, which represent, as it were, a capital stock of stored-up sunshine. Because of this capital stock of energy, we have been able to maintain an energy input into the system, particularly over the last two centuries, much larger than we would have been able to do with existing techniques if we had had to rely on the current input of available energy from the sun or the earth itself. This supplementary input, however, is by its very nature exhaustible.

The inputs and outputs of information are more subtle and harder to trace, but also represent an open system, related to, but not wholly dependent on, the transformations of matter and energy. By far the larger amount of information and knowledge is self-generated by the human society, though a certain amount of information comes into the sociosphere in the form of light from the universe outside. . . .

From the human point of view, knowledge, or information, is by far the most important of the three systems. Matter only acquires significance and only enters the sociosphere or the econosphere insofar as it becomes an object of human knowledge.

The concept of entropy, used in a somewhat loose sense, can be applied to all three of these open systems. In material systems, we can distinguish between entropic processes, which take concentrated materials and diffuse them through the oceans or over the earth's surface or into the atmosphere, and antientropic processes, which take diffuse materials and concentrate them. Material entropy can be taken as a measure of the uniformity of the distribution of elements and, more uncertainly, compounds and other structures on the earth's surface. There is, fortunately, no law of increasing material entropy, as there is in the corresponding case of energy, as it is quite possible to concentrate diffused materials if energy inputs are allowed. Thus, the processes for fixation of nitrogen from the air, processes for the extraction of magnesium or other elements from the sea, and processes for the desalinization of seawater are antientropic in the material sense, though the reduction of material entropy has to be paid for by inputs of energy and also inputs of information, or at least a stock of information in the system. In regard to matter, therefore, a closed system is conceivable, that is, a system in which there is neither increase nor decrease in material entropy. In such a system all outputs from consumption would constantly be recycled to become inputs for production, as for instance, nitrogen in the nitrogen cycle of the natural ecosystem.

In the energy system there is, unfortunately, no escape from the grim second law of thermodynamics; and if there were no energy inputs into the earth, any evolutionary or developmental process would be impossible. The large energy inputs which we have obtained from fossil fuels are strictly temporary. Even the most optimistic predictions expect the easily available supply of fossil fuels to be exhausted in a mere matter of centuries at present rates of use. If the rest of the world were to rise to American standards of power consumption, and still more if world population continues to increase, the exhaustion of fossil fuels would be even more rapid. . . .

The question of whether there is anything corresponding to entropy in the information system is a puzzling one, though of great interest. There are certainly many examples of social systems and cultures which have lost knowledge, especially in transition from one generation to the next, and in which the culture has therefore degenerated. . . . Over a great part of human history, the growth of knowledge in the earth as a whole seems to have been almost continuous, even though there have been times of relatively slow growth and times of rapid growth. As it is knowledge of certain kinds that produces the growth of knowledge in general, we have here a very subtle and complicated system, and it is hard to put one's finger on the particular elements in a culture which make knowledge grow more or less rapidly, or even which make it decline.

The closed earth of the future requires economic principles which are somewhat different from those of the open earth of the past. For the sake of picturesqueness, I am tempted to call the open economy the "cowboy economy," the cowboy being symbolic of the illimitable plains and also associated with reckless, exploitative, romantic, and violent behavior, which is characteristic of open societies. The closed economy of the future might similarly be called the "spaceman economy," in which the earth has become a single spaceship, without unlimited reservoirs of anything, either for extraction or for pollution, and in which, therefore, man must find his place in a cyclical ecological system which is capable of continuous reproduction of material form even though it cannot escape having inputs of energy. The difference between the two types of economy becomes most apparent in the attitude toward consumption. In the cowboy economy, consumption is regarded as a good thing and production likewise; and the success of the economy is measured by the amount of the throughput from the "factors of production," a part of which, at any rate, is extracted from the reservoirs of raw materials and noneconomic objects, and another part of which is output into the reservoirs of pollution. If there are infinite reservoirs from which material can be obtained and into which effluvia can be deposited, then the throughput is at least a plausible measure of the success of the economy. The gross national product is a rough measure of this total throughput. It should be possible, however, to distinguish that part of the GNP which is derived from exhaustible and that which is derived from reproducible resources, as well as that part of consumption which represents effluvia and that which represents input into the productive system again. . . .

By contrast, in the spaceman economy, throughput is by no means a desideratum, and is indeed to be regarded as something to be minimized rather than maximized. The essential measure of the success of the economy is not production and consumption at all, but the nature, extent, quality, and complexity of the total capital stock, including in this the state of the human bodies and minds included in the system. In the spaceman economy, what we are primarily concerned with is stock maintenance, and any technological change which results in the maintenance of a given total stock with a lessened throughput (that is, less production and consumption) is clearly a gain. This idea that both production and consumption are bad things rather than good things is very strange to economists, who have been obsessed with the income-flow concepts to the exclusion, almost, of capital-stock concepts.

There are actually some very tricky and unsolved problems involved in the questions as to whether human welfare or well-being is to be regarded as a stock or a flow. Something of both these elements seems actually to be involved in it, and as far as I know there have been practically no studies directed toward identifying these two dimensions of human satisfaction. Is it, for instance, eating that is a good thing, or is it being well fed? Does economic welfare involve having nice clothes, fine houses, good equipment, and so on, or is it to be measured by the depreciation and the wearing out of these things? I am inclined myself to regard the stock concept as most fundamental, that is, to think of being well fed as more important than eating, and to think even of so-called services as essentially involving the restoration of a depleting psychic capital. Thus, I have argued that we go to a concert in order to restore a psychic condition which might be called "just having gone to a concert," which, once established, tends to depreciate. When it depreciates beyond a certain point, we go to another concert in order to restore it. If it depreciates rapidly, we go to a lot of concerts; if it depreciates slowly, we go to a few. On this view, similarly, we eat primarily to restore bodily homeostasis, that is, to maintain a condition of being well fed, and so on. On this view, there is nothing desirable in consumption at all. The less consumption we can maintain a given state with, the better off we are. If we had clothes that did not wear out, houses that did not depreciate, and even if we could maintain our bodily condition without eating, we would clearly be much better off.

It is this last consideration, perhaps, which makes one pause. Would we, for instance, really want an operation that would enable us to restore all our bodily tissues by intravenous feeding while we slept? Is there not, that is to say, a certain virtue in throughput itself, in activity itself, in production and consumption itself, in raising food and in eating it? It would certainly be rash to exclude this possibility. Further interesting problems are raised by the demand for variety. We certainly do not want a constant state to be maintained; we want fluctuations in the state. Otherwise there would be no demand for variety in food, for variety in scene, as in travel, for variety in social contact, and so on. The demand for variety can, of course, be costly, and sometimes it seems to be too costly to be tolerated or at least legitimated, as in the case of marital partners, where the maintenance of a homeostatic state in the family is usually regarded as much more desirable than the variety and excessive throughput of the libertine. There are problems here which the economics profession has neglected with astonishing singlemindedness. . . . Economists continue to think and act as if production, consumption, throughput, and the GNP were the sufficient and adequate measure of economic success.

It may be said, of course, why worry about all this when the spaceman economy is still a good way off (at least beyond the lifetimes of any now living), so let us eat, drink, spend, extract, and pollute, and be as merry as we can, and let posterity worry about the spaceship earth. It is always a little hard to find a convincing answer to the man who says, "What has posterity ever done for me?" and the conservationist has always had to fall back on rather vague ethical principles postulating identity of the individual with some human community or society which extends not only back into the past but forward into the future. Unless the individual identifies with some community of this kind, conservation is obviously "irrational." Why should we not maximize the welfare of this generation at the cost of posterity? *"Après nous, le déluge"* has been the motto of not insignificant numbers or human societies. The only answer to this, as far as I can see, is to point out that the welfare of the individual depends on the extent to which he can identity himself with others, and that the most satisfactory individual identity is that which identifies not only with a community in space but also with a community extending over time from the past into the future. If this kind of identity is recognized as desirable, then posterity has a voice, even if it does not have a vote; and in a sense, if its voice can influence votes, it has votes too. This whole problem is linked up with the much larger one of the determinants of the morale, legitimacy, and "nerve" of a society, and there is a great deal of historical evidence to suggest that a society which loses its identity with posterity and which loses its positive image of the future loses also its capacity to deal with present problems, and soon falls apart.

Even if we concede that posterity is relevant to our present problems, we still face the question of time discounting and the closely related question of uncertainty discounting. It is a well-known phenomenon that individuals discount the future, even in their own lives. The very existence of a positive rate of interest may be taken as at least strong supporting evidence of this hypothesis. If we discount our own future, it is certainly not unreasonable to discount posterity's future even more, even if we do give posterity a vote. If we discount this at 5 percent per annum, posterity's vote or dollar halves every fourteen years as we look into the future, and after even a mere hundred years it is pretty small—only about one and a half cents on the dollar. If we add another 5 percent for uncertainty, even the vote of our grandchildren reduces almost to insignificance. We can argue, of course, that the ethical thing to do is not to discount the future at all, that time discounting is mainly the result of myopia and perspective, and hence is an illusion which the moral man should not tolerate. It is a very popular illusion, however, and one that must certainly be taken into consideration in the formulation of policies. It explains, perhaps, why conservationist policies almost have to be sold under some other excuse which seems more urgent, and why, indeed, necessities which are visualized as urgent, such as defense, always seem to hold priority over those which involve the future.

All these considerations add some credence to the point of view which says that we should not worry about the spaceman economy at all, and that we should just go on increasing the GNP and indeed the gross world product, or GWP, in the expectation that the problems of the future can be left to the future, that when scarcities arise, whether this is of raw materials or of pollutable reservoirs, the needs of the then present will determine the solutions of the then present, and there is no use giving ourselves ulcers by worrying about problems that we really do not have to solve. There is even high ethical authority for this point of view in the New Testament, which advocates that we should take no thought for tomorrow and let the dead bury their dead. There has always been something rather refreshing in the view that we should live like the birds, and perhaps posterity is for the birds in more senses than one; so perhaps we should all call it a day and go out and pollute something cheerfully. As an old taker of thought for the morrow, however, I cannot quite accept this solution; and I would argue, furthermore, that tomorrow is not only very close, but in many respects it is already here. The shadow of the future spaceship, indeed, is already falling over our spendthrift merriment. Oddly enough, it seems to be in pollution rather than in exhaustion that the problem is first becoming salient. Los Angeles has run out of air, Lake Erie has become a cesspool, the oceans are getting full of lead and DDT, and the atmosphere may become man's major problem in another generation, at the rate at which we are filling it up with gunk. It is, of course, true that at least on a microscale, things have been worse at times in the past. The cities of today, with all their foul air and polluted waterways, are probably not as bad as the filthy cities of the pretechnical age. Nevertheless, that fouling of the nest which has been typical of man's activity in the past on a local scale now seems to be extending to the whole world society; and one certainly cannot view with equanimity the present rate of pollution of any of the natural reservoirs, whether the atmosphere, the lakes, or even the oceans.

I would argue strongly also that our obsession with production and consumption to the exclusion of the "state" aspects of human welfare distorts the process of technological change in a most undesirable way. We are all familiar, of course, with the wastes involved in planned obsolescence, in competitive advertising, and in poor quality of consumer goods. These problems may not be so important as the "view with alarm" school indicates, and indeed the evidence at many points is conflicting. New materials especially seem to edge toward the side of improved durability, such as, for instance, neolite soles for footwear, nylon socks, wash-and-wear shirts, and so on. The case of household equipment and automobiles is a little less clear. Housing and building construction generally almost certainly has declined in durability since the Middle Ages, but this decline also reflects a change in tastes toward flexibility and fashion and a need for novelty, so that it is not easy to assess. What is clear is that no serious attempt has been made to assess the impact over the whole of economic life of changes in durability, that is, in the ratio of capital in the widest possible sense to income. I suspect that we have underestimated, even in our spendthrift society, the gains from increased durability, and that this might very well be one of the places where the price system needs correction through government-sponsored research and development. The problems which the spaceship earth is going to present, therefore, are not all in the future by any means, and a strong case can be made for paying much more attention to them in the present than we now do.

It may be complained that the considerations I have been putting forth relate only to the very long run, and they do not much concern our immediate problems. There may be some justice in this criticism, and my main excuse is that other writers have dealt adequately with the more immediate problems of deterioration in the quality of the environment. It is true, for instance, that many of the immediate problems of pollution of the atmosphere or of bodies of water arise because of the failure of the price system, and many of them could be solved by corrective taxation. If people had to pay the losses due to the nuisances which they create, a good deal more resources would go into the prevention of nuisances. These arguments involving external economies and diseconomies are familiar to economists and there is no need to recapitulate them. The law of torts is quite inadequate to provide for the correction of the price system which is required, simply because where damages are widespread and their incidence on any particular person is small, the ordinary remedies of the civil law are quite inadequate and inappropriate. There needs, therefore, to be special legislation to cover these cases, and though such legislation seems hard to get in practice, mainly because of the widespread and small personal incidence of the injuries, the technical problems involved are not insuperable. If we were to adopt in principle a law for tax penalties for social damages, with an apparatus for making assessments under it, a very large proportion of current pollution and deterioration of the environment would be prevented. There are tricky problems of equity involved, particularly where old established nuisances create a kind of "right by purchase" to perpetuate themselves, but these are problems again which a few rather arbitrary decisions can bring to some kind of solution.

The problems which I have been raising in this paper are of larger scale and perhaps much harder to solve than the more practical and immediate problems of the above paragraph. Our success in dealing with the larger problems, however, is not unrelated to the development of skill in the solution of the more immediate and perhaps less difficult problems. One can hope, therefore, that as a succession of mounting crises, especially in pollution, arouse public opinion and mobilize support for the solution of the immediate problems, a learning process will be set in motion which will eventually lead to an appreciation of and perhaps solutions for the larger ones. My neglect of the immediate problems, therefore, is in no way intended to deny their importance, for unless we make at least a beginning on a process for solving the immediate problems we will not have much chance of solving the larger ones. On the other hand, it may also be true that a long-run vision, as it were, of the deep crisis which faces mankind may predispose people to taking more interest in the immediate problems and to devote more effort for their solution. This may sound like a rather modest optimism, but perhaps a modest optimism is better than no optimism all.

Content Questions

1. For Boulding, what are the differences between "open" and "closed" systems? What arguments does he give for claiming that the earth is one or the other? (131–132)

2. What are the ways in which a system can be "open" or "closed" with respect to each of the three classes of inputs and outputs: matter, energy, and information? (132–134)

3. How can the concept of entropy be applied to open systems with respect to matter, energy, and information? Why does Boulding say that there is no law of increasing material entropy? (134)

4. Why does Boulding assert that "the closed earth of the future requires economic principles which are somewhat different from those of the open earth of the past"? (135)

5. Why does Boulding say that "the attitude toward consumption" is the feature that most distinguishes the cowboy economy from the spaceman economy? (135)

6. Why are production and consumption not the essential measures of success of the spaceman economy? (136)

7. What does Boulding mean by the distinction between a "stock" and a "flow"? Why does he consider the "stock" concept fundamental? (136)

8. Why does Boulding emphasize the importance of assessing how changes in durability and poor quality of consumer goods affect economic life? (139)

Application Questions

1. Boulding talks about antientropic processes in material systems in which diffuse materials are reconcentrated, such as desalinization of ocean waters, nitrogen fixation, and extraction of magnesium from the sea. Choose one of these examples (or make up one of your own) and estimate the amount and types of energy and information inputs necessary for reconstitution of the diffused material. Is there an increase in energy or information entropy as a result of the process? If so, is the increase in energy and information entropy in exchange for the reduction in material entropy worth it?

2. Consider how the advantages and disadvantages of durable and disposable consumer goods can be assessed, taking into account to whom or what the advantages and disadvantages accrue. Make the comparison with respect to personal satisfaction in the use of the goods, as well as to overall economic well-being.

3. Boulding suggests that tax penalties for social damages, along with an apparatus for making assessments of these damages, would prevent many problems of environmental deterioration. Describe how these assessments might be made.

Discussion Questions

1. Why does Boulding say that "there are actually some very tricky and unsolved problems involved in the questions as to whether human welfare or well-being is to be regarded as a stock or a flow"? (136)

2. Is consumption in itself desirable? Is there a difference between consumption and use?

3. Why does Boulding claim that "conservation is obviously 'irrational'" unless the individual identifies with a community that "extends not only back into the past but forward into the future"? (137)

4. Is Boulding correct in claiming that "conservationist policies almost have to be sold under some other excuse which seems more urgent"? (138) How is this assertion borne out by the current approach to the issue of global warming?

5. What connection does Boulding make between "our obsession with production and consumption to the exclusion of the 'state' aspects of human welfare" and the deterioration of the environment? (139)

Garrett Hardin

Garrett Hardin (1915–2003) attended the University of Chicago and earned his doctorate in biology from Stanford University. He was professor emeritus of human ecology and environmental studies at the University of California at Santa Barbara, where he had served on the faculty since 1946.

Hardin authored more than a dozen books based on many short papers, including "The Tragedy of the Commons," which won widespread praise when published in *Science* in 1968. In much of his subsequent writing, he developed and applied the ideas in this essay to issues concerning population, immigration, abortion, and public policy.

"The Tragedy of the Commons" takes an interdisciplinary approach to the problem of population growth. In doing so, it opens up numerous avenues of inquiry into many areas of environmental studies, including resource management, economics, population statistics, ethics, and public policy, as well as human biology and psychology. About this approach, Hardin said, "Do not underestimate its difficulties. The more specialties we try to stitch together, the greater are our opportunities to make mistakes—and the more numerous are our willing critics." "The Tragedy of the Commons" addresses what Hardin sees as a lack of attention to numerical considerations by ethicists and philosophers: "One of today's cardinal tasks is to marry the philosopher's literate ethics with the scientist's commitment to numerate analysis." This concern is critical, Hardin argues, as the earth faces problems resulting from the exponential growth of living systems but with its resources defined by relatively constant numbers.

The fundamental problem that "The Tragedy of the Commons" puts before us is the extent to which individual freedom must be sacrificed as the earth's population exceeds the environment's carrying capacity.

The Tragedy
of the Commons

At the end of a thoughtful article on the future of nuclear war, Wiesner and York[1] concluded that: "Both sides in the arms race are . . . confronted by the dilemma of steadily increasing military power and steadily decreasing national security. *It is our considered professional judgment that this dilemma has no technical solution.* If the great powers continue to look for solutions in the area of science and technology only, the result will be to worsen the situation."

I would like to focus your attention not on the subject of the article (national security in a nuclear world) but on the kind of conclusion they reached, namely that there is no technical solution to the problem. An implicit and almost universal assumption of discussions published in professional and semipopular scientific journals is that the problem under discussion has a technical solution. A technical solution may be defined as one that requires a change only in the techniques of the natural sciences, demanding little or nothing in the way of change in human values or ideas of morality.

In our day (though not in earlier times) technical solutions are always welcome. Because of previous failures in prophecy, it takes courage to assert that a desired technical solution is not possible. Wiesner and York exhibited this courage; publishing in a science journal, they insisted that the solution to the problem was not to be found in the natural sciences. They cautiously qualified their statement with the phrase, "It is our considered professional judgment. . . ." Whether they were right or not is not the concern of the present article. Rather, the concern here is with the important concept of a class of human problems which can be called "no technical solution problems," and, more specifically, with the identification and discussion of one of these.

It is easy to show that the class is not a null class. Recall the game of ticktacktoe. Consider the problem, "How can I win the game of ticktacktoe?" It is well known that I cannot, if I assume (in keeping with the conventions of game theory) that my opponent understands the game perfectly. Put another way, there is no "technical solution" to the problem. I can win only by giving a radical meaning to the word *win*. I can hit my opponent over the head; or I can drug him; or I can falsify the records. Every way in which I "win" involves, in some sense, an abandonment of the game, as we intuitively understand it. (I can also, of course, openly abandon the game—refuse to play it. This is what most adults do.)

The class of "no technical solution problems" has members. My thesis is that the "population problem," as conventionally conceived, is a member of this class. How it is conventionally conceived needs some comment. It is fair to say that most people who anguish over the population problem are trying to find a way to avoid the evils of overpopulation without relinquishing any of the privileges they now enjoy. They think that farming the seas or developing new strains of wheat will solve the problem—technologically. I try to show here that the solution they seek cannot be found. The population problem cannot be solved in a technical way, any more than can the problem of winning the game of ticktacktoe.

What Shall We Maximize?

Population, as Malthus said, naturally tends to grow "geometrically," or, as we would now say, exponentially. In a finite world this means that the per capita share of the world's goods must steadily decrease. Is ours a finite world?

A fair defense can be put forward for the view that the world is infinite; or that we do not know that it is not. But, in terms of the practical problems that we must face in the next few generations with the foreseeable technology, it is clear that we will greatly increase human misery if we do not, during the immediate future, assume that the world available to the terrestrial human population is finite. "Space" is no escape.[2]

A finite world can support only a finite population; therefore, population growth must eventually equal zero. (The case of perpetual wide fluctuations above and below zero is a trivial variant that need not be discussed.) When this condition is met, what will be the situation of mankind? Specifically, can Bentham's goal of "the greatest good for the greatest number" be realized?

No—for two reasons, each sufficient by itself. The first is a theoretical one. It is not mathematically possible to maximize for two (or more) variables at the same time. This was clearly stated by von Neumann and Morgenstern,[3] but the principle is implicit in the theory of partial differential equations, dating back at least to d'Alembert (1717–1783).

The second reason springs directly from biological facts. To live, any organism must have a source of energy (for example, food). This energy is utilized for two purposes: mere maintenance and work. For man, maintenance of life requires about 1600 kilocalories a day ("maintenance calories"). Anything that he does over and above merely staying alive will be defined as work, and is supported by "work calories" which he takes in. Work calories are used not only for what we call work in common speech; they are also required for all forms of enjoyment, from swimming and automobile racing to playing music and writing poetry. If our goal is to maximize population it is obvious what we must do: We must make the work calories per person approach as close to zero as possible. No gourmet meals, no vacations, no sports, no music, no literature, no art. . . . I think that everyone will grant, without argument or proof, that maximizing population does not maximize goods. Bentham's goal is impossible.

In reaching this conclusion, I have made the usual assumption that it is the acquisition of energy that is the problem. The appearance of atomic energy has led some to question this assumption. However, given an infinite source of energy, population growth still produces an inescapable problem. The problem of the acquisition of energy is replaced by the problem of its dissipation, as J. H. Fremlin has so wittily shown.[4] The arithmetic signs in the analysis are, as it were, reversed; but Bentham's goal is still unobtainable.

The optimum population is, then, less than the maximum. The difficulty of defining the optimum is enormous; so far as I know, no one has seriously tackled this problem. Reaching an acceptable and stable solution will surely require more than one generation of hard analytical work—and much persuasion.

We want the maximum good per person; but what is good? To one person it is wilderness, to another it is ski lodges for thousands. To one it is estuaries to nourish ducks for hunters to shoot; to another it is factory land. Comparing one good with another is, we usually say, impossible because goods are incommensurable. Incommensurables cannot be compared.

Theoretically this may be true; but in real life incommensurables *are* commensurable. Only a criterion of judgment and a system of weighting are needed. In nature the criterion is survival. Is it better for a species to be small and hideable, or large and powerful? Natural selection commensurates the incommensurables. The compromise achieved depends on a natural weighting of the values of the variables.

Man must imitate this process. There is no doubt that in fact he already does, but unconsciously. It is when the hidden decisions are made explicit that the arguments begin. The problem for the years ahead is to work out an acceptable theory of weighting. Synergistic effects, nonlinear variation, and difficulties in discounting the future make the intellectual problem difficult, but not (in principle) insoluble.

Has any cultural group solved this practical problem at the present time, even on an intuitive level? One simple fact proves that none has: there is no prosperous population in the world today that has, and has had for some time, a growth rate of zero. Any people that has intuitively identified its optimum point will soon reach it, after which its growth rate becomes and remains zero.

Of course, a positive growth rate might be taken as evidence that a population is below its optimum. However, by any reasonable standards, the most rapidly growing populations on earth today are (in general) the most miserable. This association (which need not be invariable) casts doubt on the optimistic assumption that the positive growth rate of a population is evidence that it has yet to reach its optimum.

We can make little progress in working toward optimum population size until we explicitly exorcize the spirit of Adam Smith in the field of practical demography. In economic affairs, *The Wealth of Nations* (1776) popularized the "invisible hand," the idea that an individual who "intends only his own gain," is, as it were, "led by an invisible hand to promote . . . the public interest."[5] Adam Smith did not assert that this was invariably true, and perhaps neither did any of his followers. But he contributed to a dominant tendency of thought that has ever since interfered with positive action based on rational analysis, namely, the tendency to assume that decisions reached individually will, in fact, be the best decisions for an entire society. If this assumption is correct, it justifies the continuance of our present policy of laissez faire in reproduction. If it is correct, we can assume that men will control their individual fecundity so as to produce the optimum population. If the assumption is not correct, we need to reexamine our individual freedoms to see which ones are defensible.

Tragedy of Freedom in a Commons

The rebuttal to the invisible hand in population control is to be found in a scenario first sketched in a little-known pamphlet in 1833 by a mathematical amateur named William Forster Lloyd (1795–1852).[6] We may well call it "the tragedy of the commons," using the word *tragedy* as the philosopher Whitehead used it:[7] "The essence of dramatic tragedy is not unhappiness. It resides in the solemnity of the remorseless working of things." He then goes on to say, "This inevitableness of destiny can only be illustrated in terms of human life by incidents which in fact involve unhappiness. For it is only by them that the futility of escape can be made evident in the drama."

The tragedy of the commons develops in this way. Picture a pasture open to all. It is to be expected that each herdsman will try to keep as many cattle as possible on the commons. Such an arrangement may work reasonably satisfactorily for centuries because tribal wars, poaching, and disease keep the numbers of both man and beast well below the carrying capacity of the land. Finally, however, comes the day of reckoning—that is, the day when the long-desired goal of social stability becomes a reality. At this point, the inherent logic of the commons remorselessly generates tragedy.

As a rational being, each herdsman seeks to maximize his gain. Explicitly or implicitly, more or less consciously, he asks, "What is the utility *to me* of adding one more animal to my herd?" This utility has one negative and one positive component.

1. The positive component is a function of the increment of one animal. Since the herdsman receives all the proceeds from the sale of the additional animal, the positive utility is nearly +1.

2. The negative component is a function of the additional overgrazing created by one more animal. Since, however, the effects of overgrazing are shared by all the herdsmen, the negative utility for any particular decision-making herdsman is only a fraction of -1.

Adding together the component partial utilities, the rational herdsman concludes that the only sensible course for him to pursue is to add another animal to his herd. And another; and another. . . . But this is the conclusion reached by each and every rational herdsman sharing a commons. Therein is the tragedy. Each man is locked into a system that compels him to increase his herd without limit—in a world that is limited. Ruin is the destination toward which all men rush, each pursuing his own best interest in a society that believes in the freedom of the commons. Freedom in a commons brings ruin to all.

Some would say that this is a platitude. Would that it were! In a sense, it was learned thousands of years ago, but natural selection favors the forces of psychological denial.[8] The individual benefits as an individual from his ability to deny the truth even though society as a whole, of which he is a part, suffers. Education can counteract the natural tendency to do the wrong thing, but the inexorable succession of generations requires that the basis for this knowledge be constantly refreshed.

A simple incident that occurred a few years ago in Leominster, Massachusetts, shows how perishable the knowledge is. During the Christmas shopping season the parking meters downtown were covered with plastic bags that bore tags reading: "Do not open until after Christmas. Free parking courtesy of the mayor and city council." In other words, facing the prospect of an increased demand for already scarce space, the city fathers reinstituted the system of the commons. (Cynically, we suspect that they gained more votes than they lost by this retrogressive act.)

In an approximate way, the logic of the commons has been understood for a long time, perhaps since the discovery of agriculture or the invention of private property in real estate. But it is understood mostly only in special cases which are not sufficiently generalized. Even at this late date, cattlemen leasing national land on the western ranges demonstrate no more than an ambivalent understanding, in constantly pressuring federal authorities to increase the head count to the point where overgrazing produces erosion and weed dominance. Likewise, the oceans of the world continue to suffer from the survival of the philosophy of the commons. Maritime nations still respond automatically to the shibboleth of the "freedom of the seas." Professing to believe in the "inexhaustible resources of the oceans," they bring species after species of fish and whales closer to extinction.[9]

The national parks present another instance of the working out of the tragedy of the commons. At present they are open to all, without limit. The parks themselves are limited in extent—there is only one Yosemite Valley—whereas population seems to grow without limit. The values that visitors seek in the parks are steadily eroded. Plainly, we must soon cease to treat the parks as commons or they will be of no value to anyone.

What shall we do? We have several options. We might sell them off as private property. We might keep them as public property, but allocate the right to enter them. The allocation might be on the basis of wealth, by the use of an auction system. It might be on the basis of merit, as defined by some agreed-upon standards. It might be by lottery. Or it might be on a first-come, first-served basis, administered to long queues. These, I think, are all the reasonable possibilities. They are all objectionable. But we must choose—or acquiesce in the destruction of the commons that we call our national parks.

Pollution

In a reverse way, the tragedy of the commons reappears in problems of pollution. Here it is not a question of taking something out of the commons, but of putting something in—sewage, or chemical, radioactive, and heat wastes into water; noxious and dangerous fumes into the air; and distracting and unpleasant advertising signs into the line of sight. The calculations of utility are much the same as before. The rational man finds that his share of the cost of the wastes he discharges into the commons is less than the cost of purifying his wastes before releasing them. Since this is true for everyone, we are locked into a system of "fouling our own nest," so long as we behave only as independent, rational, free-enterprisers.

The tragedy of the commons as a food basket is averted by private property, or something formally like it. But the air and waters surrounding us cannot readily be fenced, and so the tragedy of the commons as a cesspool must be prevented by different means, by coercive laws or taxing devices that make it cheaper for the polluter to treat his pollutants than to discharge them untreated. We have not progressed as far with the solution of this problem as we have with the first. Indeed, our particular concept of private property, which deters us from exhausting the positive resources of the earth, favors pollution. The owner of a factory on the bank of a stream—whose property extends to the middle of the stream—often has difficulty seeing why it is not his natural right to muddy the waters flowing past his door. The law, always behind the times, requires elaborate stitching and fitting to adapt it to this newly perceived aspect of the commons.

The pollution problem is a consequence of population. It did not much matter how a lonely American frontiersman disposed of his waste. "Flowing water purifies itself every ten miles," my grandfather used to say, and the myth was near enough to the truth when he was a boy, for there were not too many people. But as population became denser, the natural chemical and biological recycling processes became overloaded, calling for a redefinition of property rights.

How to Legislate Temperance?

Analysis of the pollution problem as a function of population density uncovers a not generally recognized principle of morality, namely: *the morality of an act is a function of the state of the system at the time it is performed.*[10] Using the commons as a cesspool does not harm the general public under frontier conditions, because there is no public; the same behavior in a metropolis is unbearable. A hundred and fifty years ago a plainsman could kill an American bison, cut out only the tongue for his dinner, and discard the rest of the animal. He was not in any important sense being wasteful. Today, with only a few thousand bison left, we would be appalled at such behavior.

In passing, it is worth noting that the morality of an act cannot be determined from a photograph. One does not know whether a man killing an elephant or setting fire to the grassland is harming others until one knows the total system in which his act appears. "One picture is worth a thousand words," said an ancient Chinese; but it may take 10,000 words to validate it. It is as tempting to ecologists as it is to reformers in general to try to persuade others by way of the photographic shortcut. But the essence of an argument cannot be photographed: it must be presented rationally—in words.

That morality is system-sensitive escaped the attention of most codi-fiers of ethics in the past. "Thou shalt not . . ." is the form of traditional ethical directives which make no allowance for particular circumstances. The laws of our society follow the pattern of ancient ethics, and therefore are poorly suited to governing a complex, crowded, changeable world. Our epicyclic solution is to augment statutory law with administrative law. Since it is practically impossible to spell out all the conditions under which it is safe to burn trash in the backyard or to run an automobile with-out smog control, by law we delegate the details to bureaus. The result is administrative law, which is rightly feared for an ancient reason—*Quis custodiet ipsos custodes?*—"Who shall watch the watchers themselves?" John Adams said that we must have "a government of laws and not men." Bureau administrators, trying to evaluate the morality of acts in the total system, are singularly liable to corruption, producing a government by men, not laws.

Prohibition is easy to legislate (though not necessarily to enforce); but how do we legislate temperance? Experience indicates that it can be accom-plished best through the mediation of administrative law. We limit possi-bilities unnecessarily if we suppose that the sentiment of *Quis custodiet* denies us the use of administrative law. We should rather retain the phrase as a perpetual reminder of fearful dangers we cannot avoid. The great chal-lenge facing us now is to invent the corrective feedbacks that are needed to keep custodians honest. We must find ways to legitimate the needed authority of both the custodians and the corrective feedbacks.

Freedom to Breed Is Intolerable

The tragedy of the commons is involved in population problems in another way. In a world governed solely by the principle of "dog eat dog"—if indeed there ever was such a world—how many children a family had would not be a matter of public concern. Parents who bred too exuberantly would leave fewer descendants, not more, because they would be unable to care adequately for their children. David Lack and others have found that such a negative feedback demonstrably controls the fecundity of birds.[11] But men are not birds, and have not acted like them for millennia, at least.

If each human family were dependent only on its own resources; *if* the children of improvident parents starved to death; *if*, thus, overbreeding brought its own "punishment" to the germ line—*then* there would be no public interest in controlling the breeding of families. But our society is deeply committed to the welfare state,[12] and, hence, is confronted with another aspect of the tragedy of the commons.

In a welfare state, how shall we deal with the family, the religion, the race, or the class (or indeed any distinguishable and cohesive group) that adopts overbreeding as a policy to secure its own aggrandizement?[13] To couple the concept of freedom to breed with the belief that everyone born has an equal right to the commons is to lock the world into a tragic course of action.

Unfortunately this is just the course of action that is being pursued by the United Nations. In late 1967, some thirty nations agreed to the following:

> The Universal Declaration of Human Rights describes the family as the natural and fundamental unit of society. It follows that any choice and decision with regard to the size of the family must irrevocably rest with the family itself, and cannot be made by anyone else.[14]

It is painful to have to deny categorically the validity of this right; denying it, one feels as uncomfortable as a resident of Salem, Massachusetts, who denied the reality of witches in the seventeenth century. At the present time, in liberal quarters, something like a taboo acts to inhibit criticism of the United Nations. There is a feeling that the United Nations is "our last and best hope," that we shouldn't find fault with it; we shouldn't play into the hands of the archconservatives. However, let us not forget what Robert Louis Stevenson said: "The truth that is suppressed by friends is the readiest weapon of the enemy." If we love the truth we must openly deny the validity of the Universal Declaration of Human Rights, even though it is promoted by the United Nations. We should also join with Kingsley Davis[15] in attempting to get Planned Parenthood-World Population to see the error of its ways in embracing the same tragic ideal.

Conscience Is Self-Eliminating

It is a mistake to think that we can control the breeding of mankind in the long run by an appeal to conscience. Charles Galton Darwin made this point when he spoke on the centennial of the publication of his grandfather's great book. The argument is straightforward and Darwinian.

People vary. Confronted with appeals to limit breeding, some people will undoubtedly respond to the plea more than others. Those who have more children will produce a larger fraction of the next generation than those with more susceptible consciences. The difference will be accentuated, generation by generation.

In C. G. Darwin's words: "It may well be that it would take hundreds of generations for the progenitive instinct to develop in this way, but if it should do so, nature would have taken her revenge, and the variety *Homo contracipiens* would become extinct and would be replaced by the variety *Homo progenitivus*."[16]

The argument assumes that conscience or the desire for children (no matter which) is hereditary—but hereditary only in the most general formal sense. The result will be the same whether the attitude is transmitted through germ cells, or exosomatically, to use A. J. Lotka's term. (If one denies the latter possibility as well as the former, then what's the point of education?) The argument has here been stated in the context of the population problem, but it applies equally well to any instance in which society appeals to an individual exploiting a commons to restrain himself for the general good—by means of his conscience. To make such an appeal is to set up a selective system that works toward the elimination of conscience from the race.

Pathogenic Effects of Conscience

The long-term disadvantage of an appeal to conscience should be enough to condemn it; but [it] has serious short-term disadvantages as well. If we ask a man who is exploiting a commons to desist "in the name of conscience," what are we saying to him? What does he hear?—not only at the moment but also in the wee small hours of the night when, half asleep, he remembers not merely the words we used but also the nonverbal communication cues we gave him unawares? Sooner or later, consciously or subconsciously, he senses that he has received two communications, and that they are contradictory: (1) (the intended communication) "If you don't do as we ask, we will openly condemn you for not acting like a responsible citizen"; (2) (the unintended communication) "If you *do* behave as we ask, we will secretly condemn you for a simpleton who can be shamed into standing aside while the rest of us exploit the commons."

Everyman then is caught in what Bateson has called a "double bind." Bateson and his coworkers have made a plausible case for viewing the double bind as an important causative factor in the genesis of schizophrenia.[17] The double bind may not always be so damaging, but it always endangers the mental health of anyone to whom it is applied. "A bad conscience," said Nietzsche, "is a kind of illness."

To conjure up a conscience in others is tempting to anyone who wishes to extend his control beyond the legal limits. Leaders at the highest level succumb to this temptation. Has any president during the past generation failed to call on labor unions to moderate voluntarily their demands for higher wages, or to steel companies to honor voluntary guidelines on prices? I can recall none. The rhetoric used on such occasions is designed to produce feelings of guilt in noncooperators.

For centuries it was assumed without proof that guilt was a valuable, perhaps even an indispensable, ingredient of the civilized life. Now, in this post-Freudian world, we doubt it.

Paul Goodman speaks from the modern point of view when he says: "No good has ever come from feeling guilty, neither intelligence, policy, nor compassion. The guilty do not pay attention to the object but only to themselves, and not even to their own interests, which might make sense, but to their anxieties."[18]

One does not have to be a professional psychiatrist to see the consequences of anxiety. We in the Western world are just emerging from a dreadful two-centuries-long Dark Ages of Eros that was sustained partly by prohibition laws, but perhaps more effectively by the anxiety-generating mechanisms of education. Alex Comfort has told the story well in *The Anxiety Makers;*[19] it is not a pretty one.

Since proof is difficult, we may even concede that the results of anxiety may sometimes, from certain points of view, be desirable. The larger question we should ask is whether, as a matter of policy, we should ever encourage the use of a technique the tendency (if not the intention) of which is psychologically pathogenic. We hear much talk these days of responsible parenthood; the coupled words are incorporated into the titles of some organizations devoted to birth control. Some people have proposed massive propaganda campaigns to instill responsibility into the nation's (or the world's) breeders. But what is the meaning of the word *responsibility* in this context? Is it not merely a synonym for the word *conscience*? When we use the word *responsibility* in the absence of substantial sanctions, are we not trying to browbeat a free man in a commons into acting against his own interest? Responsibility is a verbal counterfeit for a substantial quid pro quo. It is an attempt to get something for nothing.

If the word *responsibility* is to be used at all, I suggest that it be in the sense Charles Frankel uses it.[20] "Responsibility," says this philosopher, "is the product of definite social arrangements." Notice that Frankel calls for social arrangements—not propaganda.

Mutual Coercion Mutually Agreed Upon

The social arrangements that produce responsibility are arrangements that create coercion, of some sort. Consider bank robbing. The man who takes money from a bank acts as if the bank were a commons. How do we prevent such action? Certainly not by trying to control his behavior solely by a verbal appeal to his sense of responsibility. Rather than rely on propaganda, we follow Frankel's lead and insist that a bank is not a commons; we seek the definite social arrangements that will keep it from becoming a commons. That we thereby infringe on the freedom of would-be robbers we neither deny nor regret.

The morality of bank robbing is particularly easy to understand because we accept complete prohibition of this activity. We are willing to say, "Thou shalt not rob banks," without providing for exceptions. But temperance also can be created by coercion. Taxing is a good coercive device. To keep downtown shoppers temperate in their use of parking space, we introduce parking meters for short periods, and traffic fines for longer ones. We need not actually forbid a citizen to park as long as he wants to; we need merely make it increasingly expensive for him to do so. Not prohibition, but carefully biased options are what we offer him. A Madison Avenue man might call this persuasion; I prefer the greater candor of the word *coercion*.

Coercion is a dirty word to most liberals now, but it need not forever be so. As with the four-letter words, its dirtiness can be cleansed away by exposure to the light, by saying it over and over without apology or embarrassment. To many, the word *coercion* implies arbitrary decisions of distant and irresponsible bureaucrats; but this is not a necessary part of its meaning. The only kind of coercion I recommend is mutual coercion, mutually agreed upon by the majority of the people affected.

To say that we mutually agree to coercion is not to say that we are required to enjoy it, or even to pretend we enjoy it. Who enjoys taxes? We all grumble about them. But we accept compulsory taxes because we recognize that voluntary taxes would favor the conscienceless. We institute and (grumblingly) support taxes and other coercive devices to escape the horror of the commons.

An alternative to the commons need not be perfectly just to be preferable. With real estate and other material goods, the alternative we have chosen is the institution of private property coupled with legal inheritance. Is this system perfectly just? As a genetically trained biologist I deny that it is. It seems to me that, if there are to be differences in individual inheritance, legal possession should be perfectly correlated with biological inheritance—that those who are biologically more fit to be the custodians of property and power should legally inherit more. But genetic recombination continually makes a mockery of the doctrine of "like father, like son" implicit in our laws of legal inheritance. An idiot can inherit millions, and a trust fund can keep his estate intact. We must admit that our legal system of private property plus inheritance is unjust—but we put up with it because we are not convinced, at the moment, that anyone has invented a better system. The alternative of the commons is too horrifying to contemplate. Injustice is preferable to total ruin.

It is one of the peculiarities of the warfare between reform and the status quo that it is thoughtlessly governed by a double standard. Whenever a reform measure is proposed it is often defeated when its opponents triumphantly discover a flaw in it. As Kingsley Davis has pointed out,[21] worshippers of the status quo sometimes imply that no reform is possible without unanimous agreement, an implication contrary to historical fact. As nearly as I can make out, automatic rejection of proposed reforms is based on one of two unconscious assumptions: (1) that the status quo is perfect; or (2) that the choice we face is between reform and no action, if the proposed reform is imperfect, we presumably should take no action at all, while we wait for a perfect proposal.

But we can never do nothing. That which we have done for thousands of years is also action. It also produces evils. Once we are aware that the status quo is action, we can then compare its discoverable advantages and disadvantages with the predicted advantages and disadvantages of the proposed reform, discounting as best we can for our lack of experience. On the basis of such a comparison, we can make a rational decision which will not involve the unworkable assumption that only perfect systems are tolerable.

Recognition of Necessity

Perhaps the simplest summary of this analysis of man's population problems is this: the commons, if justifiable at all, is justifiable only under conditions of low population density. As the human population has increased, the commons has had to be abandoned in one aspect after another.

First we abandoned the commons in food gathering, enclosing farmland and restricting pastures and hunting and fishing areas. These restrictions are still not complete throughout the world.

Somewhat later we saw that the commons as a place for waste disposal would also have to be abandoned. Restrictions on the disposal of domestic sewage are widely accepted in the Western world; we are still struggling to close the commons to pollution by automobiles, factories, insecticide sprayers, fertilizing operations, and atomic energy installations.

In a still more embryonic state is our recognition of the evils of the commons in matters of pleasure. There is almost no restriction on the propagation of sound waves in the public medium. The shopping public is assaulted with mindless music, without its consent. Our government is paying out billions of dollars to create a supersonic transport which will disturb 50,000 people for every one person who is whisked from coast to coast three hours faster. Advertisers muddy the airwaves of radio and television and pollute the view of travelers. We are a long way from outlawing the commons in matters of pleasure. Is this because our Puritan inheritance makes us view pleasure as something of a sin, and pain (that is, the pollution of advertising) as the sign of virtue?

Every new enclosure of the commons involves the infringement of somebody's personal liberty. Infringements made in the distant past are accepted because no contemporary complains of a loss. It is the newly proposed infringements that we vigorously oppose; cries of "rights" and "freedom" fill the air. But what does "freedom" mean? When men mutually agreed to pass laws against robbing, mankind became more free, not less so. Individuals locked into the logic of the commons are free only to bring on universal ruin; once they see the necessity of mutual coercion, they become free to pursue other goals. I believe it was Hegel who said, "Freedom is the recognition of necessity."

The most important aspect of necessity that we must now recognize is the necessity of abandoning the commons in breeding. No technical solution can rescue us from the misery of overpopulation. Freedom to breed will bring ruin to all. At the moment, to avoid hard decisions many of us are tempted to propagandize for conscience and responsible parenthood. The temptation must be resisted, because an appeal to independently acting consciences selects for the disappearance of all conscience in the long run, and an increase in anxiety in the short.

The only way we can preserve and nurture other and more precious freedoms is by relinquishing the freedom to breed, and that very soon. "Freedom is the recognition of necessity"—and it is the role of education to reveal to all the necessity of abandoning the freedom to breed. Only so, can we put an end to this aspect of the tragedy of the commons.

Notes

1. J. B. Wiesner and H. F. York, *Sci. Amer.* 211 (No. 4), 27 (1964).
2. G. Hardin, *J. Hered.* 50, 68 (1959); S. von Hoerner, *Science* 137, 18 (1962).
3. J. von Neumann and O. Morgenstern, *Theory of Games and Economic Behavior* (Princeton Univ. Press, Princeton, N.J., 1944), p. 11.
4. J. H. Fremlin, *New Sci.*, No. 415 (1964), p. 285.
5. A. Smith, *The Wealth of Nations* (Modern Library, New York, 1937), p. 423.
6. W. F. Lloyd, *Two Lectures on the Checks to Population* (Oxford Univ. Press, Oxford, England, 1833), reprinted (in part) in *Population, Evolution, and Birth Control,* G. Hardin, ed. (Freeman, San Francisco, 1964), p. 37.
7. A. N. Whitehead, *Science and The Modern World* (Mentor, New York, 1948), p. 17.
8. G. Hardin, ed. *Population, Evolution, and Birth Control* (Freeman, San Francisco, 1964), p. 56.
9. S. McVay, *Sci. Amer.* 216 (No. 8), 13 (1966).
10. J. Fletcher, *Situation Ethics* (Westminster, Philadelphia, 1966).
11. D. Lack, *The Natural Regulation of Animal Numbers* (Clarendon Press, Oxford, 1954).
12. H. Girvetz, *From Wealth to Welfare* (Stanford Univ. Press, Stanford, Calif., 1950).
13. G. Hardin, *Perspec. Biol. Med. 6,* 366 (1963).
14. U Thant, *Int. Planned Parenthood News,* No. 168 (February 1968), p. 3.
15. K. Davis, *Science* 158, 730 (1967).
16. S. Tax, ed., *Evolution After Darwin* (Univ. of Chicago Press, Chicago, 1960), vol. 2, p. 469.
17. G. Bateson, D. D. Jackson, J. Haley, J. Weakland, *Behav. Sci.* 1, 251 (1956).
18. P. Goodman, *New York Rev. Books* 10 (8), 22 (23 May 1968).
19. A. Comfort, *The Anxiety Makers* (Nelson, London, 1967).
20. C. Frankel, *The Case for Modern Man* (Harper, New York, 1955), p. 203.
21. J. D. Roslansky, *Genetics and the Future of Man* (Appleton-Century-Crofts, New York, 1966), p. 177.

Content Questions

1. What arguments does Hardin use to claim that the world's optimum population size cannot be the same as the maximum population? (149–150)

2. According to Hardin, what kinds of criteria can apply in comparing goods, both in nature and in deliberate human assessments, given the premise that goods are incommensurable? (150)

3. Why does Hardin characterize the predicament of using the commons beyond its carrying capacity as a "tragedy," rather than a "problem"? (151)

4. What distinction is Hardin making about private property when he claims that "the tragedy of the commons as a food basket is averted by private property," but that "our particular concept of private property, which deters us from exhausting the positive resources of the earth, favors pollution"? (153–154)

5. By what argument does Hardin show that an appeal to conscience in the matter of population control will lead to a "self-eliminating" result? (156–157)

6. What arguments does Hardin make to show that the population problem is in the class of "no technical solution" problems? (148, 162)

Application Questions

1. What is the analogy between the example of the overuse of the commons and the problem of population growth? How far does the analogy hold?

2. Why does Hardin say that Adam Smith's idea of the invisible hand "has ever since interfered with positive action based on rational analysis"? What arguments would support "our present policy of laissez faire in reproduction" that Hardin calls into question? (151)

3. Does Hardin mean for us to think of the measures proposed by organizations such as Planned Parenthood as futile attempts to find a technical solution (for example, birth control) to a problem that can have no such solution?

Discussion Questions

1. What does Hardin mean when he states that "it is when the hidden decisions are made explicit that the arguments begin" about the comparison of goods? (150)

2. Is Hardin saying that the freedom of the commons consists of completely unrestrained individual behavior by each of the users? Is this consistent with his claim that "social stability" precedes the accelerated use of the commons? (151) Is self-interest the only motivation in how the commons is used?

3. What does Hardin mean when he says that the morality of an act depends on *"the state of the system at the time it is performed"*? In the example of the bison hunter, is it convincing that the hunter "was not in any important sense being wasteful"? (154)

4. Does commitment to the welfare state inevitably support the freedom to breed without limit?

5. If the education of each generation is possible, would appealing to conscience or a sense of responsibility concerning breeding inevitably result in the elimination of conscientious individuals?

6. What does Hardin mean when he says that, "as a genetically trained biologist," he denies that one of our chosen alternatives to the commons—private property plus inheritance—is perfectly just? (160) How can scientific knowledge establish whether a social arrangement is or is not just?

7. Can a rational decision—such as the "mutual coercion" Hardin suggests with regard to the population problem—be at the same time a form of injustice? (159–160)

8. How does Hegel's remark that "freedom is the recognition of necessity" apply to the population problem? Are there ways in which the surrender of one kind of freedom results in another freedom?

Barry Commoner

When Barry Commoner (1917–) wrote *The Closing Circle: Nature, Man, and Technology* (1971), from which the following selection is taken, he had already been active in environmental politics for almost two decades. Born in Brooklyn, Commoner received his Ph.D. from Harvard University in 1941 and joined the faculty of Washington University in St. Louis, Missouri, in 1947, teaching there until 1981. Building upon his original research on the physicochemical basis of biological processes, Commoner became concerned in the early 1950s with the worldwide infiltration of strontium 90—a byproduct of open-air nuclear tests—into the living tissues of plants and animals. In 1958, along with other scientists, he founded the Greater St. Louis Citizens' Committee for Nuclear Information. This committee pioneered the scientists' information movement, which is devoted to educating the public about environmental problems.

In his acclaimed book *Science and Survival* (1966), Commoner wrote, "The separation of the laws of nature among the different sciences is a human conceit; nature itself is an integrated whole." From a platform of solid scientific research, writing, speaking, and membership in such organizations as the Scientists' Institute for Public Information, Commoner became one of the most articulate advocates for safeguarding the environment against technologies and economic systems that disregard this wholeness. In 1980, he was the Citizens' Party's U.S. presidential candidate in a campaign emphasizing the social cost of environmental problems. Commoner now continues his research at the Center for Biology of Natural Systems at Queens College, CUNY, in the Critical Genetics Project, which provides the general public with information about genetic engineering and biotechnology.

The Closing Circle

(selection)

Any living thing that hopes to live on the earth must fit into the ecosphere or perish. The environmental crisis is a sign that the finely sculptured fit between life and its surroundings has begun to corrode. As the links between one living thing and another, and between all of them and their surroundings, begin to break down, the dynamic interactions that sustain the whole have begun to falter and, in some places, stop.

Why, after millions of years of harmonious coexistence, have the relationships between living things and their earthly surroundings begun to collapse? Where did the fabric of the ecosphere begin to unravel? How far will the process go? How can we stop it and restore the broken links?

Understanding the ecosphere comes hard because, to the modern mind, it is a curiously foreign place. We have become accustomed to think of separate, singular events, each dependent upon a unique, singular cause. But in the ecosphere every effect is also a cause: an animal's waste becomes food for soil bacteria; what bacteria excrete nourishes plants; animals eat the plants. Such ecological cycles are hard to fit into human experience in the age of technology, where machine A always yields product B, and product

This selection is taken from chapter 1, "The Environmental Crisis," chapter 9, "The Technological Flaw," and chapter 10, "The Social Issues."

B, once used, is cast away, having no further meaning for the machine, the product, or the user.

Here is the first great fault in the life of man in the ecosphere. We have broken out of the circle of life, converting its endless cycles into man-made, linear events: oil is taken from the ground, distilled into fuel, burned in an engine, converted thereby into noxious fumes, which are emitted into the air. At the end of the line is smog. Other man-made breaks in the ecosphere's cycles spew out toxic chemicals, sewage, heaps of rubbish—testimony to our power to tear the ecological fabric that has, for millions of years, sustained the planet's life.

Suddenly we have discovered what we should have known long before: that the ecosphere sustains people and everything that they do; that anything that fails to fit into the ecosphere is a threat to its finely balanced cycles; that wastes are not only unpleasant, not only toxic, but, more meaningfully, evidence that the ecosphere is being driven toward collapse.

If we are to survive, we must understand *why* this collapse now threatens. Here, the issues become far more complex than even the ecosphere. Our assaults on the ecosystem are so powerful, so numerous, so finely interconnected, that although the damage they do is clear, it is very difficult to discover how it was done. By which weapon? In whose hand? Are we driving the ecosphere to destruction simply by our growing numbers? By our greedy accumulation of wealth? Or are the machines which we have built to gain this wealth—the magnificent technology that now feeds us out of neat packages, that clothes us in man-made fibers, that surrounds us with new chemical creations—at fault?

~ ~ ~

We know that *something* went wrong in the country after World War II, for most of our serious pollution problems either began in the postwar years or have greatly worsened since then. While two factors frequently blamed for the environmental crisis, population and affluence, have intensified in that time, these increases are much too small to account for the 200 to 2,000 percent rise in pollution levels since 1946. The product of these two factors, which represents the total output of goods (total production equals population times production per capita), is also insufficient to account for the intensification of pollution. Total production—as measured by GNP—has increased by 126 percent since 1946, while most pollution levels have risen by at least several times that rate. Something else besides growth in population and affluence must be deeply involved in the environmental crisis.

"Economic growth" is a popular whipping boy in certain ecological circles. As indicated earlier, there are good theoretical grounds why economic growth *can* lead to pollution. The rate of exploitation of the ecosystem, which generates economic growth, cannot increase indefinitely without overdriving the system and pushing it to the point of collapse. However, this theoretical relationship does not mean that any increase in economic activity automatically means more pollution. What happens to the environment depends on *how* the growth is achieved. During the nineteenth century the nation's economic growth was in part sustained by rapacious lumbering, which denuded whole hillsides and eroded the soil. On the other hand, the economic growth that in the 1930s began to lift the United States out of the Great Depression was enhanced by an ecologically sound measure, the soil conservation program. This program helped to restore the fertility of the depleted soil and thereby contributed to economic growth. Such ecologically sound economic growth not only avoids environmental deterioration, but can even reverse it. For example, improved conservation of pasturelands, which has been economically beneficial in the western part of the Missouri River drainage basin, seems to have reduced the level of nitrate pollution in that stretch of the river. In contrast, further downstream, in Nebraska, agricultural growth has been achieved counterecologically by intensifying the use of fertilizer, which leads to serious nitrate pollution problems.

In other words, the fact that the economy has grown—that GNP has increased—tells us very little about the possible environmental consequences. For that, we need to know *how* the economy has grown.

The growth of the United States economy is recorded in elaborate detail in a variety of government statistics—huge volumes tabulating the amounts of various goods produced annually, the expenditures involved, the value of the goods sold, and so forth. Although these endless columns of figures are rather intimidating, there are some useful ways to extract meaningful facts from them. In particular, it is helpful to compute the rate of growth of each productive activity, a procedure that nowadays can be accomplished by committing the tables of numbers to an appropriately programmed computer. In order to compare one kind of economic activity with another, it is useful to arrange the computer to yield a figure for the percentage increase, or decrease, in production or consumption.

Not long ago, two of my colleagues and I went through the statistical tables and selected from them the data for several hundred items, which together represent a major and representative part of overall United States agricultural and industrial production. For each item, the average annual percentage change in production or consumption was computed for the years since 1946, or since the earliest date for which the statistics were available. Then we computed the overall change for the entire twenty-five-year period—a twenty-five-year growth rate. When this list is rearranged in decreasing order of growth rate, a picture of *how* the United States economy has grown since World War II begins to emerge.

The winner of this economic sweepstakes, with the highest postwar growth rate, is the production of nonreturnable soda bottles, which has increased about 53,000 percent in that time. The loser, ironically, is the horse; work animal horsepower has declined by 87 percent of its original postwar value. The runners-up are an interesting but seemingly mixed bag. In second place is production of synthetic fibers, up 5,980 percent; third is mercury used for chlorine production, up 3,930 percent; succeeding places are held as follows: mercury used in mildew-resistant paint, up 3,120 percent; air conditioner compressor units, up 2,850 percent; plastics, up 1,960 percent; fertilizer nitrogen, up 1,050 percent; electric housewares (such as can openers and corn poppers), up 1,040 percent; synthetic organic chemicals, up 950 percent; aluminum, up 680 percent; chlorine gas, up 600 percent; electric power, up 530 percent; pesticides, up 390 percent; wood pulp, up 313 percent; truck freight, up 222 percent; consumer electronics (television sets, tape recorders), up 217 percent; motor fuel consumption, up 190 percent; cement, up 150 percent.

Then there is a group of productive activities that, as indicated earlier, have grown at about the pace of the population (i.e., up about 42 percent): food production and consumption, total production of textiles and clothes, household utilities, and steel, copper, and other basic metals.

Finally, there are the losers, which increase more slowly than the population or actually shrink in total production: railroad freight, up 17 percent; lumber, down 1 percent; cotton fiber, down 7 percent; returnable beer bottles, down 36 percent; wool, down 42 percent; soap, down 76 percent; and, at the end of the line, work animal horsepower, down 87 percent.

What emerges from all these data is striking evidence that while production for most basic needs—food, clothing, housing—has just about kept up with the 40 to 50 percent or so increase in population (that is, production *per capita* has been essentially constant), the *kinds* of goods produced to meet these needs have changed drastically. New production technologies have displaced old ones. Soap powder has been displaced by synthetic detergents; natural fibers (cotton and wool) have been displaced by synthetic ones; steel and lumber have been displaced by aluminum, plastics, and concrete; railroad freight has been displaced by truck freight; returnable bottles have been displaced by nonreturnable ones. On the road, the low-powered automobile engines of the 1920s and 1930s have been displaced by high-powered ones. On the farm, while per capita production has remained about constant, the amount of harvested acreage has decreased; in effect, fertilizer has displaced land. Older methods of insect control have been displaced by synthetic insecticides, such as DDT, and for controlling weeds the cultivator has been displaced by the herbicide spray. Range feeding of livestock has been displaced by feedlots.

In each of these cases, what has changed drastically is the technology of production rather than overall output of the economic good. Of course, part of the economic growth in the United States since 1946 has been based on some newly introduced goods: air conditioners, television sets, tape recorders, and snowmobiles, all of which have increased absolutely without displacing an older product.

Distilled in this way, the mass of production statistics begins to form a meaningful pattern. In general, the growth of the United States economy since 1946 has had a surprisingly small effect on the degree to which individual needs for basic economic goods have been met. That statistical fiction, the "average American," now consumes, each year, about as many calories, protein, and other foods (although somewhat less of vitamins); uses about the same amount of clothes and cleaners; occupies about the same amount of newly constructed housing; requires about as much freight; and drinks about the same amount of beer (twenty-six gallons per capita!) as he did in 1946. However, his food is now grown on less land with much more fertilizer and pesticides than before; his clothes are more likely to be made of synthetic fibers than of cotton or wool; he launders with synthetic detergents rather than soap; he lives and works in buildings that depend more heavily on aluminum, concrete, and plastic than on steel and lumber; the goods he uses are increasingly shipped by truck rather than rail; he drinks beer out of nonreturnable bottles or cans rather than out of returnable bottles or at the tavern bar. He is more likely to live and work in air-conditioned surroundings than before. He also drives about twice as far as he did in 1946, in a heavier car, on synthetic rather than natural rubber tires, using more gasoline per mile, containing more tetraethyl lead, fed into an engine of increased horsepower and compression ratio.

These primary changes have led to others. To provide the raw materials needed for the new synthetic fibers, pesticides, detergents, plastics, and rubber, the production of synthetic organic chemicals has also grown very rapidly. The synthesis of organic chemicals uses a good deal of chlorine. Result: chlorine production has increased sharply. To make chlorine, an electric current is passed through a salt solution by way of a mercury electrode. Consequently, mercury consumption for this purpose has increased—by 3,930 percent in the twenty-five-year postwar period. Chemical products, along with cement for concrete and aluminum (also winners in the growth race), use rather large amounts of electric power. Not surprisingly then, that item, too, has increased considerably since 1946.

All this reminds us of what we have already been told by advertising—which incidentally has *also* grown; for example, the use of newsprint for advertising has grown faster than its use for news—that we are blessed with an economy based on very modern technologies. What the advertisements do not tell us—as we are urged to buy synthetic shirts and detergents, aluminum furniture, beer in no-return bottles, and Detroit's latest creation—is that *all this "progress" has greatly increased the impact on the environment.*

This pattern of economic growth is the major reason for the environmental crisis. A good deal of the mystery and confusion about the sudden emergence of the environmental crisis can be removed by pinpointing, pollutant by pollutant, how the postwar technological transformation of the United States economy has produced not only the much-heralded 126 percent rise in GNP, but also, at a rate about ten times faster than the growth of GNP, the rising levels of environmental pollution.

What is needed, and what—it is to be hoped—will be worked out before long, is an ecological analysis of every major aspect of the production, use, and disposition of goods. What is needed is a kind of "ecological impact inventory" for each productive activity, which will enable us to attach a sort of pollution price tag to each product. We would then know, for example, for each pound of detergent: how much air pollution is generated by the electric power and fuel burned to manufacture its chemical ingredients; how much water pollution is due to the mercury "loss" by the factory in the course of manufacturing the chlorine needed to produce it; the water pollution due to the detergent and phosphate entering sewage systems; the ecological effect of fluoride and arsenic (which may contaminate the phosphate), and of mercury, which might contaminate any alkali used to compound the detergent. Such pollution price tags are needed for all major products if we are to judge their relative *social* value. The foregoing account shows how far we are from this goal, and once again reminds us how blind we are about the environmental effects of modern technology.

It is useful, at this point, to return to a question asked earlier: what are the relative effects of the three factors that might be expected to influence the intensity of environmental pollution—population size, degree of affluence, and the tendency of the productive technology to pollute? A rather simple mathematical relationship connects the amount of pollutant emitted into the environment to these factors: pollutant emitted is equal to the product of the three factors—population times the amount of a given economic good per capita times output of pollutant per unit of the economic good produced. In the United States, all three factors have changed since 1946. By comparing these changes with the concurrent increase in total pollutant output, it is possible to assign to each of the three factors the fraction of the overall increase in pollutant output for which it is responsible. When this computation is carried out for the economic goods considered above—agricultural production (pollutant outputs: nitrogen fertilizer, pesticides), cleaners (pollutant output: phosphate), passenger car travel (pollutant outputs: lead and nitrogen oxides), and beer consumption (pollutant output: beer bottles)—a rather clear picture emerges.

The increase in population accounts for from 12 to 20 percent of the various increases in total pollutant output since 1946. The affluence factor (i.e., amount of economic good per capita), accounts for from 1 to 5 percent of the total increase in pollutant output, except in the case of passenger travel, where the contribution rises to about 40 percent of the total. This reflects a considerable increase in vehicle miles traveled per capita. However, as already pointed out, a good deal of this increase does not reflect improved welfare, but rather the unfortunate need for increased travel incident upon the decay of the inner cities and the growth of suburbs.

The technology factor—that is, the increased output of pollutants per unit production resulting from the introduction of new productive technologies since 1946—accounts for about 95 percent of the total output of pollutants, except in the case of passenger travel, where it accounts for about 40 percent of the total.

The foregoing conclusions are based on those instances in which quantitative data on pollution output of various productive activities are available. However, from the qualitative evidence on other pollution problems discussed earlier, it is already apparent that they follow a similar pattern: most of the sharp increase in pollution levels is due not so much to population or affluence as to changes in productive technology.

The overall evidence seems clear. The chief reason for the environmental crisis that has engulfed the United States in recent years is the sweeping transformation of productive technology since World War II. The economy has grown enough to give the United States population about the same amount of basic goods, per capita, as it did in 1946. However, productive technologies with intense impacts on the environment have displaced less destructive ones. The environmental crisis is the inevitable result of this counterecological pattern of growth.

⌒ ⌒ ⌒

If technology is indeed to blame for the environmental crisis, it might be wise to discover wherein its "inventive genius" has failed us—and to correct that flaw—before entrusting our future survival to technology's faith in itself. It would be prudent, then, to examine the past record of technological efforts and to discover why they have failed so often in the environment.

The technology of sewage treatment is a good example. The basic problem has already been described earlier. When sewage, which contains considerable organic matter, is dumped into a river or lake, it generates an inordinate demand for oxygen, which is consumed as the bacteria of decay convert organic matter to inorganic breakdown products. As a result, this practice has commonly depleted the oxygen supply of surface waters, killing off the bacteria of decay and thereby halting the aquatic cycle of self-purification. Enter the sanitation technologist. First, the technological problem is defined: how can the oxygen demand of sewage be reduced before it enters surface waters? Then, the means are designed: the bacteria of decay are domesticated by establishing them in a treatment plant, artificially supplied with sufficient oxygen to accommodate the entering organic matter. What is released from the treatment plant is largely the inorganic residue of bacterial action. Since these have no oxygen demand, the problem, as stated, has been solved; modern sewage treatment technology has been created.

This, briefly, is the technological scenario—a story, which, in confirmation of the technological faith, seems to end happily. Unfortunately, offstage, in nature's rivers and streams, the scenario does not work out so well. The treated sewage effluents are now rich in the inorganic residues of decay—carbon dioxide, nitrate, and phosphate—which in the natural cycle support the growth of algae. Now heavily fertilized, the algae bloom furiously, soon die, releasing organic matter, which regenerates the oxygen demand that sewage technology had removed. The technologist's success is undone. The reason for this failure is clear: the technologist defined his problem too narrowly, taking into his field of vision only one segment of what in nature is an endless cycle that will collapse if stressed *anywhere*. This same fault lies behind every ecological failure of modern technology: attention to a single facet of what in nature is a complex whole.

These pollution problems arise not out of some minor inadequacies in the new technologies, but because of their very success in accomplishing their designed aims. A modern sewage treatment plant causes algal overgrowths and resultant pollution *because* it produces, as it is designed to do, so much plant nutrient in its effluent. Modern, highly concentrated, nitrogen fertilizers result in the drainage of nitrate pollutants into streams and lakes just *because* they succeed in the aim of raising the nutrient level of the soil. The modern high-compression gasoline engine contributes to smog and nitrate pollution *because* it successfully meets its design criterion—the development of a high level of power. Modern synthetic insecticides kill birds, fish, and useful insects just *because* they are successfully absorbed by insects and kill them, as they are intended to do. Plastics clutter the landscape *because* they are unnatural, synthetic substances designed to resist degradation—precisely the properties that are the basis of their technological value.

Here we can begin to sense an explanation of the contradiction between the supposed infallibility of technology and its evident failures in the environment. The new technologies were, in fact, *not* failures—when tested against their stated aims. Thus the stated aim of nuclear weapons technology—to explode bombs—has been brilliantly achieved; thousands of Japanese graves and the radioactivity of our bones, after all, testify to that. In the same sense, a sewage treatment plant is a success, for it does, after all, achieve its goal of reducing the biological oxygen demand of sewage. Similarly, nitrogen fertilizer does accomplish what the agronomist set out to achieve—an increased crop yield. Synthetic pesticides do kill insects, detergents do wash clothes, and plastics do effectively contain beer cans.

It becomes clear, then, that we are concerned not with some fault in technology, which is only coincident to its value, but with a failure that derives from its basic *success* in industrial and agricultural production. If the ecological failure of modern technology is due to its success in accomplishing what it sets out to do, then the fault lies in its *aims.*

Why, then, should modern technology be guided by aims that are so consistently off the ecological mark? Again we can turn to Galbraith for help. Here is Galbraith's definition of technology, especially as it relates to production:

> Technology means the systematic application of scientific or other organized knowledge to practical tasks. *Its most important consequence, at least for purpose of economics, is in forcing the division and subdivision of any such task into its component parts. Thus, and only thus, can organized knowledge be brought to bear on performance.* Specifically, there is no way that organized knowledge can be brought to bear on the production of an automobile as a whole or even on the manufacture of a body or chassis. It can only be applied if the task is so subdivided that it begins to be coterminous with some established area of scientific or engineering knowledge. Though metallurgical knowledge cannot be applied to the manufacture of the whole vehicle, it can be used in the design of the cooling system or the engine block. While knowledge of mechanical engineering cannot be brought to bear on the manufacture of the vehicle, it can be applied to the machining of the crankshaft. While chemistry cannot be applied to the composition of the car as a whole, it can be used to decide on the composition of the finish or trim. . . . Nearly all of the consequences of technology, and much of the shape of modern industry, derive from this need to divide and subdivide tasks.

Now the reason for the ecological failure of technology becomes clear: unlike the automobile, the ecosystem cannot be subdivided into manageable parts, for its properties reside in the whole, in the connections between the parts. A process that insists on dealing only with the separated parts is bound to fail. Galbraith's description of how technology is applied to the production of an automobile—fragment by fragment—is precisely how it has been used in the series of blunders that have generated the environmental crisis. It explains why technology can design a useful fertilizer, a powerful automobile, or an efficient nuclear bomb. But since technology, as presently construed, cannot cope with the *whole* system on which the fertilizer, the automobile, or the nuclear bomb intrudes, disastrous ecological surprises—water pollution, smog, and global radioactive fallout—are inevitable. Ecological failure is apparently a necessary consequence of the nature of modern technology, as Galbraith defines it.

Add to this the faith "that problems have solutions before there is knowledge of how they are to be solved" and it becomes clear why in the age of technology we have acted blindly, massively, on nature *before* we were aware of the consequences. In popular imagery the technologist is often seen as a modern wizard, a kind of scientific sorcerer. It now appears that he is less sorcerer than sorcerer's apprentice.

Ecological survival does not mean the abandonment of technology. Rather, it requires that technology be derived from a scientific analysis that is appropriate to the natural world on which technology intrudes.

This suggests that behind the ecological failure of modern technology lies a corresponding failure in its scientific base. For, to cite Galbraith once more, the fragmented nature of technology is dictated by the need to make the technological task "coterminous with some established area of scientific or engineering knowledge." The fault in technology, then, appears to derive from the fragmented nature of its scientific base.

There is, indeed, a specific fault in our system of science, and in the resultant understanding of the natural world, which, I believe, helps to explain the ecological failure of technology. This fault is reductionism, the view that effective understanding of a complex system can be achieved by investigating the properties of its isolated parts. The reductionist methodology, which is so characteristic of much of modern research, is not an effective means of analyzing the vast natural systems that are threatened by degradation. For example, water pollutants stress a total ecological web and its numerous organisms; the effects on the whole natural system are not adequately described by laboratory studies of pure cultures of separate organisms. The leading exponent of the opposite approach, *holism*, is René Dubos of Rockefeller University, who has done such excellent work in analyzing the interdependence between man and nature.

The reductionist approach has had a particularly adverse effect on what we know about the biological systems that are at risk in the environment. Biology has become a flourishing and well-supported science in the United States; it is producing a wealth of new knowledge and is training many scientists skilled in its new methodology. But modern biological research is now dominated by the conviction that the most fruitful way to understand life is to discover a specific molecular event that can be identified as "the mechanism" of a particular biological process. The complexities of soil biology or the delicate balance of the nitrogen cycle in a river, which are not reducible to simple molecular mechanisms, are now often regarded as uninteresting relics of some ancient craft. In the pure glow of molecular biology, studying the biology of sewage is a dull and distasteful exercise hardly worth the attention of a "modern" biologist.

This helps to explain a curious paradox in the status of environmental science in the United States. Since World War II there has been an unprecedented growth of biological research; yet we remain astonishingly ignorant of the profound changes that, during that same period, have occurred in our own biological surroundings. For example, we lack historical data regarding the levels of lead, mercury, cadmium, and other metallic pollutants in the soil, water, and air; national measurements of smog and other urban air pollutants began only recently and are still inadequate. In the absence of such baseline data, it is difficult to interpret the present pollution levels. I once asked a government research official to explain this deficiency. The answer was forthright: proposals for research to measure the levels of environmental pollutants were nearly always rejected under the rubric "pedestrian research." After all, what could such data contribute to "fundamental" biological knowledge, which was always construed in terms of molecular theories exclusively derived from test-tube data? Fortunately, in the last few years, in direct response to the environmental crisis, the National Science Foundation has taken the leadership to institute a wholly new kind of program of research support: Research Applied to National

Needs. That we must now develop a major new research program on "national needs," is tragic evidence that previous programs have failed to meet them.

Nor is reductionism limited to biology; it is, rather, the dominant viewpoint of modern science as a whole. It often leads sociologists to become psychologists, psychologists to become physiologists, physiologists to become cellular biologists, and turns cellular biologists into chemists, chemists into physicists, and physicists into mathematicians. Reductionism tends to isolate scientific disciplines from each other, and all of them from the real world. In each case, the discipline appears to be moving away from observation of the natural, real object: biologists tend to study not the natural living organism, but cells and ultimately molecules isolated from them. One result of this approach is that communication among the disciplines becomes difficult unless the subject is reduced to the simplest common denominator; the biologist is unable to communicate with the chemist unless he reduces his analytical biological problem to a molecular one. But the problem is then likely to become irrelevant to the real world. The failure of communication among such specialized basic sciences is an important source of difficulty in understanding environmental problems. For example, the chemists who developed the processes for synthesizing branched chain detergents might have been forewarned about the ultimate failure of their products if they had been in close contact with biochemists—who already knew that such branched molecules tend to resist enzymatic attack and would therefore persist in disposal systems.

Reductionism has also tended to isolate scientific disciplines from the problems that affect the human condition. Such problems, environmental degradation for example, involve inherently complex systems. Life, as we live it, is not encompassed by a single academic discipline. Real problems that touch our lives and impinge on what we value rarely fit into the neat categories of the college catalog, such as physical chemistry, nuclear physics, or molecular biology.

For example, to encompass in our minds the terrifying deterioration of our cities, we need to know not only the principles of economics, architecture, and social planning, but also the physics and chemistry of the air, the biology of water systems, and the ecology of the domestic rat and the cockroach. In a word, we need to understand science and technology that is *relevant* to the human condition.

179

However, we in the scientific community have been brought up in a different tradition. We have a justified pride in our intellectual independence and know—for we often have to battle to maintain it—how essential this independence is to the search for truth. But scientists may sometimes tend to translate intellectual independence into a kind of mandatory avoidance of all problems that do not arise in their own minds—an approach that may cut them off from the real and urgent needs of society, and often from their students as well. As a result, science has become too isolated from the real problems of the world and a poor instrument for understanding the threats to its survival.

In sum, we can trace the origin of the environmental crisis through the following sequence. Environmental degradation largely results from the introduction of new industrial and agricultural production technologies. These technologies are ecologically faulty because they are designed to solve singular, separate problems and fail to take into account the inevitable "side effects" that arise because, in nature, no part is isolated from the whole ecological fabric. In turn, the fragmented design of technology reflects its scientific foundation, for science is divided into disciplines that are largely governed by the notion that complex systems can be understood only if they are first broken into their separate component parts. This reductionist bias has also tended to shield basic science from a concern for real-life problems, such as environmental degradation.

The isolation of science from such practical problems has another unfortunate consequence. Most people are less interested in the discipline of science than they are in its practical effects on their daily lives. And the separation between science and the problems that concern people has tended to limit what most people know about the scientific background of environmental issues. Yet such *public* knowledge is essential to the solution of every environmental problem. For these depend not only on scientific data, but ultimately on a public judgment which balances the benefits to be gained from a particular technology against the associated environmental hazards.

In effect, the citizen faces an important question about modern technology: does it pay? Whether we ask this in the direct language of profit and loss or in the more abstract language of social welfare, the question is crucial. Sooner or later, every human endeavor—if it is to continue—must pass this simple test: is it worth what it costs?

However, no scientific principle can guide the choice between some number of kilowatt-hours of electric power and some number of cases of thyroid cancer, or between some number of bushels of corn and some number of cases of infant methemoglobinemia. These are *value* judgments; they are determined not by scientific principle, but by the value that we place on economic advantage and on human life or by our belief in the wisdom of committing the nation to mass transportation or to biological warfare. These are matters of morality, of social and political judgment. In a democracy they belong not in the hands of "experts," but in the hands of the people and their elected representatives.

The environmental crisis is the legacy of our unwitting assault on the natural systems that support us. It represents hidden costs that are mounting toward catastrophe. If it is to be resolved, these costs must be made explicit and balanced against the benefits of technology in open, public debate. But this debate will not come easily. For the public has little access to the necessary scientific data. Much of the needed information has been, and remains, wrapped in government secrecy. Unearthing the needed information and disseminating it to the public is, I believe, the unique responsibility of the scientific community. For to exercise its right of conscience, the public must have the relevant scientific facts in understandable terms. As the custodians of this knowledge, we in the scientific community owe it to our fellow citizens to help inform them about the crisis in the environment.

Content Questions

1. Why does Commoner say that the ecosphere is a "curiously foreign place" to the modern mind? (167)

2. What does Commoner mean when he says that we have converted "endless cycles into man-made, linear events"? (168)

3. Why are the increases in population and affluence not adequate in accounting for increases in pollution levels since 1946, according to Commoner? (168)

4. Why does Commoner claim that "what happens to the environment depends on *how* the growth is achieved"? (169)

5. In Commoner's statistical analysis of the increase in various goods produced, why is it significant that "food production and consumption, total production of textiles and clothes, household utilities, and steel, copper, and other basic metals" have grown at about the same pace as the population? (170)

6. What changes in the technology of production does Commoner claim are responsible for the increase in pollution levels? (171)

7. What does Commoner mean when he says that "the technologist defined his problem too narrowly"? (175)

8. Why does Commoner claim that pollution problems were not the result of the failure of new technologies, but rather the result of their success? (175)

9. What does Commoner think are the aims of modern technology? (176)

10. What does Commoner mean by "reductionism"? (177)

11. Why does Commoner say that "the failure of communication among such specialized basic sciences is an important source of difficulty in understanding environmental problems"? (179)

Application Questions

1. When Commoner performed the statistical analysis of production activity detailed in *The Closing Circle,* he had available to him data from 1946 through the late 1960s. Outline how you could make similar comparisons for the subsequent period, from 1970 through 2000. Determine how absolute production and pollutants per unit of production have changed over this thirty-year period. Also determine if the types of pollutants have changed.

2. One of the environmental problems that has become prominent since Commoner wrote *The Closing Circle* is global warming. What biophysical systems would you analyze to establish the reality of this phenomenon (not all scientists recognize it), and to confirm that it is the result of human activity? What technological "successes," in Commoner's terms, might account for global warming?

Discussion Questions

1. What does Commoner mean when he refers to something fitting into the ecosphere?

2. How can we judge the relative social value of products in relation to the cost to be paid in increased environmental impact?

3. Why does Commoner claim that there are properties and connections between the parts of the ecosystem that cannot be revealed through subdivision into "manageable parts"? (177)

4. Is technology always an intrusion into the natural world?

5. What does Commoner mean when he says that "the discipline appears to be moving away from observation of the natural, real object"? (179) What gives one object of investigation more reality than another?

6. Why does Commoner claim that "*public* knowledge is essential to the solution of every environmental problem"? (180) How much and what kind of scientific knowledge should the public have in order to judge well?

7. How are value judgments different from judgments determined by scientific principles? Why does Commoner claim that value judgments "belong not in the hands of 'experts,' but in the hands of the people and their elected representatives"? (181)

Lewis Thomas

Lewis Thomas (1913–1993), born in Flushing, New York, was a medical doctor, distinguished biomedical investigator, dean of two medical schools, and president of the Memorial Sloan-Kettering Cancer Center.

Thomas authored several books, including *The Lives of a Cell: Notes of a Biology Watcher* (1974), which won the National Book Award and from which this selection is taken. Many of the essays in *The Lives of a Cell* first appeared in the *New England Journal of Medicine*. Thomas's written observations demonstrate a profound grasp of biological intricacies, but his scientific knowledge never overshadows his wonder at the mystery of life or his compassion for the earth and all living things.

In a 1992 interview, Thomas declared that "symbiosis is the rule rather than the freak exception," a challenge to the Darwinian legacy of competition that informed most biological research and theory for nearly a century. Thomas went on to say that "the earth itself behaves a lot like an organism," as James E. Lovelock contended more than twenty years earlier. In the selection that follows, Thomas speaks of the earth as being alive: it breathes and, from space, "has the organized, self-contained look of a live creature, full of information, marvelously skilled in handling the sun." For Thomas, the earth is the "only exuberant thing in this part of the cosmos." He uses poetic language and anthropomorphic imagery to describe the earth and convey scientific information. His descriptions, whether metaphorical or real, lead readers to question how art and aesthetics influence not only the ways scientists construct theories, but also the ways people perceive and conceive of the earth.

The World's Biggest
Membrane

Viewed from the distance of the moon, the astonishing thing about the earth, catching the breath, is that it is alive. The photographs show the dry, pounded surface of the moon in the foreground, dead as an old bone. Aloft, floating free beneath the moist, gleaming membrane of bright blue sky, is the rising earth, the only exuberant thing in this part of the cosmos. If you could look long enough, you would see the swirling of the great drifts of white cloud, covering and uncovering the half-hidden masses of land. If you had been looking for a very long, geologic time, you could have seen the continents themselves in motion, drifting apart on their crustal plates, held afloat by the fire beneath. It has the organized, self-contained look of a live creature, full of information, marvelously skilled in handling the sun.

It takes a membrane to make sense out of disorder in biology. You have to be able to catch energy and hold it, storing precisely the needed amount and releasing it in measured shares. A cell does this, and so do the organelles inside. Each assemblage is poised in the flow of solar energy, tapping off energy from metabolic surrogates of the sun. To stay alive, you have to be able to hold out against equilibrium, maintain imbalance, bank against entropy, and you can only transact this business with membranes in our kind of world.

When the earth came alive it began constructing its own membrane, for the general purpose of editing the sun. Originally, in the time of prebiotic elaboration of peptides and nucleotides from inorganic ingredients in the water on the earth, there was nothing to shield out ultraviolet radiation except the water itself. The first thin atmosphere came entirely from the degassing of the earth as it cooled, and there was only a vanishingly small trace of oxygen in it. Theoretically, there could have been some production of oxygen by photodissociation of water vapor in ultraviolet light, but not much. This process would have been self-limiting, as Urey showed, since the wavelengths needed for photolysis are the very ones screened out selectively by oxygen; the production of oxygen would have been cut off almost as soon as it occurred.

The formation of oxygen had to await the emergence of photosynthetic cells, and these were required to live in an environment with sufficient visible light for photosynthesis but shielded at the same time against lethal ultraviolet. Berkner and Marshall calculate that the green cells must therefore have been about ten meters below the surface of water, probably in pools and ponds shallow enough to lack strong convection currents (the ocean could not have been the starting place).

You could say that the breathing of oxygen into the atmosphere was the result of evolution, or you could turn it around and say that evolution was the result of oxygen. You can have it either way. Once the photosynthetic cells had appeared, very probably counterparts of today's blue-green algae, the future respiratory mechanism of the earth was set in place. Early on, when the level of oxygen had built up to around 1 percent of today's atmospheric concentration, the anaerobic life of the earth was placed in jeopardy, and the inevitable next stage was the emergence of mutants with oxidative systems and ATP [adenosine triphosphate]. With this, we were off to an explosive developmental stage in which great varieties of respiring life, including the multicellular forms, became feasible.

Berkner has suggested that there were two such explosions of new life, like vast embryological transformations, both dependent on threshold levels of oxygen. The first, at 1 percent of the present level, shielded out enough ultraviolet radiation to permit cells to move into the surface layers of lakes, rivers, and oceans. This happened around 600 million years ago, at the beginning of the Paleozoic era, and accounts for the sudden abundance of marine fossils of all kinds in the record of this period. The second burst occurred when oxygen rose to 10 percent of the present level. At this time, around 400 million years ago, there was a sufficient canopy to allow life out of the water and onto the land. From here on it was clear going, with nothing to restrain the variety of life except the limits of biologic inventiveness.

It is another illustration of our fantastic luck that oxygen filters out the very bands of ultraviolet light that are most devastating for nucleic acids and proteins, while allowing full penetration of the visible light needed for photosynthesis. If it had not been for this semipermeability, we could never have come along.

The earth breathes, in a certain sense. Berkner suggests that there may have been cycles of oxygen production and carbon dioxide consumption, depending on relative abundances of plant and animal life, with the ice ages representing periods of apnea. An overwhelming richness of vegetation may have caused the level of oxygen to rise above today's concentration, with a corresponding depletion of carbon dioxide. Such a drop in carbon dioxide may have impaired the "greenhouse" property of the atmosphere, which holds in the solar heat otherwise lost by radiation from the earth's surface. The fall in temperature would in turn have shut off much of living, and, in a long sigh, the level of oxygen may have dropped by 90 percent. Berkner speculates that this is what happened to the great reptiles; their size may have been all right for a richly oxygenated atmosphere, but they had the bad luck to run out of air.

Now we are protected against lethal ultraviolet rays by a narrow rim of ozone, thirty miles out. We are safe, well ventilated, and incubated, provided we can avoid technologies that might fiddle with that ozone, or shift the levels of carbon dioxide. Oxygen is not a major worry for us, unless we let fly with enough nuclear explosives to kill off the green cells in the sea; if we do that, of course, we are in for strangling.

It is hard to feel affection for something as totally impersonal as the atmosphere, and yet there it is, as much a part and product of life as wine or bread. Taken all in all, the sky is a miraculous achievement. It works, and for what it is designed to accomplish it is as infallible as anything in nature. I doubt whether any of us could think of a way to improve on it, beyond maybe shifting a local cloud from here to there on occasion. The word *chance* does not serve to account well for structures of such magnificence. There may have been elements of luck in the emergence of chloroplasts, but once these things were on the scene, the evolution of the sky became absolutely ordained. Chance suggests alternatives, other possibilities, different solutions. This may be true for gills and swim bladders and forebrains, matters of detail, but not for the sky. There was simply no other way to go.

We should credit it for what it is: for sheer size and perfection of function, it is far and away the grandest product of collaboration in all of nature.

It breathes for us, and it does another thing for our pleasure. Each day, millions of meteorites fall against the outer limits of the membrane and are burned to nothing by the friction. Without this shelter, our surface would long since have become the pounded powder of the moon. Even though our receptors are not sensitive enough to hear it, there is comfort in knowing that the sound is there overhead, like the random noise of rain on the roof at night.

Content Questions

1. In his opening line, Thomas asserts that the earth is "alive." (187) For Thomas, how does one define or recognize life?

2. What does Thomas mean when he says that "it takes a membrane to make sense out of disorder in biology"? (187)

3. In what "certain sense" does the earth "breathe"? (189)

4. Thomas uses the words *luck* or *chance* several times to describe complex evolutionary events, trends, or developments, but he categorically denies the role of chance in the construction of the atmosphere. Why? What is unique about the atmosphere that cannot be accounted for by chance? Why is it "absolutely ordained"? (189–190)

Application Questions

1. What is a membrane and why is it the distinguishing factor of life for a living organism or entity?

2. What is the role of chance or luck in evolution and what is the role of necessity or inevitability?

3. Why, chemically and physically, could life not have begun in the ocean, according to Thomas?

4. Why are imbalance, disequilibrium, and a trend toward increasing organization or information *(negentropy)* hallmarks of life or living systems? How are these related to one another? What is their relationship to energy?

5. Thomas claims that "to stay alive, you have to be able to hold out against equilibrium, maintain imbalance, [and] bank against entropy." What does he mean by this? (187)

6. Thomas describes aerobic organisms (organisms with "oxidative systems and ATP") as mutants. Why are they (we) mutants? (188)

7. According to Thomas, "You could say that the breathing of oxygen into the atmosphere was the result of evolution, or you could turn it around and say that evolution was the result of oxygen." (188) Why are both claims possible?

Discussion Questions

1. Is Thomas's live earth purposive? Does it possess intent or sentience? Is it a creature in the usual sense that we understand the word?

2. When Thomas describes the earth as being alive and breathing, is he speaking metaphorically, or does he mean that the earth is actually a living being that breathes?

3. If we believe that the earth is alive, that it breathes, and that the chemical composition of its atmosphere is the result of collaboration between the earth's living and nonliving systems, what effect might this have on human actions that affect the atmosphere or the life that creates and sustains it?

4. Is Thomas's essay scientific? Why or why not?

5. Why is it hard to "feel affection" for the atmosphere? (189)

6. What does Thomas mean when he says that the sky is "the grandest product of collaboration in all of nature"? (190)

Annie Dillard

Annie Dillard (1945–) was born in Pittsburgh, Pennsylvania. She received an M.A. from Hollins College, where she studied English, theology, and creative writing.

Pilgrim at Tinker Creek, from which the following selection is taken, was published in 1974, and critics immediately compared the power and sensibility of the book to Henry David Thoreau's *Walden* (1854). Dillard spent four seasons on Tinker Creek in the Roanoke Valley of Virginia, connecting her detailed observations of that place to her knowledge of theology, philosophy, natural science, and physics. She explores similar themes in her books *Holy the Firm* (1977) and *Teaching a Stone to Talk* (1982).

In addition to her explorations of nature, Dillard has published poetry, memoirs, literary criticism, novels, and an autobiography. A voracious bibliophile, often reading more than 100 books a year, she cites Ann Haven Morgan's *The Field Book of Ponds and Streams* (1930) as an important early influence, along with the poetry of Ralph Waldo Emerson. Dillard teaches literature and writing at Wesleyan University in Connecticut. *Pilgrim at Tinker Creek* was awarded the Pulitzer Prize for nonfiction in 1975.

Intricacy

A rosy, complex light fills my kitchen at the end of these lengthening June days. From an explosion on a nearby star eight minutes ago, the light zips through space, particle-wave, strikes the planet, angles on the continent, and filters through a mesh of land dust: clay bits, sod bits, tiny wind-borne insects, bacteria, shreds of wing and leg, gravel dust, grits of carbon, and dried cells of grass, bark, and leaves. Reddened, the light inclines into this valley over the green western mountains; it sifts between pine needles on northern slopes, and through all the mountain blackjack oak and haw, whose leaves are unclenching, one by one, and making an intricate, toothed and lobed haze. The light crosses the valley, threads through the screen on my open kitchen window, and gilds the painted wall. A plank of brightness bends from the wall and extends over the goldfish bowl on the table where I sit. The goldfish's side catches the light and bats it my way; I've an eyeful of fish-scale and star.

This Ellery cost me twenty-five cents. He is a deep red orange, darker than most goldfish. He steers short distances mainly with his slender red lateral fins; they seem to provide impetus for going backward, up, or down. It took me a few days to discover his ventral fins; they are completely transparent and all but invisible—dream fins. He also has a short anal fin, and a tail that is deeply notched and perfectly transparent at the two tapered

This selection is taken from chapter 8, "Intricacy," from Pilgrim at Tinker Creek.

tips. He can extend his mouth, so that it looks like a length of pipe; he can shift the angle of his eyes in his head so he can look before and behind himself, instead of simply out to his side. His belly, what there is of it, is white ventrally, and a patch of this white extends up his sides—the variegated Ellery. When he opens his gill slits he shows a thin crescent of silver where the flap overlapped—as though all his brightness were sunburn.

For this creature, as I said, I paid twenty-five cents. I had never bought an animal before. It was very simple; I went to a store in Roanoke called "Wet Pets"; I handed the man a quarter, and he handed me a knotted plastic bag bouncing with water in which a green plant floated and the goldfish swam. This fish, two bits' worth, has a coiled gut, a spine radiating fine bones, and a brain. Just before I sprinkle his food flakes into his bowl, I rap three times on the bowl's edge; now he is conditioned, and swims to the surface when I rap. And, he has a heart.

Once, years ago, I saw red blood cells whip, one by one, through the capillaries in a goldfish's transparent tail. The goldfish was etherized. Its head lay in a wad of wet cotton wool; its tail lay on a tray under a dissecting microscope, one of those wonderful light-gathering microscopes with two eyepieces like a stereoscope in which the world's fragments—even the skin on my finger—look brilliant with myriads of colored lights, and as deep as any alpine landscape. The red blood cells in the goldfish's tail streamed and coursed through narrow channels invisible save for glistening threads of thickness in the general translucency. They never wavered or slowed or ceased flowing, like the creek itself; they streamed redly around, up, and on, one by one, more, and more, without end. (The energy of that pulse reminds me of something about the human body: if you sit absolutely perfectly balanced on the end of your spine, with your legs either crossed tailor fashion or drawn up together, and your arms forward on your legs, then even if you hold your breath, your body will rock with the energy of your heartbeat, forward and back, effortlessly, for as long as you want to remain balanced.) Those red blood cells are coursing in Ellery's tail now, too, in just that way, and through his mouth and eyes as well, and through mine. I've never forgotten the sight of those cells; I think of it when I see the fish in his bowl; I think of it lying in bed at night, imagining that if I concentrate enough I might be able to feel in my fingers' capillaries the small knockings and flow of those circular dots, like a string of beads drawn through my hand.

Something else is happening in the goldfish bowl. There on the kitchen table, nourished by the simple plank of complex light, the plankton is blooming. The water yellows and clouds; a transparent slime coats the leaves of the water plant, elodea; a blue-green film of single-celled algae clings to the glass. And I have to clean the doggone bowl. I'll spare you the details: it's the plant I'm interested in. While Ellery swims in the stoppered sink, I rinse the algae down the drain of another sink, wash the gravel, and rub the elodea's many ferny leaves under running water until they feel clean.

The elodea is not considered much of a plant. Aquarists use it because it's available and it gives off oxygen completely submersed; laboratories use it because its leaves are only two cells thick. It's plentiful, easy to grow, and cheap—like the goldfish. And, like the goldfish, its cells have unwittingly performed for me on a microscope's stage.

I was in a laboratory, using a very expensive microscope. I peered through the deep twin eyepieces and saw again that color-charged, glistening world. A thin, oblong leaf of elodea, a quarter of an inch long, lay on a glass slide sopping wet and floodlighted brilliantly from below. In the circle of light formed by the two eyepieces trained at the translucent leaf, I saw a clean mosaic of almost colorless cells. The cells were large—eight or nine of them, magnified 450 times, packed the circle—so that I could easily see what I had come to see: the streaming of chloroplasts.

Chloroplasts bear chlorophyll; they give the green world its color, and they carry out the business of photosynthesis. Around the inside perimeter of each gigantic cell trailed a continuous loop of these bright green dots. They spun like paramecia; they pulsed, pressed, and thronged. A change of focus suddenly revealed the eddying currents of the river of transparent cytoplasm, a sort of "ether" to the chloroplasts, or "spacetime," in which they have their tiny being. Back to the green dots: they shone, they swarmed in ever-shifting files around and around the edge of the cell; they wandered, they charged, they milled, raced, and ran at the edge of apparent nothingness, the empty-looking inner cell; they flowed and trooped greenly, up against the vegetative wall.

All the green in the planted world consists of these whole, rounded chloroplasts wending their ways in water. If you analyze a molecule of chlorophyll itself, what you get is 136 atoms of hydrogen, carbon, oxygen, and nitrogen arranged in an exact and complex relationship around a central ring. At the ring's center is a single atom of magnesium. Now, if you remove the atom of magnesium and in its exact place put an atom of iron, you get a molecule of hemoglobin. The iron atom combines with all the other atoms to make red blood, the streaming red dots in the goldfish's tail.

It is, then, a small world there in the goldfish bowl, and a very large one. Say the nucleus of any atom in the bowl were the size of a cherry pit: its nearest electron would revolve around it 175 yards away. A whirling air in his swim bladder balances the goldfish's weight in the water; his scales overlap, his feathery gills pump and filter; his eyes work, his heart beats, his liver absorbs, his muscles contract in a wave of extending ripples. The daphnias he eats have eyes and jointed legs. The algae the daphnias eat have green cells stacked like checkers or winding in narrow ribbons like spiral staircases up long columns of emptiness. And so on diminishingly down. We have not yet found the dot so small it is uncreated, as it were, like a metal blank, or merely roughed in—and we never shall. We go down landscape after mobile, sculpture after collage, down to molecular structures like a mob dance in Brueghel, down to atoms airy and balanced as a canvas by Klee, down to atomic particles, the heart of the matter, as spirited and wild as any El Greco saints. And it all works. "Nature," said Thoreau in his journal, "is mythical and mystical always, and spends her whole genius on the least work." The creator, I would add, churns out the intricate texture of least works that is the world with a spendthrift genius and an extravagance of care. This is the point.

Content Questions

1. What similarity does Dillard see between herself and the goldfish? Why is this observation important? (196)

2. Why does Dillard keep elodea in the goldfish bowl? What is a chloroplast and what is its function? (197)

3. In terms of molecular structure, what difference is there between chlorophyll and hemoglobin? How are they similar? Why does Dillard describe these details? (197)

Application Questions

1. Dillard offers a poetic and scientifically accurate, but brief, account of the function of chloroplasts. Give a more detailed account of how chloroplasts function in plant cell metabolism. What is their role in the energy pyramid, in converting sunlight to other forms of life-sustaining energy?

2. Describe how the fishbowl "ecosystem" works. Is it a closed or open system? Why does Dillard have to clean out the bowl periodically? Why don't we have to clean out ponds or lakes?

Discussion Questions

1. What does Dillard mean when she describes the light entering her kitchen as "complex"? (195)

2. Why does Dillard stress the fact that the goldfish cost twenty-five cents?

3. What does Dillard mean when she says that "we have not yet found the dot so small it is uncreated"? (198)

4. Why does Dillard place landscape and molecular structure in the same sentence with sculpture and collage, and with the artists Brueghel, Klee, and El Greco? (198)

5. What is Dillard adding to Thoreau's statement about nature? (198)

James E. Lovelock

James E. Lovelock (1919–) was born in Letchworth, England. Trained as a chemist, medical physician, and biophysicist, he has worked as a geophysiologist (studying the science of the earth's systems) and an environmentalist, as well as designed and developed scientific instruments.

Inspiration for his Gaia hypothesis came in the 1960s while Lovelock was working with a team of NASA researchers to develop a way to test for life on other planets. His notion of Gaia was simple, direct, and testable: If a planet were lifeless, its atmospheric composition could be explained by physics and chemistry alone, and it would be close to a state of chemical equilibrium. If the planet bore life, however, organisms would need to use the atmosphere as a source of raw materials and a repository for wastes. These uses would not only change the planet's composition but also leave it in a state far from equilibrium. This realization prompted Lovelock to hypothesize that the totality of life on earth constitutes "a self-regulating system able to keep its climate and chemical composition comfortable for the organisms that inhabit it." In a deliberately provocative move, he called this hypothesis Gaia, after the ancient Greek earth goddess.

Lovelock published his hypothesis and the evidence for it in *Gaia: A New Look at Life on Earth* (1979), from which the following selection is taken. Despite its wide and persistent public appeal, Lovelock's hypothesis was roundly criticized by scientists and other experts for its narrative style, evocative language, mythological associations, blatant anthropomorphism, and apparent teleology. Now, more than twenty years since its introduction, the hypothesis has been substantially restated: "Regulation, at a state fit for life, is a property of the whole evolving system of life, air, ocean, and rocks." It is now tentatively accepted as a theory, though subject to further testing.

The Recognition of Gaia

I first put forward the Gaia hypothesis at a scientific meeting about the origins of life on earth which took place in Princeton, New Jersey, in 1968. Perhaps it was poorly presented. It certainly did not appeal to anyone except Lars Gunnar Sillen, the Scandinavian chemist now sadly dead. Lynn Margulis, of Boston University, had the task of editing our various contributions, and four years later in Boston Lynn and I met again and began a most rewarding collaboration which, with her deep knowledge and insight as a life scientist, was to go far in adding substance to the wraith of Gaia, and which still happily continues.

We have since defined Gaia as a complex entity involving the earth's biosphere, atmosphere, oceans, and soil; the totality constituting a feedback or cybernetic system which seeks an optimal physical and chemical environment for life on this planet. The maintenance of relatively constant conditions by active control may be conveniently described by the term "homeostasis."

The Gaia of this book is a hypothesis but, like other useful hypotheses, she has already proved her theoretical value, if not her existence, by giving rise to experimental questions and answers which were profitable exercises

This selection is taken from Gaia: A New Look at Life on Earth, *chapter 1, "Introductory," and chapter 3, "The Recognition of Gaia."*

in themselves. If, for example, the atmosphere is, among other things, a device for conveying raw materials to and from the biosphere, it would be reasonable to assume the presence of carrier compounds for elements essential in all biological systems, for example, iodine and sulfur. It was rewarding to find evidence that both were conveyed from the oceans, where they are abundant, through the air to the land surface, where they are in short supply. The carrier compounds, methyl iodide and dimethyl sulfide respectively, are directly produced by marine life. Scientific curiosity being unquenchable, the presence of these interesting compounds in the atmosphere would no doubt have been discovered in the end and their importance discussed without the stimulus of the Gaia hypothesis. But they were actively sought as a result of the hypothesis and their presence was consistent with it.

If Gaia exists, the relationship between her and man, a dominant animal species in the complex living system, and the possibly shifting balance of power between them, are questions of obvious importance. I have discussed them in later chapters, but this book is written primarily to stimulate and entertain. The Gaia hypothesis is for those who like to walk or simply stand and stare, to wonder about the earth and the life it bears, and to speculate about the consequences of our own presence here.

~ ~ ~

Picture a clean-swept sunlit beach with the tide receding; a smooth, flat plain of golden glistening sand where every random grain has found due place and nothing more can happen.

Beaches are, of course, in reality seldom absolutely flat, smooth, and undisturbed, or at least not for long. The golden reaches of sand are continually resculpted by fresh winds and tides. Yet events may still be circumscribed. We may still be in a world where change is no more than the shifting profile of the windswept dunes; or no more than the ebb and flow of the tide, creating and erasing its own ripples in the sand.

Now let us suppose that our otherwise immaculate beach contains one small blot on the horizon: an isolated heap of sand which at close range we recognize instantly to be the work of a living creature. There is no shadow of a doubt, it is a sandcastle. Its structure of piled, truncated cones reveals the bucket technique of building. The moat and drawbridge, with its etched facsimile of a portcullis already fading as the drying wind returns the grains to their equilibrium state, are also typical. We are programmed, so to speak, for instant recognition of a sandcastle as a human artifact, but if more proof were needed that this heap of sand is no natural phenomenon, we should point out that it does not fit with the conditions around it. The rest of the beach has been washed and brushed into a smooth carpet; the sandcastle has still to crumble; and even a child's fortress in the sand is too intricate in the design and relationship of its parts, too dearly purpose-built, to be the chance structure of natural forces.

Even in this simple world of sand and sandcastles there are clearly four states: the inert state of featureless neutrality and complete equilibrium (which can never be found in reality on earth so long as the sun shines and gives energy to keep the air and sea in motion, and thus shift the grains of sand); the structured but still lifeless "steady state," as it is called, of a beach of rippled sand and wind-piled dunes; the beach when exhibiting a product of life in the sandcastle; and finally the state when life itself is present on the scene in the form of the builder of the castle.

The third order of complexity represented by the sandcastle, between the abiological, or nonliving, steady state and that when life is present, is important in our quest for Gaia. Though lifeless themselves, the constructions made by a living creature contain a wealth of information about the needs and intentions of their builder. The clues to Gaia's existence are as transient as our sandcastle. If her partners in life were not there, continually repairing and recreating, as children build fresh castles on the beach, all Gaia's traces would soon vanish.

How, then, do we identify and distinguish between the works of Gaia and the chance structures of natural forces? And how do we recognize the presence of Gaia herself? Fortunately we are not, like those demented hunters of the Snark, entirely without a chart or means of recognition; we have some clues. At the end of the last century Boltzman made an elegant redefinition of entropy as a measure of the probability of a molecular distribution. It may seem at first obscure, but it leads directly to what we seek. It implies that wherever we find a highly improbable molecular assembly it is probably life or one of its products, and if we find such a distribution to be global in extent then perhaps we are seeing something of Gaia, the largest living creature on earth.

But what, you may ask, is an improbable distribution of molecules? There are many possible answers, such as the rather unhelpful ones: an ordered distribution of improbable molecules (like you, the reader), or an improbable distribution of common molecules (as, for example, the air). A more general answer, and one useful in our quest, is a distribution which is sufficiently different from the background state to be recognizable as an entity. Another general definition of an improbable molecular distribution is one which would require the expenditure of energy for its assembly from the background of molecules at equilibrium. (Just as our sandcastle is recognizably different from its uniform background, and the extent to which it is different or improbable is a measure of the entropy reduction or purposeful life-activity that it represents.)

We now begin to see that the recognition of Gaia depends upon our finding on a global scale improbabilities in the distribution of molecules so unusual as to be different and distinguishable, beyond reasonable doubt, from both the steady state and the conceptual equilibrium state.

It will help us in our quest to start with a clear idea of what the earth would be like, both in the equilibrium state and in the lifeless steady state. We also need to know what is meant by chemical equilibrium.

The state of disequilibrium is one from which, in principle at least, it should be possible to extract some energy, as when a grain of sand falls from a high spot to a low one. At equilibrium, all is level and no more energy is available. In our small world of sand grains the fundamental particles were effectively all of the same, or of very similar, material. In the real world there are one hundred or more chemical elements with the capacity to join together in many different ways. A few of them—carbon, hydrogen, oxygen, nitrogen, phosphorus, and sulfur—are capable of interacting and interlinking to an almost infinite extent. However, we know more or less the proportions of all the elements in the air, the sea, and the surface rocks. We also know the amount of energy released when each of these elements combines with another and when their compounds combine in their turn. So if we assume that there is a constant random source of disturbance, like a fitful wind in our sand world, we can calculate what will be the distribution of chemical compounds when the state of lowest energy is reached— in other words that state from which no further energy can be gained by chemical reactions. When we do this calculation, with of course the aid of a computer, we find that our chemical equilibrium world is approximately as shown in table 1.

The distinguished Swedish chemist Sillen was the first to calculate what would be the result of bringing the substances of the earth to thermodynamic equilibrium. Many others have done so since and have substantially confirmed his work. It is one of those exercises where the imagination can be set free through the assistance of a computer as a faithful and willing slave to perform the many tedious calculations.

Table 1   A comparison of the composition of the oceans and the air of the present world and of a hypothetical chemical equilibrium world

	PRINCIPAL COMPONENTS PERCENTAGE		
	Substance	Present world	Equilibrium world
AIR	Carbon dioxide	0.03	98
	Nitrogen	78	1
	Oxygen	21	0
	Argon	1	1
OCEAN	Water	96	85
	Salt	3.5	13

On the scale of the earth itself, we must swallow some formidable academic unrealities to reach the equilibrium state. We have to imagine that somehow the world has been totally confined within an insulated vessel, like a cosmic Dewar flask, kept at 15°C. The whole planet is then uniformly mixed until all possible chemical reactions have gone to completion, and the energy they released has been removed so as to keep the temperature constant. We might finish with a world covered with a layer of ocean, devoid of waves or ripples, above which there would be an atmosphere rich in carbon dioxide and devoid of oxygen and nitrogen. The sea would be very salty and the sea bed would consist of silica, silicates, and clay minerals.

The exact chemical composition and form of our chemical equilibrium world is less important than the fact that in such a world there is no source of energy whatever: no rain, no waves or tides, and no possibility of a chemical reaction which would yield energy. It is very important for us to understand that such a world—warm, damp, with all of the ingredients of life at hand—could never bear life. Life requires a constant energy flux from the sun to sustain it.

This abstract equilibrium world differs from a possibly real but lifeless earth in the following significant ways: the real earth would be spinning and in orbit around the sun and subject therefore to a powerful flux of radiant energy, which would include some radiation capable of splitting molecules at the atmosphere's outer reaches. It would also have a hot interior, maintained by the disintegration of radioactive elements left over from whatever cataclysmic nuclear explosion produced the debris from which the earth was formed. There would be clouds and rain, and possibly some land. Assuming the present solar output, polar ice caps would be unlikely, for this steady-state lifeless world would be richer in carbon dioxide and consequently lose heat less readily than does the real world we live in today.

In a real but lifeless world a little oxygen might appear, as water decomposed at the outer reaches of the atmosphere and the light hydrogen atoms escaped to space. Just how much oxygen is very uncertain and a matter of debate. It would depend on the rate at which reducing materials entered from below the crust and also on how much hydrogen was returned from space. We can be sure, though, that if oxygen were present it would be no more than a trace, as is found on Mars now. In this world, power would be available, since windmills and water wheels would function, but chemical energy would be very hard to find. Nothing remotely like a fire could be lit. Even if traces of oxygen did accumulate in the atmosphere, there would be no fuel to burn in it. Even if fuel were available, at least 12 percent oxygen in the air is needed to start a fire, and this is far, far more than the trace amount of a lifeless world.

Although the lifeless steady-state world differs from the imaginary equilibrium world, the difference between them is very much less than that between either of them and our living world of today. The wide differences in the chemical composition of the air, sea, and land are the subjects of later chapters. For the present, the point of interest is that everywhere on the earth today chemical power is available and in most places a fire can be lit. Indeed, it would require only an increase of about 4 percent in the atmospheric level of oxygen to bring the world into danger of conflagration. At 25 percent oxygen level even damp vegetation will continue to burn once combustion has started, so that a forest fire started by a lightning flash would burn fiercely till all combustible material was consumed. Those science-fiction stories of other worlds with bracing atmospheres due to the richer oxygen content are fiction indeed. A landing of the heroes' spaceship would have destroyed the planet.

My interest in fires and the availability of chemical free energy is not due to some quirk or pyromanic tendency, it is because recognizability in chemical terms can be measured by the intensity of free energy (for example, the power available from lighting a fire). By this measure alone our world, even the nonliving part of it, is recognizably very different from the equilibrium and steady-state worlds. Sandcastles would vanish from the earth in a day if there were no children to build them. If life were extinguished, the available free energy for fighting fires would vanish just as soon, comparatively, as oxygen vanished from the air. This would happen over a period of a million years or so, which is as nothing in the life of a planet.

The keynote, then, of this argument is that just as sandcastles are almost certainly not accidental consequences of natural but nonliving processes like wind or waves, neither are the chemical changes in the composition of the earth's surface and atmosphere which make the lighting of fires possible. All right, you may say, you are establishing a convincing case for the idea that many of the nonliving features of our world, like the ability to light a fire, are a direct result of the presence of life, but how does this help us to recognize the existence of Gaia? My answer is that where these profound disequilibriums are global in extent, like the presence of oxygen and methane in the air or wood on the ground, then we have caught a glimpse of something global in size which is able to sustain and keep constant a highly improbable distribution of molecules.

The lifeless worlds which I have modeled for comparison with our present living world are not very sharply defined, and geologists might query the distribution of elements and compounds. Certainly there is room for debate on how much nitrogen a nonliving world would possess. It will be particularly interesting to learn more about Mars and its nitrogen content, and whether this gas is chemically bound on the surface as nitrate or some other nitrogen compound, or whether it has, as Professor Michael McElroy of Harvard University has suggested, escaped to space. Mars may well be a prototype nonliving steady-state world.

Because of these uncertainties, let us consider two other ways of constructing a steady-state lifeless world and then see how they compare with the model world we have already discussed. Let us assume that Mars and Venus are indeed lifeless, and interpolate between them, in place of our present Earth, a hypothetical lifeless planet. Its chemical and physical features, in relation to its neighbors, can perhaps best be imagined in terms of a fictional country sited halfway between Finland and Libya. The atmospheric compositions of Mars, our present Earth, Venus, and our hypothetical abiological Earth are listed in table 2.

Another way is to assume that one of those predictions of imminent doom for our planet came true and that all life on earth ceased, down to the last spore of some deep-buried anaerobic bacteria. So far, no doom scenario yet imagined has the slightest chance of achieving such a degree of destruction, but let us assume that it could. In order to carry out our experiment properly and trace the changing chemical scene during the earth's transition from a healthy, life-bearing world to a dead planet, we need to find a process which will remove life from the scene without altering the physical environment. Contrary to the forebodings of many environmentalists, finding a suitable killer turns out to be an almost insoluble problem. There is the alleged threat posed by chlorofluorocarbons to the ozone layer, which if depleted would allow a flood of lethal ultraviolet radiation from the sun to "destroy all life on earth." The complete or partial removal of the ozone layer could have unpleasant consequences for life as we know it. Many species, including man, would be discomforted and some would be destroyed. Green plants, the primary producers of food and oxygen, might suffer but, as has been recently shown, some species of blue-green algae, the primary power transformers of ancient times and modern shores, are highly resistant to shortwave ultraviolet radiation. Life on this planet is a very tough, robust, and adaptable entity and we are but a small part of it. The most essential part is probably that which dwells on the floors of the continental shelves and in the soil below the surface. Large plants and animals are relatively unimportant. They are comparable rather to those elegant salesmen and glamorous models used to display a firm's products, desirable perhaps, but not essential. The tough and reliable workers composing the microbial life of the soil and seabeds are the ones who keep things

Table 2

	PLANET			
	Venus	Earth without life	Mars	Earth as it is
Carbon dioxide (%)	98	98	95	0.03
Nitrogen (%)	1.9	1.9	2.7	78
Oxygen (%)	trace	trace	0.13	21
Argon (%)	0.1	0.1	2	1
Surface temperatures (°C)	477	290±50	-53	13
Total pressure (bars)	90	60	0064	1.0

moving, and they are protected against any conceivable level of ultraviolet light by the sheer opacity of their environment.

Nuclear radiation has lethal possibilities. If a nearby star becomes a supernova and explodes, would not the flood of cosmic rays sterilize the earth? Or what if all the nuclear weapons stockpiled on earth were exploded almost simultaneously in a global war? Again, we and the larger animals and plants might be seriously affected, but it is doubtful whether unicellular life would for the most part even notice such an event. There have been many investigations of the ecology of Bikini Atoll to see if the high level of radioactivity, resulting from the bomb tests there, had adversely affected the life of that coral island. The findings show that, in spite of the continuing radioactivity in the sea and on land, this has had little effect on the normal ecology of the area, except in places where the explosions had blown away the top soil and left bare rock behind.

Toward the end of 1975, the National Academy of Sciences of the United States issued a report prepared by an eight-man committee of their own distinguished members, assisted by forty-eight other scientists chosen from those expert in the effects of nuclear explosions and all things subsequent to them. The report suggested that if half of all of the nuclear weapons in the world's arsenals, about 10,000 megatons, were used in a nuclear war, the effects on most of the human and man-made ecosystems of the world would be small at first and would become negligible within thirty years. Both aggressor and victim nations would of course suffer catastrophic local devastation, but areas remote from the battle and, especially important in the biosphere, marine and coastal ecosystems would be minimally disturbed.

To date, there seems to be only one serious scientific criticism of the report, namely, of the claim that the major global effect would be the partial destruction of the ozone layer by oxides of nitrogen generated in the heat of the nuclear explosions. We now suspect that this claim is false and that stratospheric ozone is not much disturbed by oxides of nitrogen. There was, of course, at the time of the report a strange and disproportionate concern in America about stratospheric ozone. It might in the end prove to be prescient, but then as now it was a speculation based on very tenuous evidence. In the 1970s it still seems that a nuclear war of major proportions, although no less horrific for the participants and their allies, would not be the global devastation so often portrayed. Certainly it would not much disturb Gaia.

211

The report itself was criticized then as now on political and moral grounds. It was judged irresponsible, as it might even encourage the bomb-happy among the military planners to let fly.

It seems that to delete life from our planet without changing it physically is well-nigh impossible. We are left for our experiment with only science-fictional possibilities, so let us construct a doom scenario in which all life on earth down to that last deep-buried spore is indeed annihilated.

Dr. Intensli Eeger is a dedicated scientist, employed by an efficient and successful agricultural research organization. He is much distressed by those appalling pictures of starving children shown in the Oxfam appeals. He is determined to devote his scientific skills and talents to the task of increasing the world's food production, especially in those underdeveloped regions which gave rise to the Oxfam pictures. His work plan is based on the idea that food production in these countries is hindered by, among other things, a lack of fertilizers, and he knows that the industrial nations would find it difficult to produce and deliver simple fertilizers such as nitrates and phosphates in sufficient quantities to be of any use. He also knows that the use of chemical fertilizers alone has drawbacks. He plans instead to develop by genetic manipulation a greatly improved strain of nitrogen-fixing bacteria. By this means, nitrogen in the air could be transferred directly to the soil without the need for a complex chemical industry, and also without disturbing the natural chemical balance of the soil.

Dr. Eeger had spent many years of patient trial with many promising strains which did wonders on the laboratory field plots but which failed when transferred to the tropical test grounds. He persisted until one day he heard by chance from a visiting agriculturalist that a strain of maize had been developed in Spain which flourished in soil poor in phosphate. Dr. Eeger had a hunch. He guessed that maize would be unlikely to flourish in such a soil without assistance. Was it possible that it had acquired a cooperative bacterium which, like that which lives on the roots of clover and can fix nitrogen from the air, had somehow contrived to gather what phosphate there was in the soil for the benefit of the maize?

Dr. Eeger spent his next holiday in Spain, close to the agricultural center where the work on maize was being done, having previously arranged to visit his Spanish colleagues and discuss the problem. They met and talked, and exchanged samples. On returning to his laboratory, Dr. Eeger cultivated the maize and from it extracted a motile microorganism with a capacity to gather phosphate from soil particles far more efficiently than any other organism he had ever known. It was not difficult for a man of his skills to contrive the adaptation of this new bacterium so that it could live comfortably with many other food crops and particularly with rice, the most important food source in the tropical regions. The first trials of cereals treated with *Phosphomonas eegarii* at the English test site were astonishingly successful. Yields of all the crops they tried were substantially increased. Moreover, no harmful or adverse effects were found in any of the tests.

The day came for the tropical trial at the field station in northern Queensland. A culture of *P. eegarii* was without ceremony sprayed in diluted form upon a small patch of experimental rice paddy. But here the bacterium forsook its contrived marriage with the cereal plants and formed a more exciting but adulterous union with a tough and self-sufficient blue-green alga growing on the water surface of the paddy field. They grew happily together, doubling in numbers every twenty minutes in the warm tropical environment, the air and soil providing all they needed. Small predatory organisms would normally have ensured a check on such a development, but this combination was not to be stopped. Its capacity to gather phosphorus rendered the environment barren for everything else.

Within hours, the rice paddy and those around it took on the appearance of a ripe duck pond covered with lurid iridescent green scum. It was realized that something had gone badly wrong and the scientists soon uncovered the association of *P. eegarii* and the alga. Foreseeing the dangers with rare promptness, they arranged that the entire paddy area and the water channels leading from it be treated with a biocide and the growth destroyed.

That night, Dr. Eeger and his Australian colleagues went late to bed, tired and worried. The dawn fulfilled their worst fears. The new bloom, like some living verdigris, covered the surface of a small stream a mile away from the paddies and only a few miles from the sea. Again, every agent of destruction was applied wherever the new organism might have traveled. The director of the Queensland station tried desperately but in vain to persuade the government to evacuate the area at once and use a hydrogen bomb to sterilize it before the spread was beyond all possibility of control.

In two days, the algal bloom had started to spread into the coastal waters, and by then it was too late. Within a week, the green stain was clearly visible to airline passengers flying six miles above the Gulf of

Carpentaria. Within six months, more than half of the ocean and most of the land surfaces were covered with a thick green slime which fed voraciously on the dead trees and animal life decaying beneath it.

By this time Gaia was mortally stricken. Just as we all too frequently die through the uncontrolled growth and spread of an errant version of our own cells, so the cancerous algal-bacterial association had displaced all the intricate variety of cells and species which make up the healthy living planet. The near-infinity of creatures performing essential cooperative tasks was displaced by a greedy, uniform green scum, knowing nothing but an insatiable urge to feed and grow.

Viewed from space, the earth had changed to a blotchy green and faded blue. With Gaia moribund, the cybernetic control of the earth's surface composition and atmosphere at an optimum value for life had broken down. Biological production of ammonia had long ceased. Decaying matter, including vast quantities of the alga itself, produced sulfur compounds that oxidized to sulfuric acid in the atmosphere. So the rain fell ever more acid upon the land and steadily denied that habitat to the usurper. The lack of other essential elements began to exert its effect and gradually the algal bloom faded until it survived only in a few marginal habitats, where nutrients were for a while still available.

Now let us see how this stricken earth would move slowly but inexorably toward a barren steady state, although the time scale might be of the order of a million years or more. Thunderstorms and radiation from the sun and space would continue to bombard our defenseless world and would now sever the more stable chemical bonds, enabling them to recombine in forms closer to equilibrium. At first, the most important of these reactions would be that between oxygen and the dead organic matter. Half of it might be oxidized, while the rest would be covered with mud and sand and buried. This process would remove only a small percentage of the oxygen. More slowly and surely it would also combine with the reduced gases from volcanoes and with the nitrogen of the air. As the nitric and sulfuric acid rain washed the earth, some of the vast store of carbon dioxide fixed by life as limestone and chalk would be returned as gas to the atmosphere.

As explained in the previous chapter, carbon dioxide is a greenhouse gas. With small quantities, its effect on the temperature of the air is proportional to the amount added or, as the mathematicians would say, there is a linear effect. However, once the carbon dioxide concentration in the air approaches or exceeds 1 percent, new nonlinear effects come into play and the heating greatly increases. In the absence of a biosphere to fix carbon dioxide, its concentration in the atmosphere would probably exceed the critical figure of 1 percent. The earth would then heat up rapidly to a temperature near to that of boiling water. Increasing temperatures would speed up chemical reactions and accelerate their progression toward chemical equilibrium. Meantime, all traces of our algal destroyer would finally have vanished, sterilized by the boiling seas.

In our present world, the very low temperatures at about seven miles above the earth's surface freeze out water vapor until there is only about one part in a million left. The escape of this tiny portion upwards, where it may dissociate to produce oxygen, is so slow as to be of no consequence. However, the violent weather of a world of boiling seas would probably generate thunder clouds penetrating as far as the upper atmosphere and causing there a rise in temperature and humidity. This in turn might encourage the more rapid decomposition of water, the escape of hydrogen so formed into space, and a greater production of oxygen. The release of more oxygen would ensure the ultimate removal of virtually all nitrogen from the air. The atmosphere would eventually consist of carbon dioxide and steam, with a little oxygen (probably less than 1 percent) and the rare gas argon and its relatives, which have no chemical role to play. Earth would become permanently cocooned in brilliant white cloud—a second Venus, although not quite as hot.

The rundown to equilibrium could follow a very different path. If, during its period of insatiable growth, the alga had greatly depleted atmospheric carbon dioxide, the earth might have been set on a course of irreversible cooling. Just as an excess of carbon dioxide leads to overheating, so its removal from the atmosphere could lead to runaway freezing. Ice and snow would cover most of the planet, freezing to death the last of that overambitious life form. The chemical combination of nitrogen and oxygen would still take place, but rather more slowly. The end result would be a more or less frozen planet with a thin low-pressure atmosphere of carbon dioxide and argon, and with mere traces of oxygen and nitrogen. In other words, like Mars, although not quite as cold.

We cannot be certain which way things would go. What is certain is that with Gaia's intelligence network and intricate system of checks and balances totally destroyed, there would be no going back. Our lifeless Earth, no longer a colorful misfit, a planet that broke all the rules, would fall soberly into line, in barren steady state, between its dead brother and sister, Mars and Venus.

It is necessary for me to remind you that the foregoing is fiction. It may be scientifically plausible as a model, but then only if the postulated bacterial association could exist, remain stable, and exert its aggression without check or hindrance. The genetic manipulation of microorganisms for the benefit of mankind has been a busy activity ever since they were domesticated for such purposes as cheese- and winemaking. As everyone who is a practitioner of these arts and indeed every farmer will confirm, domestication does not favor survival under wild conditions. So strongly expressed, however, has been public concern over the dangers of genetic manipulations involving DNA itself, that it was good to have no less an authority than John Postgate confirm that this brief essay in science fiction is indeed just a flight of fancy. In real life, there must be many taboos written into the genetic coding, the universal language shared by every living cell. There must also be an intricate security system to ensure that exotic outlaw species do not evolve into rampantly criminal syndicates. Vast numbers of viable genetic combinations must have been tried out, through countless generations of microorganisms, during the history of life.

Perhaps our continuing orderly existence over so long a period can be attributed to yet another Gaian regulatory process, which makes sure that cheats can never become dominant.

Content Questions

1. What is the significance of iodine and sulfur in the earth's atmosphere? How does their presence support the Gaia hypothesis? (204)

2. What does Lovelock mean when he suggests that it is a lack of "fit" between a structure or process and "the conditions around it" that indicates the presence of life? (205)

3. What are the four possible states of the world? (205)

4. How do we "identify and distinguish between the works of Gaia and the chance structures of natural forces"? (205)

5. Why is it the case that "wherever we find a highly improbable molecular assembly it is probably life or one of its products"? And if we "find such a distribution to be global in extent," why are we "perhaps . . . seeing something of Gaia"? (205)

6. What is an "improbable distribution of molecules"? (205)

7. How is persistent atmospheric disequilibrium a sign of life? (206)

Application Questions

1. The Gaia hypothesis is now considered to be the "Gaia theory" and has been restated as follows: "Regulation, at a state fit for life, is a property of the whole evolving system of life, air, ocean, and rocks." What is the difference between the Gaia hypothesis and the Gaia theory? What is the difference between a hypothesis and a theory in general?

2. Is the Gaia hypothesis testable? Can it lead to predictions? Does Lovelock provide any examples of tests or predictions in the selection? Is the Gaia theory testable? Does it lead to predictions?

3. Why, if life were extinguished, would the available free energy for lighting fires vanish? In other words, what is the connection between energy and life?

4. In light of current information about the health of the earth's ecosystems, is Lovelock's optimism about the resilience, toughness, and adaptability of life on earth justified?

5. Lovelock assures us that his fictional scenario involving Dr. Intensli Eeger's genetically manipulated bacterium is impossible because the "postulated bacterial association" could not "exist, remain stable, and exert its aggression without check or hindrance." (216) Can you find examples in the environment around you that bear out his reassurance? Can you find examples that do not?

6. Using Lovelock's definition of life—or more precisely his atmospheric chemical "markers" of it—how could a NASA scientist test for life on another planet without actually landing on that planet and looking for it?

7. Why is earth "a planet that broke all the rules"? (216) What rules?

8. What does Lovelock mean when he says that "perhaps our continuing orderly existence over so long a period can be attributed to yet another Gaian regulatory process, which makes sure that cheats can never become dominant"? (216)

9. Why doesn't an exclusively geochemical explanation of the earth's atmosphere account for its condition? That is, what does the presence of life enable us to explain that the lack of it does not?

10. Is free energy a sign of life or a precondition of it?

Discussion Questions

1. What is Gaia? Is Gaia the same as the earth? Why or why not?

2. Lovelock claims that "we recognize instantly . . . the work of a living creature." (204) What do we recognize, exactly, and why do we recognize it?

3. Is Lovelock claiming that Gaia is sentient? That Gaia is purposive or teleological?

4. Lovelock asserts that "if Gaia exists, the relationship between her and man, a dominant animal species in the complex living system, and the possibly shifting balance of power between them, are questions of obvious importance." (204) What are the questions of importance? Why?

5. If we assent to Lovelock's hypothesis, what are the consequences, if any, for human action? Do we have ethical "duties" to Gaia and her constituent elements?

6. Lovelock states that "large plants and animals are relatively unimportant, . . . desirable perhaps, but not essential" to the continued existence of Gaia. (210) What does he mean by this? If this is the case, should we be concerned about saving endangered species and ecosystems?

7. How do we "recognize" Gaia?

8. What is the role of aesthetics, or an appreciation for beauty, in the formulation of a scientific explanation or theory? Does it play a role in the recognition of and appreciation for Gaia?

Bill McKibben

A freelance writer and environmentalist, Bill McKibben (1960–) was a staff writer for the *New Yorker* magazine from 1982 to 1987. He has published hundreds of articles in such venues as the *Atlantic Monthly, Audubon, Outside,* the *New York Times,* the *New York Review of Books, Natural History, Esquire,* and *Rolling Stone.* His books include *The Age of Missing Information* (1992), which examines the link between mass media and environmental deterioration, and *Hope, Human, and Wild: True Stories of Living Lightly on the Earth* (1995), which explores sustainable alternatives to the problematic link in wealthy countries between consumerism and the "good life" it is supposed to entail. In 2003, he published *Enough: Setting Limits on Human Genetic Technologies* (2003).

McKibben's first book, *The End of Nature* (1989), from which this selection is taken, offers a comprehensive account of global environmental problems and makes the controversial assertion that human actions are bringing about the end of nature. Since then, he has written several other books on religion and nature, and remains committed to challenging the existing political and economic order that he believes is the root of both the environmental and spiritual crises.

McKibben currently resides in Vermont, where he is a visiting scholar at Middlebury College's Environmental Studies Program. He is also a lay leader of a small Methodist church in New York's Adirondack Mountains.

The End of Nature

(selection)

Almost every day, I hike up the hill out my back door. Within a hundred yards the woods swallow me up, and there is nothing to remind me of human society—no trash, no stumps, no fence, not even a real path. Looking out from the high places, you can't see road or house; it is a world apart from man. But once in a while someone will be cutting wood farther down the valley, and the snarl of a chain saw will fill the woods. It is harder on those days to get caught up in the timeless meaning of the forest, for man is nearby. The sound of the chain saw doesn't blot out all the noises of the forest or drive the animals away, but it does drive away the feeling that you are in another, separate, timeless, wild sphere.

Now that we have changed the most basic forces around us, the noise of that chain saw will always be in the woods. We have changed the atmosphere, and that will change the weather. The temperature and rainfall are no longer to be entirely the work of some separate, uncivilizable force, but instead in part a product of our habits, our economies, our ways of life. Even in the most remote wilderness, where the strictest laws forbid the felling of a single tree, the sound of that saw will be clear, and a walk in the woods will

This selection is taken from part 1, "The End of Nature," and part 2, "A Path of More Resistance."

be changed—tainted—by its whine. The world outdoors will mean much the same thing as the world indoors, the hill the same thing as the house.

An idea, a relationship, can go extinct, just like an animal or a plant. The idea in this case is "nature," the separate and wild province, the world apart from man to which he adapted, under whose rules he was born and died. In the past, we spoiled and polluted parts of that nature, inflicted environmental "damage." But that was like stabbing a man with toothpicks: though it hurt, annoyed, degraded, it did not touch vital organs, block the path of the lymph or blood. We never thought that we had wrecked nature. Deep down, we never really thought we could: it was too big and too old; its forces—the wind, the rain, the sun—were too strong, too elemental.

But, quite by accident, it turned out that the carbon dioxide and other gases we were producing in our pursuit of a better life—in pursuit of warm houses and eternal economic growth and of agriculture so productive it would free most of us from farming—*could* alter the power of the sun, *could* increase its heat. And that increase could change the patterns of moisture and dryness, breed storms in new places, breed deserts. Those things may or may not have yet begun to happen, but it is too late to altogether prevent them from happening. We have produced the carbon dioxide—we are ending nature.

If nature were about to end, we might muster endless energy to stave it off; but if nature has already ended, what are we fighting for? Before any redwoods had been cloned or genetically improved, one could understand clearly what the fight against such tinkering was about. It was about the idea that a redwood was somehow sacred, that its fundamental identity should remain beyond our control. But once that barrier has been broken, what is the fight about, then? It's not like opposing nuclear reactors or toxic waste dumps, each one of which poses new risks to new areas. This damage is to an idea, the idea of nature, and all the ideas that descend from it. It is not cumulative. Wendell Berry once argued that without a "fascination" with the wonder of the natural world "the energy needed for its preservation will never be developed"—that "there must be a mystique of the rain if we are ever to restore the purity of the rainfall." This makes sense when the problem is transitory—sulfur from a smokestack drifting over the Adirondacks. But how can there be a mystique of the rain now that every drop—even the drops that fall as snow on the Arctic, even the drops that fall deep in the remaining forest primeval—bears the permanent stamp of man? Having lost its separateness, it loses its special power. Instead of being a category like God—something beyond our control—it is now a category like the defense budget or the minimum wage, a problem we must work out. This in itself changes its meaning completely, and changes our reaction to it.

A few weeks ago, on the hill behind my house, I almost kicked the biggest rabbit I had ever seen. She had nearly finished turning white for the winter, and we stood there watching each other for a pleasant while, two creatures linked by curiosity. What will it mean to come across a rabbit in the woods once genetically engineered "rabbits" are widespread? Why would we have any more reverence or affection for such a rabbit than we would for a Coke bottle?

The end of nature probably also makes us reluctant to attach ourselves to its remnants, for the same reason that we usually don't choose friends from among the terminally ill. I love the mountain outside my back door—the stream that runs along its flank, and the smaller stream that slides down a quarter-mile mossy chute, and the place where the slope flattens into an open plain of birch and oak. But I know that some part of me resists getting to know it better—for fear, weak-kneed as it sounds, of getting hurt. If I knew as well as a forester what sick trees looked like, I fear I would see them everywhere. I find now that I like the woods best in winter, when it is harder to tell what might be dying. The winter woods might be perfectly healthy come spring, just as the sick friend, when she's sleeping peacefully, might wake up without the wheeze in her lungs.

Writing on a different subject, the bonds between men and women, Allan Bloom describes the difficulty of maintaining a committed relationship in an age when divorce—the end of that relationship—is so widely accepted: "The possibility of separation is already the fact of separation, inasmuch as people today must plan to be whole and self-sufficient and cannot risk interdependence." Instead of working to strengthen our attachments, our energies "are exhausted in preparation for independence." How much more so if that possible separation is definite, if that hurt and confusion is certain. I love winter best now, but I try not to love it too much, for fear of the January perhaps not so distant when the snow will fall as warm rain. There is no future in loving nature.

And there may not even be much past. Though Thoreau's writings grew in value and importance the closer we drew to the end of nature, the time fast approaches when he will be inexplicable, his notions less sensible to future men than the cave paintings are to us. Thoreau writes, on his climb up Katahdin, that the mountain "was vast, Titanic, and such as man never inhabits. Some part of the beholder, even some vital part, seems to escape through the loose grating of his ribs. . . . Nature has got him at a disadvantage, caught him alone, and pilfers him of some of his divine faculty. She does not smile on him as in the plains. She seems to say sternly, why came ye here before your time. This ground is not prepared for you." This sentiment describes perfectly the last stage of the relationship of man to nature—though we had subdued her in the low places, the peaks, the poles, the jungles still rang with her pure message. But what sense will this passage make in the years to come, when Katahdin, the "cloud factory," is ringed by clouds of man's own making? When the massive pines that ring its base have been genetically improved for straightness of trunk and "proper branch drop," or, more likely, have sprung from the cones of genetically improved trees that began a few miles and a few generations distant on some timber plantation? When the moose that ambles by is part of a herd whose rancher is committed to the enlightened, Gaian notion that "conservation and profit go hand in hand"?

Thoreau describes an afternoon of fishing at the mouth of Murch Brook, a dozen miles from the summit of Katahdin. Speckled trout "swallowed the bait as fast as we could throw in; and the finest specimens . . . that I have ever seen, the largest one weighing three pounds, were heaved upon the shore." He stood there to catch them as "they fell in a perfect shower" around him. "While yet alive, before their tints had faded, they glistened like the fairest flowers, the product of primitive rivers; and he could hardly trust his senses, as he stood over them, that these jewels should have swam away in that Aboljacknagesic water for so long, some many dark ages— these bright fluviatile flowers, seen of Indians only, made beautiful, the Lord only knows why, to swim there!" But through biotechnology we have already synthesized growth hormone for trout. Soon pulling them from the water will mean no more than pulling cars from an assembly line. We won't have to wonder why the Lord made them beautiful and put them there; we will have created them to increase protein supplies or fish-farm profits. If we want to make them pretty, we may. Soon Thoreau will make no sense. And when that happens, the end of nature—which began with our alteration of the atmosphere, and continued with the responses to our precarious situation of the "planetary managers" and the "genetic engineers"—will be final. The loss of memory will be the eternal loss of meaning.

In the end, I understand perfectly well that defiance may mean prosperity and a sort of security—that more dams will help the people of Phoenix, and that genetic engineering will help the sick, and that there is so much progress that can still be made against human misery. And I have no great desire to limit my way of life. If I thought we could put off the decision, foist it on our grandchildren, I'd be willing. As it is, I have no plans to live in a cave, or even an unheated cabin. If it took ten thousand years to get where we are, it will take a few generations to climb back down. But this could be the epoch when people decide at least to go no farther down the path we've been following—when we make not only the necessary technological adjustments to preserve the world from overheating but also the necessary mental adjustments to ensure that we'll never again put our good ahead of everything else's. This is the path I choose, for it offers at least a shred of hope for a living, eternal, meaningful world.

The reasons for my choice are as numerous as the trees on the hill outside my window, but they crystallized in my mind when I read a passage from one of the brave optimists of our managed future. "The existential philosophers—particularly Sartre—used to lament that man lacked an essential purpose," writes Walter Truett Anderson. "We find now that the human predicament is not quite so devoid of inherent purpose after all. To be caretakers of a planet, custodians of all its life forms and shapers of its (and our own) future is certainly purpose enough." This intended rallying cry depresses me more deeply than I can say. That is our destiny? To be "caretakers" of a managed world, "custodians" of all life? For that job security we will trade the mystery of the natural world, the pungent mystery of our own lives and of a world bursting with exuberant creation? Much better, Sartre's neutral purposelessness. But much better than that, another vision, of man actually living up to his potential.

As birds have flight, our special gift is reason. Part of that reason drives the intelligence that allows us, say, to figure out and master DNA, or to build big power plants. But our reason could also keep us from following blindly the biological imperatives toward endless growth in numbers and territory. Our reason allows us to conceive of our species as a species, and to recognize the danger that our growth poses to it, and to feel something for the other species we threaten. Should we so choose, we could exercise our reason to do what no other animal can do: we could limit ourselves voluntarily, *choose* to remain God's creatures instead of making ourselves gods. What a towering achievement that would be, so much more impressive than the largest dam (beavers can build dams) because so much harder. Such restraint—not genetic engineering or planetary management—is the real challenge, the hard thing. Of course we can splice genes. But can we *not* splice genes?

The momentum behind our impulse to control nature may be too strong to stop. But the likelihood of defeat is not an excuse to avoid trying. In one sense it's an aesthetic choice we face, much like Thoreau's, though what is at stake is less the shape of our own lives than the very practical question of the lives of all the other species and the creation they together constitute. But it is, of course, for our benefit, too. Jeffers wrote, "Integrity is wholeness, the greatest beauty is / organic wholeness of life and things, the divine beauty of the universe. Love that, not man / Apart from that, or else you will share man's pitiful confusions, or drown in despair when his days darken." The day has come when we choose between that wholeness and man in it or man apart, between that old clarity or new darkness.

The strongest reason for choosing man apart is, as I have said, the idea that nature has ended. And I think it has. But I cannot stand the clanging finality of the argument I've made, any more than people have ever been able to stand the clanging finality of their own deaths. So I hope against hope. Though not in our time, and not in the time of our children, or their children, if we now, *today*, limited our numbers and our desires and our ambitions, perhaps nature could someday resume its independent working. Perhaps the temperature could someday adjust itself to its own setting, and the rain fall of its own accord.

Time, as I said at the start of this essay, is elusive, odd. Perhaps the ten thousand years of our encroaching, defiant civilization, all eternity to us and a yawn to the rocks around us, could give way to ten thousand years of humble civilization when we choose to pay more for the benefits of nature, when we rebuild the sense of wonder and sanctity that could protect the natural world. At the end of that span we would still be so young, and perhaps ready to revel in the timelessness that surrounds us. I said, much earlier, that one of the possible meanings of the end of nature is that God is dead. But another, if there was or is any such thing as God, is that he has granted us free will and now looks on, with great concern and love, to see how we exercise it: to see if we take the chance offered by this crisis to bow down and humble ourselves, or if we compound original sin with terminal sin.

And if what I fear indeed happens? If the next twenty years sees us pump ever more gas into the sky, and if it sees us take irrevocable steps into the genetically engineered future, what solace then? The only ones in need of consolation will be those of us who were born in the transitional decades, too early to adapt completely to a brave new ethos.

I've never paid more than the usual attention to the night sky, perhaps because I grew up around cities, on suburban blocks lined with streetlights. But last August, on a warm Thursday afternoon, my wife and I hauled sleeping bags high into the mountains and laid them out on a rocky summit and waited for night to fall and the annual Perseid meteor shower to begin. After midnight, it finally started in earnest—every minute, every thirty seconds, another spear of light shot across some corner of the sky, so fast that unless you were looking right at it you had only the sense of a flash. Our bed was literally rock hard, and when, toward dawn, an unforecast rain soaked our tentless clearing, it was cold—but the night was glorious, and I've since gotten a telescope. When, in *Paradise Lost*, Adam asks about the movements of the heavens, Raphael refuses to answer. "Let it speak," he says, "the Maker's high magnificence, who built / so spacious, and his line stretcht out so far; / That man may know he dwells not in his own; / An edifice too large for him to fill, / Lodg'd in a small partition, and the rest / Ordain'd for uses to his Lord best known." We may be creating microscopic nature; we may have altered the middle nature all around us; but this vast nature above our atmosphere still holds mystery and wonder. The occasional satellite does blip across, but it is almost a self-parody. Someday, man may figure out a method of conquering the stars, but at least for now when we look into the night sky, it is as Burroughs said: "We do not see ourselves reflected there—we are swept away from ourselves, and impressed with our own insignificance."

As I lay on the mountaintop that August night I tried to pick out the few constellations I could identify—Orion's Belt, the Dippers. The ancients, surrounded by wild and even hostile nature, took comfort in seeing the familiar above them—spoons and swords and nets. But we will need to train ourselves not to see those patterns. The comfort we need is inhuman.

Content Questions

1. What is the "timeless meaning of the forest" and why would human presence prevent one from getting "caught up" in it? (223)

2. In what way can an idea or a relationship go extinct? (224)

3. What is the "idea of nature" and what other ideas "descend" from it? (224)

4. How was nature "a category like God" and why is it now "a category like the defense budget or the minimum wage"? (224–225)

5. McKibben claims that our actions have changed the "meaning" of nature. (225) What, for McKibben, is the meaning of nature?

6. McKibben admits, "I have no great desire to limit my way of life." (227) Then he says that "this could be the epoch when people decide at least to . . . make not only the necessary technological adjustments to preserve the world from overheating but also the necessary mental adjustments to ensure that we'll never again put our good ahead of everything else's." (227) Is he contradicting himself here?

7. What does McKibben mean when he says that we should "rebuild the sense of wonder and sanctity that could protect the natural world"? (228)

8. Why is the choice to restrain "our impulse to control nature" an "aesthetic choice"? (228)

9. What does McKibben mean by "the end of nature"? (228) How are we ending it?

Application Questions

1. What is biotechnology? Investigate some of the ways people have altered genotypes throughout history and then compare these with the biotechnology and genetic engineering projects of today. Discuss some of the benefits and dangers of manipulating the genetic code of animals (including humans) and plants; be sure to consider social (ethical, economic, political) as well as ecological impacts.

2. Go outside, somewhere near your school or home. Can you identify anything that is completely natural? If something is not completely natural, does this change how you feel about it?

3. What do we mean when we say that something is polluted? When is something polluted or damaged and when is it merely affected or altered?

Discussion Questions

1. Does McKibben consider humans and our works to be a "part of" or "apart from" nature?

2. Can you tell from the selection how McKibben defines nature and the natural?

3. Why *wouldn't* we have as much reverence and respect for a genetically engineered rabbit as we would for a "natural" one? (225)

4. Can science and a spiritual approach to nature coexist? Do we need more than science to save nature?

5. McKibben states that "our special gift is reason" and that this reason, paradoxically, is what enables us to both exceed the limits of nature as well as restrain ourselves from doing so. (227) Do you agree that it is reason that will determine our choice of futures or is it something else?

Gary Snyder

Gary Snyder (1930–) is a prominent poet, environmental activist, Zen Buddhist, and teacher of literature and wilderness thought. He lives in the foothills of Sierra Nevada in Northern California. A pioneer in the Western study of Buddhism and Asian poetry, he spent twelve years in Japan, including three years in a Zen monastery. His prize-winning poetry (*Turtle Island* won the Pulitzer Prize in 1975) and his essays collected in *The Practice of the Wild* (1990), *A Place in Space* (1995), and *The Gary Snyder Reader* (1999) have inspired and sustained a generation of ecologists and environmentalists.

Snyder was born in San Francisco and first came to prominence in the 1950s with the beat poets, creating a West Coast literary community with Allen Ginsberg and Jack Kerouac, who made Snyder the hero of his novel *The Dharma Bums* (1958). Over the next five decades, Snyder's reputation grew in stature, so much so that he is now recognized as a major American writer and cultural icon. In 1966, he was awarded the poetry prize from the National Institute of Arts and Letters.

Since 1985, Snyder has taught at the University of California, Davis, where he was a central force in starting the Nature and Culture Program, as well as the summer writing conference "The Art of the Wild." He has published sixteen books of poetry and prose and received both the Bollingen Poetry Prize and the Robert Kirsch Lifetime Achievement Award from the *Los Angeles Times*.

The Words
Nature, Wild, and Wilderness

Take *nature* first. The word *nature* is from Latin *natura*, "birth, constitution, character, course of things"—ultimately from *nasci*, to be born. So we have *nation, natal, native, pregnant*. The probable Indo-European root (via Greek *gna*—hence cognate, agnate) is *gen* (Sanskrit *jan*), which provides *generate* and *genus*, as well as *kin* and *kind*.

The word gets two slightly different meanings. One is "the outdoors"— the physical world, including all living things. Nature by this definition is a norm of the world that is apart from the features or products of civilization and human will. The machine, the artifact, the devised, or the extraordinary (like a two-headed calf) is spoken of as "unnatural." The other meaning, which is broader, is "the material world or its collective objects and phenomena," including the products of human action and intention. As an agency, nature is defined as "the creative and regulative physical power which is conceived of as operating in the material world and as the immediate cause of all its phenomena." Science and some sorts of mysticism rightly propose that *everything* is natural. By these lights there is nothing unnatural about New York City, or toxic wastes, or atomic energy, and nothing—by definition—that we do or experience in life is "unnatural."

(The "supernatural"? One way to deal with it is to say that "the supernatural" is a name for phenomena which are reported by so few people as to leave their reality in doubt. Nonetheless these events—ghosts, gods,

235

magical transformations, and such—are described often enough to make them continue to be intriguing and, for some, credible.)

The physical universe and all its properties—I would prefer to use the word *nature* in this sense. But it will come up meaning "the outdoors" or "other-than-human" sometimes even here.

The word *wild* is like a gray fox trotting off through the forest, ducking behind bushes, going in and out of sight. Up close, first glance, it is "wild"— then farther into the woods next glance it's "wyld" and it recedes via Old Norse *villr* and Old Teutonic *wilthijaz* into a faint pre-Teutorilc *ghweltijos* which means, still, wild, and maybe wooded (*wald*), and lurks back there with possible connections to *will*, to Latin *silva* (forest, sauvage), and to the Indo-European root *ghwer*, base of Latin *ferus* (feral, fierce), which swings us around to Thoreau's "awful ferity" shared by virtuous people and lovers. The Oxford English Dictionary has it this way:

Of animals—not tame, undomesticated, unruly.

Of plants—not cultivated.

Of land—uninhabited, uncultivated.

Of foodcrops—produced or yielded without cultivation.

Of societies—uncivilized, rude, resisting constituted government.

Of individuals—unrestrained, insubordinate, licentious, dissolute, loose. "Wild and wanton widowes"—1614.

Of behavior—violent, destructive, cruel, unruly.

Of behavior—artless, free, spontaneous. "Warble his native wood-notes wild"—John Milton.

Wild is largely defined in our dictionaries by what—from a human standpoint—it is not. It cannot be seen by this approach for what it *is*. Turn it the other way:

Of animals—free agents, each with its own endowments, living within natural systems.

Of plants—self-propagating, self-maintaining, flourishing in accord with innate qualities.

Of land—a place where the original and potential vegetation and fauna are intact and in full interaction and the landforms are entirely the result of nonhuman forces. Pristine.

Of foodcrops—food supplies made available and sustainable by the natural
  excess and exuberance of wild plants in their growth and in the production
  of quantities of fruit or seeds.

Of societies—societies whose order has grown from within and is maintained
  by the force of consensus and custom rather than explicit legislation.
  Primary cultures, which consider themselves the original and eternal
  inhabitants of their territory. Societies which resist economic and political
  domination by civilization. Societies whose economic system is in
  a close and sustainable relation to the local ecosystem.

Of individuals—following local custom, style, and etiquette without
  concern for the standards of the metropolis or nearest trading post.
  Unintimidated, self-reliant, independent. "Proud and free. "

Of behavior—fiercely resisting any oppression, confinement, or exploitation.
  Far-out, outrageous, "bad," admirable.

Of behavior—artless, free, spontaneous, unconditioned. Expressive, physical,
  openly sexual, ecstatic.

Most of the senses in this second set of definitions come very close to
being how the Chinese define the term *Tao,* the *way* of Great Nature: elud-
ing analysis, beyond categories, self-organizing, self-informing, playful,
surprising, impermanent, insubstantial, independent, complete, orderly,
unmediated, freely manifesting, self-authenticating, self-willed, complex,
quite simple. Both empty and real at the same time. In some cases we might
call it sacred. It is not far from the Buddhist term *dharma* with its original
senses of forming and firming.

The word *wilderness,* earlier *wyldernesse,* Old English *wildeornes,* possibly
from "wild-deer-ness" (*deor,* deer and other forest animals) but more likely
"wildern-ness," has the meanings:

A large area of wild land, with original vegetation and wildlife, ranging
  from dense jungle or rainforest to arctic or alpine "white wilderness."

A wasteland, as an area unused or useless for agriculture or pasture.

A space of sea or air, as in Shakespeare, "I stand as one upon a Rock,
  environ'd with a Wilderness of Sea" *(Titus Andronicus).* The oceans.

A place of danger and difficulty: where you take your own chances,
  depend on your own skills, and do not count on rescue.

This world as contrasted with heaven. "I walked through the wildernesse
  of this world" *(The Pilgrim's Progress).*

A place of abundance, as in John Milton, "a wildernesse of sweets."

Milton's usage of wilderness catches the very real condition of energy and richness that is so often found in wild systems. "A wildernesse of sweets" is like the billions of herring or mackerel babies in the ocean, the cubic miles of krill, wild prairie grass seed (leading to the bread of this day, made from the germs of grasses)—all the incredible fecundity of small animals and plants, feeding the web. But from another side, wilderness has implied chaos, eros, the unknown, realms of taboo, the habitat of both the ecstatic and the demonic. In both senses it is a place of archetypal power, teaching, and challenge.

⌢ ⌢ ⌢

So we can say that New York City and Tokyo are "natural" but not "wild." They do not deviate from the laws of nature, but they are habitat so exclusive in the matter of who and what they give shelter to, and so intolerant of other creatures, as to be truly odd. Wilderness is a *place* where the wild potential is fully expressed, a diversity of living and nonliving beings flourishing according to their own sorts of order. In ecology we speak of "wild systems." When an ecosystem is fully functioning, all the members are present at the assembly. To speak of wilderness is to speak of wholeness. Human beings came out of that wholeness, and to consider the possibility of reactivating membership in the Assembly of All Beings is in no way regressive.

Content Questions

1. What definitions of *nature* does Snyder provide? What are the differences between these definitions? (235)

2. What are the meanings of *Tao* and *dharma?* (237)

3. Why are New York City and Tokyo " 'natural' but not 'wild' "? (238)

4. What distinctions does Snyder make between the terms *nature, wild,* and *wilderness?*

Application Question

Choose a very familiar location and try to describe it in three parallel ways according to Snyder's terms: as *natural,* as *wild,* and as *wilderness.* Which terms are the most useful, and which are less useful? Why?

Discussion Questions

1. Which of Snyder's definitions of *nature* is more useful to environmental science? Why?

2. Why is Snyder dissatisfied with the Oxford English Dictionary's definition of *wild?* How does his definition depart from the dictionary's? What does Snyder's definition of *wild* say about his way of looking at the world?

3. What does Snyder mean and what does he imply when he speaks of "wilderness" in terms of John Milton's "wildernesse of sweets" and "the habitat of both the ecstatic and the demonic"? (237–238)

4. What does Snyder suggest by saying that we must reactivate "membership in the Assembly of All Beings"? Why is reinstating this membership "in no way regressive"? (238)

Terry Tempest Williams

Terry Tempest Williams (1955–) is a naturalist, writer, and political activist. She earned an M.A. in environmental education from the University of Utah. Williams has taught on the Navajo Reservation at Montezuma Creek in Utah, been a naturalist-in-residence at the Utah Museum of Natural History, and served as a visiting professor of English at the University of Utah.

An award-winning author, Williams has published numerous books and essays exploring the relationship—for good or ill—between human communities and the natural world. In *Refuge: An Unnatural History of Family and Place* (1991), Williams chronicles the parallel events of cancer caused by nuclear fallout and the flooding of a migratory bird refuge in northern Utah. In both instances, natural events—cancer and floods—are complicated by "unnatural" human interference—nuclear radiation and dams.

A lifelong resident of Utah, Williams possesses an intimate knowledge of place that informs her commitment to both the land and the human communities that live on it. For Williams, their fates are inextricably, though not always clearly, intertwined; one cannot pursue the well-being of one without considering that of the other. She describes herself as "a Mormon woman who grew up in the Great Basin and now lives in the Colorado Plateau. These are the lenses of culture, gender, and geography that I see out of." Her work reflects her identity and history, and she sees these biases as necessary assets in both her writing and activism.

Water Songs

Lee Milner and I stood in front of the diorama of the black-crowned night heron at the American Museum of Natural History in New York City. *Nycticorax nycticorax:* a long-legged bird common in freshwater marshes, swamps, and tidal flats, ranging from Canada to South America.

We each had our own stories. My tales were of night herons at the Bear River Migratory Bird Refuge in Utah—the way they fly with their heads sunken in line with their backs, their toes barely projecting beyond their tail, the way they roost in trees with their dark green feathered robes. Lee painted them at Pelham Bay Park on the northern edge of the Bronx, where, she says, "they fly about you like moths." Both of us could recreate their steady wingbeats with our hands as they move through crepuscular hours.

Two women, one from Utah and one from the Bronx, brought together by birds.

We were also colleagues at the American Museum. I was there as part of an exchange program from the Utah Museum of Natural History, on staff for six weeks. Lee was hired to manage the Alexander M. White Natural Science Center while the program director was on medical leave. The center is a special hands-on exhibit where children can learn about nature in New York City.

We worked together each day, teaching various school groups about the natural history in and around their neighborhoods. In between the toad, turtle, and salamander feedings, we found time to talk. Lee was passionate about her home. She would pull out maps of Pelham Bay Park and run her fingers over every slough, every clump of cattails and stretch of beach that was part of this ecosystem. She would gesture with her body the way the light shifts, exposing herons, bitterns, and owls. And she spoke with sadness about being misunderstood, how people outside the Bronx did not recognize the beauty.

I wasn't sure I did.

Lee and her father had just moved to Co-op City, and she described the view from their apartment as perfect for looking out over cattails. She promised to take me to Pelham Bay before I left.

The opportunity finally came. Our aquarium had been having bacteria problems that had killed some of the organisms. We decided we could use some more intertidal creatures: crabs, shrimp, and maybe some barnacles. We needed to go collecting. Pelham Bay was the place.

David Spencer, another instructor, agreed to come along. The plan was to meet Lee at Co-op City in the morning. David and I packed our pails, nets, and collecting gear before leaving the museum for the bus. Our directions were simple—one crosstown transfer, a few blocks up, and we were on the Fordham Road bus to Co-op City.

The idea of finding anything natural in the built environment passing my window seemed unnatural. All I could see was building after building, and beyond that, mere shells of buildings burnt out and vacant with empty lots mirroring the human deprivation.

"South Bronx," remarked David as he looked out his window.

Two elderly women sitting across from us, wrapped in oversized wool coats, their knees slightly apart, smiled at me. I looked down at my rubber boots with my old khakis tucked inside, my binoculars around my neck and the large net I was holding in the aisle—how odd I must look. I was about to explain when their eyes returned to their hands folded neatly across their laps. I asked David, who was reading, if he felt the slightest bit silly or self-conscious.

"No," he said. "Nothing surprises New Yorkers." He returned to his book.

We arrived at Co-op City. Lee was there to meet us. I was not prepared for the isolating presence of these high-rise complexes that seemed to grow out of the wetlands. Any notion of community would have to be vertical.

From her apartment, Lee had a splendid view of the marshes.

Through the haze, I recognized the Empire State Building and the twin towers of the World Trade Center. The juxtaposition of concrete and wetlands was unsettling. They did nothing to inspire each other.

"The water songs of the red-winged blackbirds are what keep me here," Lee said as we walked toward Pelham Bay. "I listen to them each morning before I take the train into the city. These open lands hold my sanity."

"Do other tenants of Co-op City look at the marsh this way?" David asked.

"Most of them don't see the marsh at all," she replied.

I was trying hard not to let the pristine marshes I knew back home interfere with what was before us. The cattails were tattered and limp. Water stained with oil swirled around the stalks. It smelled of sewage. Our wetlands are becoming urban wastelands. This one, at least, had not completely been dredged, drained, or filled.

It was midwinter, an overcast sky. The mood was sinister. But I trusted Lee, and the deeper we entered into Pelham Bay Park, the more hauntingly beautiful it became, in spite of the long shadows and thin silhouettes of men behind bushes.

"This is a good place for us to collect," she said, putting down her bucket at the estuary.

Within minutes, we were knee-deep in tide pools and sloughs. My work was hampered by the muck that leached into the water. I could not see, much less find, what one would naturally assume to be there. More oil slicks. Iridescent water. Yellow foam. I kept coming up with gnarled oysters with abnormal growths on their shells. I handed an oyster dripping with black ooze to David.

"Eat this," I said.

"Not until you lick off your fingers first," he replied, wiping the animal clean.

These wetlands did not sparkle and sing. They were moribund.

Lee didn't see them this way. She knew too much to be defensive, yet recognized her place as their defender and saw the beauty inherent in marshes as systems of regeneration. She walked toward us with a bucket of killifish, some hermit crabs, and one ghost shrimp.

"Did you see the night heron?" she asked.

I had not seen anything but my own fears fly by with a few gulls.

We followed her through a thicket of hardwoods to another clearing. She motioned us down in the grasses.

"See him?" she whispered.

On the edge of the rushes stood the black-crowned night heron. Perfectly still. His long white plumes, like the misplaced hairs of an old man, hung down from the back of his head, undulating in the breeze. We could see his red eye reflected in the slow, rippling water.

Lee Milner's gaze through her apartment window out over the cattails was not unlike the heron's. It will be this stalwartness in the face of terror that offers wetlands their only hope. When she motioned us down in the grasses to observe the black-crowned night heron still fishing at dusk, she was showing us the implacable focus of those who dwell there.

This is our first clue to residency.

Somehow, I felt more at home. Seeing the heron oriented me. I relaxed. We watched the mysterious bird until he finally outpatienced us. We left to collect a few more organisms before dark.

I made a slight detour. I wanted to walk on the beach during sunset. There was no one around. The beach was desolate, with the exception of a pavilion. It stood on the sand like a forgotten fortress. Graffiti looking more like Japanese characters than profanities streaked the walls. The windows, without glass, appeared as holes in a decaying edifice. In the middle of the promenade was a beautiful mosaic sundial. Someone had cared about this place.

In spite of the cold, I took off my boots and stockings and rolled up the cuffs of my pants. I needed to feel the sand and the surf beneath my feet. The setting sun looked like the tip of a burning cigarette through the fog. Up ahead, a black body lay stiff on the beach. It was a Labrador. Small waves rocked the dead dog back and forth. I turned away.

Lee and David were sitting on the pavilion stairs watching more night herons crisscross the sky. Darkness was settling in. Lee surmised we had wandered a good six miles or so inside the park. Even she did not think we should walk back to Co-op City after sunset. They had found a phone booth while I was out walking and had called a cab.

"So are we being picked up here?" I asked.

They looked at each other and shook their heads.

"We have a problem," David said. "No one will come get us."

"What do you mean?"

"The first company we dialed thought we were a prank call," said Lee. "Sure, you're out at Pelham Bay. Sure, y'all want a ride into the city. No cabby in hell's dumb enough to fall for that one . . . click."

"And the second company hung up on us," David said. "At least the third cab operation offered us an alternative. They said our only real option was to call for a registered car."

"Let's do it," I said.

"We would have except we've run out of change," Lee replied.

I handed her what I had in my pockets. She called a gypsy cab service.

Waiting for our hired car's headlights to appear inside this dark urban wilderness was the longest thirty minutes I can remember. We stood on the concrete steps of the pavilion like statues, no one saying a word. I thought to myself, "we could be in Greece, we could be in a movie, we could be dead."

The registered car slowly pulled up and stopped. The driver pushed the passenger's door open with his foot. Because of all of our gear, I sat in front. Our driver could barely focus on our faces, let alone speak. I noticed his arms ravaged with needle tracks, how his entire body shook.

Eight silent miles. Thirty dollars. I gave him a generous tip and later felt guilty, knowing where the money would go. David and I hugged Lee, thanked her, and took the specimens, buckets, screens, and nets with us as we caught the bus back to Manhattan. The hour-long ride back to the city allowed me to settle into my fatigue. I dreamed of the pavilion, the stiff black dog, and the long-legged birds who live there.

David tapped me on the shoulder. I awoke startled. Disoriented.

"Next stop is ours," he said.

We got off the bus and walked over to Madison and Seventy-ninth Street to catch the crosstown bus back to the museum. We kept checking the fish to see if they were safe, surprised to see them surviving at all given the amount of sloshing that had occurred throughout the day.

As we stood on the corner waiting, a woman stopped. "Excuse me," she said. "I like your look. Do you mind me asking where you purchased your trousers and boots? And the binoculars are a fabulous accessory."

I looked at David who was grinning.

"Utah," I said in a tired voice. "I bought them all in Utah."

"I see . . ." the woman replied. "I don't know that shop." She quickly disappeared into a gourmet deli.

Back at the museum, the killifish were transferred safely into the aquarium with the shrimp and crabs. Before we left, I placed the oysters in their own tank for observation. With our faces to the glass, we watched the aquariums for a few minutes to make certain all was in order. Life appeared fluid. We turned off the lights and left. In the hallway, we heard music. Cocktail chatter. It was a fundraising gala in the African Hall. We quietly slipped out. No one saw us enter or leave.

Walking home on Seventy-seventh Street, I became melancholy. I wasn't sure why. Usually after a day in the field I am exhilarated. I kept thinking about Lee, who responds to Pelham Bay Park as a lover, who rejects this open space as a wicked edge for undesirables, a dumping ground for toxins or occasional bodies. Pelham Bay is her home, the landscape she naturally comprehends, a sanctuary she holds inside her unguarded heart. And suddenly, the water song of the red-winged blackbirds returned to me, the songs that keep her attentive in a city that has little memory of wildness.

Content Questions

1. Williams says that "the idea of finding anything natural in the built environment passing my window seemed unnatural." (244) What does she mean?

2. What does Williams mean when she says that "any notion of community would have to be vertical"? (244) What kind of community is she talking about?

3. Initially, Williams is dismayed by the marshes of Pelham Bay Park. According to her, they "did not sparkle and sing. They were moribund." (245) What makes Williams feel this way? Does her attitude change in the end?

4. While in Pelham Bay Park, Williams says that she "had not seen anything but [her] own fears fly by." (245) What fears is she talking about? Why would "stalwartness in the face of terror" offer the wetlands their "only hope"? (246)

5. What is the "first clue to residency" and why is residency important? (246)

Application Questions

1. Williams says that she feels more at home once she sees the heron in the marshes; seeing the bird orients her. How do you orient yourself in your environment? What landmarks, events, or animals mark a place as home for you?

2. How are marshes "systems of regeneration"? (245) What special ecological functions and services do saltwater marshes perform?

3. Find a place that is predominantly urban or "built." Describe the nature you find there. What is your response to it?

4. The purpose of the visit to Pelham Bay is to collect specimens for the American Museum's Natural Science Center. How can places like museums, science centers, zoos, parks, and botanical gardens educate people about nature?

Discussion Questions

1. What is the role of storytelling in environmental science?

2. Is it possible to learn about nature in a city?

3. What does Lee mean when she says that most of the residents in Co-op City don't see the marsh at all? What does it take to "see" a landscape?

4. Williams compares the marshes of Pelham Bay to the "pristine" marshes she knows back home in Utah. (245) To be natural, does the environment have to be pristine?

5. Williams says that Lee "knew too much to be defensive, yet recognized her place as [the wetlands'] defender and saw the beauty inherent in marshes as systems of regeneration." (245) What is the connection, if any, between knowledge, the recognition of beauty, and activism?

6. What is the significance of Williams's exchange with the woman who "likes her look" and wants to know where she purchased her clothes and "accessories"? (247)

7. What is an "urban wilderness"? (247) Is it a contradiction in terms? Can a city be wild? Can it have a "memory of wildness"? (248) How?

R. Edward Grumbine

R. Edward Grumbine (1953–) studied environmental science and policy at Antioch Graduate School and the University of Montana. Since 1982, he has been the director of the Sierra Institute Wilderness Field Studies Program at the University of California, Santa Cruz, where he also teaches wilderness history and the natural history of California. Grumbine's writing has appeared in a range of periodicals, including scientific journals such as *Conservation Biology* and popular publications such as *High Country News*. He is currently examining ecological change over the last thirty years in the Olympic Peninsula, the Great Smoky Mountains, and Utah's Canyonlands.

Grumbine has been a strong advocate for public land management policy based on the holistic approach of conservation biology. This approach seeks to maintain and preserve biodiversity by concentrating on entire ecosystems rather than individual species. At the same time, advocates of conservation biology view the practice of their science as advancing an explicit agenda of goals and values. In his book *Ghost Bears: Exploring the Biodiversity Crisis (1992),* Grumbine focuses on the fate of the endangered grizzly bear. In it, he shows how understanding the connections between conservation biology, environmental laws, land management practices, and environmental values can lead to a radical reordering of the concepts on which our institutions and policies are based. Grumbine emphasizes the importance of bringing the values of the "deep ecology" movement into mainstream environmental policy.

The Politics of Wilderness and the Practice of the Wild

Smoke in the chill gray air.

We climbed up the steep road from the coast accompanied by a change in the weather and an onshore breeze. In the center of a jumble of cinder block buildings, vintage house trailers, and rusting hulks of dead automobiles stood the wood slab roundhouse. Weedy blackberries rambled nearby. At first, not knowing back from front, we couldn't find the door. But soon the entranceway, a passage constructed on the north side and filled with firewood, drew us in.

Upon entering the roundhouse, the Kashaya Pomo of north coastal California turn in a circle clockwise. But if you're a first-time visitor, they don't expect you to follow this ritual. Nor do they come right out and tell you about it. If you don't detect it for yourself, it might never be explained. So it's good to pay close attention and not hesitate to inquire about appropriate roundhouse behavior.

As our eyes adjusted to the light from the fire pit near the door, we could see about fifteen people seated on rough benches that curved around the inside walls. Crackle of fire and murmur of voices, people were saying hello, visiting, gossiping quietly.

We looked for our friend, Lorin Smith, who had invited us to the fall Acorn Festival. Lorin is a retired state park ranger and the spiritual leader (*yomta* or doctor) of the Kashaya people. He was sitting on a special chair (special because it was the only seat in the house with back support) against the east wall. He greeted us and we visited, after placing our potluck food on the tables in the rear. Other people stood and ate, as the kids eyed the desserts.

The Acorn Festival is the most important public ceremony that the Kashaya Pomo conduct. Anyone may come to celebrate the harvest and the beginning of the winter rainy season. Over the next few hours, people continued to drift in. Most of those present were Anglo. There were perhaps ten to fifteen Pomo.

I noticed the centerpost. It was massive, over four feet thick, from the hard-packed earthen floor up to the roof beams. It was smooth and dark-cured from years of smoke. Lorin told me that the elders found it in an old clear-cut left for slash. It was hauled to the new roundhouse site by truck, but the Pomo raised it in place by hand.

The ceremony began without any obvious sign. A Pomo woman stood up and greeted everyone. There were thirty or forty people in the round-house now, though one hundred and fifty could have fit in with room to spare. The woman invited everyone to join in the singing and dancing. Though there was little sense of formality to her remarks, it was clear that the Pomo were following certain procedures.

A chorus of male and female singers sang repetitive lyrics over the beat of clacker sticks. (The Pomo do not use drums.) Smoke curled around the centerpost and flew out the smoke hole. Clacker stick sounds rattled up to the roof beams. Some of the songs were accompanied by dances. At times, men and women would dance together; other songs were danced by the women alone. I was surprised that Lorin did little singing and danced only once. But for this he put on a fancy western shirt, held oak boughs in his hands, and danced solo.

The Pomo accepted us as neighbors and friends. Songs were shared and dance steps were explained briefly. During the dances people talked, sang along, moved around a bit, and went outside to pee. It wasn't like being in church or sitting zazen. After some time I was less sure of where I was, what kind of person I was supposed to be, and when events were supposed to begin and end. But though my boundaries were being stretched, I was not concerned. The centerpost held up the world and it was firm, stout, and round.

The ceremony ended with Pomo and Christian prayers of thanksgiving: to acorns, the forest, the fire, the roundhouse, to the singers and dancers, to

Great Spirit, and to God. We said goodbye and drifted out the door—cold night, waxing moon, and thousands of stars dancing across the roundhouse of the sky.

Later, I couldn't get over the fact that the chorus was composed mainly of white people. Most of the participants were Anglo, too. The roundhouse sat in the middle of a postage-stamp reservation surrounded by non-Indian cutover timber company land. The Pomo had been so accommodating, so gracious. But they were hanging on by the skin of their teeth—the rusting trailers and junked cars proved that. What did the people do for work? With so few Pomo participating, how could the songs and dances survive? Did the people have some strategy for survival or were they merely resigned to the overwhelming presence of white voices singing their songs to keep them alive?

⌣ ⌣ ⌣

A month later and fifteen hundred miles away, I sat on a comfortable sofa by a roaring fireplace in the meeting room of a guest ranch in the heart of the Greater Yellowstone Ecosystem. Snow lay on the ground outside and daylight faded against the Gallatin Range. Next to me on an end table sat an expensive cast bronze of an Indian warrior on horseback. I was a member of a group of environmental activists gathered from around the country to discuss forest reform strategy. What might be done to increase pressure on Congress to protect wilderness areas and biodiversity?

I had been asked to explain how ecology and conservation biology might provide new strategies to aid the cause. First, I described why setting up a nature reserve system in the United States had failed. Parks were too few and too small to prevent extinctions over time. Political dealmaking could not encompass the biological needs of species and the ecosystems they depended upon. Second, I outlined how conservation biology principles could be used to expand current proposals for new parks and wilderness. Science could also be summoned to argue for Endangered Species Act reauthorization. I proposed that the goal of saving wild places might be replaced with the goal of protecting ecological integrity. This new goal would include maintaining and restoring viable populations of all native species, representative samples of all U.S. ecosystems, and ecosystem patterns and processes. I concluded by suggesting that if ecological integrity became the new watchword of the environmental movement, we might be able to

255

protect many more acres of wildlands than if we focused only on roadless areas.

During the talk my thoughts strayed outside. Hiking up the Yellowstone River the previous day I had seen a bald eagle fishing the shallows and a dead elk whose hindquarters bore the marks of coyote scavenging for a meal. What if, somehow, the people in this group could sway the political process so that the goal of ecological integrity might become manifest? What if a hundred greater ecosystems as healthy as Yellowstone returned to life across the continent? Why not a Greater Tall Grass Prairie in Minnesota? A Greater Northern Forest Ecosystem stretching from the coast to the interior? A Greater Gila-Cochise Ecosystem in the Southwest? A Greater . . .

I felt energized as my talk ended. But the group's response astonished me. Though many appeared to be in general agreement, several participants raised challenging questions.

"With all this emphasis on biology, where are the environmental ethics in your position? I don't see protecting wilderness as having much to do at all with what you've just said."

"What is your standard? What do you believe is worth fighting for?"

"This science is all fine and good, but do you believe in wilderness or not?"

Flustered, I attempted to explain that the goal of protecting ecological integrity was shot through with values. And that, using the Greater Yellowstone Ecosystem as an example, more lands might be protected if activists looked beyond the remaining pool of roadless lands and instead based their strategy on the biological needs of grizzly bears. But my response was hardly compelling to the group. We broke for lunch.

～ ～ ～

Months later, I am reminded of the roadhouse, set among cutover forests and decrepit government housing, and how what happened with the Pomo is related to the politics of wilderness and the prospects for protecting biodiversity. Pomo behavior during the Acorn Festival offers signs of wildness and hope for the future. There were several tokens present that night: fire, darkness, an earthen circle in the round. But I had experienced these before and in wilder places—campfires under the great western sky out in the back of the beyond. What impressed me were signs that we label "cultural" but in fact are also "wild." The Pomo constructed time so loosely that I felt at times like I was backfloating in an immense ocean. The evening did not so much progress as unfold. The most important ceremony of the year was conducted as informally as I might brush my teeth or sweep the kitchen floor. There was, however, focus to events: the fire was fed, songs began and ended, people danced certain steps, the earth's bounty was remembered. The roundhouse created a boundary and also brought in the world outside so that a great intermingling was possible.

But the Pomo are not flourishing. There was no acorn mush to be eaten at the Acorn Festival. The Pomo have, quite literally, lost their major source of nourishment. Words to songs were forgotten too often. This was an embarrassment to the Pomo, not a product of informality. Most troubling was the lack of Pomos participating. The roundhouse's celebrants were mostly non-Indian. This was acknowledged by the lead woman singer at the ceremony's close: "You people here are helping us, you know, to keep the songs and prayers alive."

And the Greater Yellowstone participants were helping to keep diversity alive. But unlike the Kashaya people, the group gathered at the ranch had been socialized to separate culture from nature and people from places. Evidence of this culture/nature divide is demonstrated by the questions at the meeting. The Yellowstone activists could not break with the wilderness tradition that depends upon pristine nature as a source of human inspira- tion—in contrast to developed lands devoid of any wild qualities. That tradition, as worthy as it has been, rests upon one of the key assumptions of history: culture can only be opposed to wildness. This assumption is not inconsequential. It allows most citizens of industrial societies to inhabit a world that is, by any reckoning of the facts, being destroyed by industrial imperialism. Wilderness reserves and protected areas are expected to offer a balance to environmental destruction and escape for the weary urbanite. Yet many activists, who do care enough to fight industrial power, unwittingly maintain the people/nature fence. They wish to perpetuate, instead of extend, the wilderness philosophy and tactics inherited from nineteenth- century Romantic ideals of the balance of nature. But this balance has never existed.

Consider the terms *biodiversity* and *sustainability*. Where have they come from and why have they appeared today? The answer is that they have appeared today because they are disappearing so rapidly. Conservation biology has grown in direct proportion to the increasing rate and scale of extinctions and habitat destruction. Debate over what is sustainable behavior has emerged as people confront hard evidence that such behavior no longer exists in many places. The biodiversity crisis is forcing Americans and others to reevaluate not only their political commitments but also the cultural assumptions upon which these strategies are based.

During my time with the Pomo, sustainability and wildness were never discussed. In Yellowstone we talked incessantly about these two matters. But we could not agree that the American idea of wilderness is an article of faith born of the very power that is destroying wildlands. This same power favors balance over uncertainty and surprise, *Homo sapiens* over all the diversity of life, brotherhood over sisterhood, one dominant culture over multicultural variety, economic well-having over ecological well-being, and the politics of wilderness over the practice of the wild. The radical Western split between nature and culture allows us to presume that ecological sources may be transformed into natural resources for human use only, that a human house cannot be round and wild, and that a mountain lion's home range is immaterial to the dedication of wildlands. But what if natural resources don't exist? What if legally defined wilderness areas are figments of our cultural imagination?

~ ~ ~

What is *wild?* Wildness escapes easy definition. While wilderness in America is most often a place, wildness is the force behind places or, as Tom Lyons says, "the overarching reality that transcends all plans and creations." A biologist might study natural selection and adaptive behavior in the field, but the process of evolution is wild.

Humans, too, are wild. Wildness in people might be characterized as the self-regulating aspects of *body* interacting with the unconscious depths of *mind* with each of these in constant contact with *environment*. In the roundhouse, potluck food graced the tables in back. Acorn boughs were laid against the walls. Humans sang and danced. Neighbors were recognized, received, and respected. Wildness was flowing without legal proclamation.

Classified wilderness areas may allow wild nature to live and breathe to the extent that these places are less subject to human control. Being in wilderness gives us the opportunity to connect with wildness and collapse the culturally relative categories of modern existence. Wilderness and wildness intersect where a river, mountain, elk, or Indian paintbrush spark awareness in us that helps to break down the fence between people and nature.

But the fence between culture and nature is difficult to reduce. It springs out of a fundamental paradox of human existence: the distinction between self and other. This boundary appears to go beyond history at least as far back as the beginning of the Neolithic era. The Pomo recognize it; so do all modern peoples. We cannot deny the distinctions between humans and other species, coyotes and spiders, or any member of earth's community of life. But we can decide what to make of these differences. Up to the present day, our choices have been poorly made. When confronted with otherness, we have chosen opposition over accord. Taking conflict as our standard, we have separated culture from nature and wilderness from wildness. To paraphrase writer Barbara Allen, we haven't lost our relationship with wild nature, we have simply invented it in terms that do not allow us to sustain cooperative relations with it.

In adapting culture to fit the "rules" of wildness, humans may choose between fear of nature or solidarity with it. But these choices are never cut-and-dried. They are always tangled up with such ongoing human predicaments as the need for individuals and groups within societies to come to terms with answers to the questions that cultures have already imposed. Even if every wilderness activist replaced the idea of wilderness with the goal of protecting ecological integrity, Congress and the general public might be unwilling to go along. Not every Pomo who lives at Kashaya associates with the roundhouse. Each individual must furthermore define through personal (and cultural) experience just how wide the boundaries of the self may be extended toward others. Here the deep ecology movement has offered wilderness advocates many powerful examples. But answers to these questions are always provisional. In an evolving world, ecosystem edges are always in flux and human borders are continually subject to negotiation.

~ ~ ~

How might we begin to integrate wild culture with wild nature? Ironically, the first step in protecting wildness is to continue to focus on increasing the size and number of protected areas—that is, wilderness. These lands are the last surviving remnants of wild diversity and they are faced with imminent development. But protection of biodiversity should be emphasized over preservation of scenic lands and recreational opportunities. Given the politics of wilderness protection in the United States, the best hope for success will be to ground such an approach in science. A conservation biology platform would include: habitat protection for viable populations of all native species; areas sized large enough to encompass natural disturbance regimes; a management timeline that allows for the continuing evolution of species and ecosystems; and human use integrated into the system of protected areas that would provide for *Homo sapiens* within the foregoing constraints. The hope of protecting large wildlands is that this strategy would slow the rate of the biodiversity crisis while also providing people with experiences that could feed the nature/culture system both ways—sustaining wildness at the core of protected lands as well as at the center of human communities. The promise of this strategy is that as humans begin to gain direct experience with ecosystems by working to protect biodiversity, wildness may explicitly become part of culture again.

〜 〜 〜

Deep in wild mountains, a ghost bear burrows into a hillside for winter's sleep. She has never encountered a human being, so people say her kind do not live there.

In the slow-moving shallows of a Georgia river, a few freshwater mussels congregate on the backside of a boulder. They are endangered, the last of their species, and their stretch of stream is about to host another new tract of suburban houses.

In the roundhouse each fall, people still sing and bless the oak trees. They dance and invite neighbors to the feast. Sometimes the singers forget the words and the dancers must stop to remember steps before they begin anew. I don't know the words to the songs or the steps to the dance, but I pay attention as best I can, hum along, and shuffle to the beat. For the Pomo, as for many people today, the fit between culture and nature appears unsustainable. But the centerpost, deep in earth and shaped by human hands, holds up the roof of the world. The great sky is just outside. It is inside, too. I can see it through the smoke hole.

Content Questions

1. At the Yellowstone meeting, what distinction is Grumbine making between wilderness protection and protection of ecological integrity? (255)

2. What does Grumbine mean when he says that "political dealmaking could not encompass the biological needs of species and the ecosystems they depended upon"? (255)

3. In spite of the impoverished condition of the Pomo, why does Grumbine say that their behavior during the Acorn Festival "offers signs of wildness and hope for the future"? (256)

4. What, according to Grumbine, is the "not inconsequential" assumption of the Yellowstone participants with regard to the culture/nature divide? (257)

5. How does Grumbine account for the appearance of the terms *biodiversity* and *sustainability*? (257)

6. According to Grumbine, how is the American idea of wilderness related to the power that is destroying the wildlands? (258)

7. How does Grumbine define *wildness* and *wilderness*? (258)

8. What connection does Grumbine claim exists between the distinction of nature/culture and self/other? (259)

9. Why does Grumbine say that the choices humans make between fear of nature and solidarity with nature are "never cut-and-dried"? (259)

10. What argument does Grumbine make for saying that "protection of biodiversity should be emphasized over preservation of scenic lands and recreational opportunities"? (259–260)

Application Questions

1. Grumbine suggests that designated administrative units for ecosystem management should be divided not by political boundaries but rather by watersheds, ecosystems, or other natural units. Choose one of his examples and outline the principles and goals of this kind of management in terms of ecological boundaries, data collecting and monitoring, and the place of humans in the ecosystem. Also, discuss what changes in the current bureaucratic structure might be necessary for the implementation and success of ecosystem management.

2. Grumbine speaks of "sustaining wildness at the core of protected lands as well as at the center of human communities." (260) Discuss how these two things could be accomplished both through ecosystem management practices and through cultural practices analogous to those of the Pomo.

Discussion Questions

1. What is the distinction between the politics of wilderness and the practice of the wild? What does Grumbine mean by "practice"?

2. What does Grumbine mean when he says "though my boundaries were being stretched, I was not concerned. The centerpost held up the world and it was firm, stout, and round"? (254) Why is the centerpost so important to his perspective on the Pomo?

3. Why did the other participants at the Yellowstone meeting challenge Grumbine by asking whether he believed in wilderness or not?

4. In what way can some of the things we label cultural also be wild?

5. What does Grumbine mean by the biodiversity crisis, and why does he claim that it is "forcing Americans and others to reevaluate not only their political commitments but also the cultural assumptions upon which these strategies are based"? (258)

6. How is being in the wilderness related to connecting with wildness and collapsing "the culturally relative categories of modern existence"? (258)

7. In addition to science, what does Grumbine think is necessary for biology-based ecosystem management to flourish? How is the integration of "wild culture with wild nature" important to this? (259)

Jan Zita Grover

Jan Zita Grover (1945–) grew up in San Francisco and began caring for people with
AIDS in the early days of the epidemic, continuing as an AIDS worker for eight years.
She then traveled to northwestern Wisconsin in an effort to restore her spirit,
and eventually took up residence in a rustic cabin. She found herself in the "sand
counties"—the landscape of Aldo Leopold's *A Sand County Almanac.* Grover
soon drew a parallel between the ravaged land of northwestern Wisconsin and
the ravaged bodies of the people she had cared for in San Francisco. Her first
book, *North Enough: AIDS and Other Clear-Cuts* (1997), vividly links these two devas-
tations. It won the Minnesota Book Award for creative nonfiction in 1998.

In prose that is both lyrical and uncompromising, Grover asks us to examine our
conventional view of nature's aesthetic appeal, pointing instead to a different kind
of beauty that might influence what we think and do about the conservation
of certain landscapes and resources. Her second book, *Northern Waters* (1999),
is about—among many other things—her love of fly fishing. Grover is also a
contributing editor for the *Women's Review of Books.*

This selection was first published in *New American Nature Writing 1996.* A
revised version appears in *North Enough: AIDS and Other Clear-Cuts.*

Cutover

It's the sort of logged out, burned over district that makes westward migration seem like a good idea. A land so used, so brutalized, that to stay with it, to endure it, must often have seemed like a penance. Miles of black oak and jack pine, much of it dead and down. Sand roads lined with scrub. Beaten-down trailers and perpetually unfinished houses, their composition walls dulling to gray as the seasons pass. Hills and grades scraped nude, gullies branded into the thin sand soils by ATVs. A place visited mostly when the bogs freeze over and hunters from cities to the south—the Twins, Milwaukee, Chicago—spread across the scratchy hills in search of bear and whitetails. The white and red pine here is anything but natural, the result of Civilian Conservation Corps reforestation in the 1930s, when much of the Cutover was replanted to pine as the only practicable solution to the region's depopulation and failure as farmland.

The Wisconsin Cutover is a profoundly altered land, a profoundly damaged culture. Logged over two to three times between 1860 and 1920, the northern tier of Wisconsin's counties became all but depopulated by humans and forests alike. Sold in the 1910s and 1920s to naive would-be farmers by the railroad and timber companies that had felled the forests, the Cutover's soils were too thin, its growing season too short for farming. By 1921, taxes on a million acres in the Cutover were delinquent and over 40 percent of the tax deeds remained unsold. By 1927, over 2.5 million acres

265

were in tax delinquency and 80 percent of tax deeds were unsold. In 1927, the University of Wisconsin Experiment Station reported that the total acreage under cultivation in the "resettled" Cutover was only 6 percent.

Up here in the extreme northwestern corner of Wisconsin, on the pine barrens of Douglas County, there's seemingly a bar for every resident—bars hidden back on sand roads, bars tucked back in the trees. My neighbor says the impressive ratio of bars to people gives fresh meaning to the term "Build it, and they will come."

They're out there for a reason.

The Cutover isn't pristine wilderness. It's the topography of more than a century of relentless abuse and adaptation to that abuse. The long glacial hills sliding away from the road are densely covered in knee-high popple. Beyond lie moraines bereft even of seedlings, a denuded pine barrens of sandy orange soil, piled slash, and the crisscross indicia of earthmovers' treads. Stumps like broken yellow beaver teeth. Only under snow cover is it conventionally beautiful. I could call it damaged, but that would be to emphasize only its scars; what surprises and moves me is the nimbleness and unexpectedness of its recovery.

The sand road to the last cabin the agent shows me winds past pulp tree plantations of jack pine. Turning onto County Road 50, we dip past thickets of oak and popple toward a low, boggy appendix of Crystal Lake. This is no managed landscape. Instead, it bears all the signs of a neglect neither benign nor malign, merely indifferent. Downed pine and oak everywhere. The few small birch choked by anonymous, weedy shrubs. With the exception of several near-dead red pines, not a tree is over fifteen feet tall, so the landscape looks dwarfed, ignoble. A dead porcupine lies across the road, its viscera turned out on the tar surface like items at a yard sale. The hole in its abdomen is as smoothly incised as an eye tuck.

We flash past him, my doubts increasing. Up ahead someone has planted idiot strips of young red and white pine. Their soughing beauty makes the jack pine and black oak behind them look even more scrofulous and less North Woods–idyllic.

The northern black oak (*Quercus ellipsoidalis*) of the Great Lakes states isn't meant to stand alone; it's a forest player, inconspicuous and comfortable en masse. It doesn't spread like the bur oak of the prairies, luxuriating in wild space. Instead, it reaches, in an apologetic, arthritic way, just high enough to wave its tips at the sun and provide room beneath for browse. Lichens crowd its trunk and branches; its brittle twigs snap easily in wind, returning accommodatingly to the ground. Tree fanciers have nothing good to say about it. Donald Culross Peattie, author of the magisterial *A Natural History of Western and Eastern Trees*, is typical in his dismissal: he calls the black oak "peculiarly unkempt and formless in its winter nakedness," a graceless tree "you will never see it in cultivation . . . for it has no charms to recommend it."

The jack pine, the black oak's companion in northern Wisconsin, grows with equal humility: here "a mere runt as to height and grace, a weed in the opinion of the lumberman, fit for nothing but pulpwood," sniffs Peattie. Farther north, it's a straight, stately tree, but here on Superior's south shore, jack pine looks self-effacing. It lacks the breathtaking height of reds and whites; as it ages, its branches rise popplelike toward the sky, diminishing its profile. At sixty, a jack pine is ancient, ready to fall; at sixty, a red or white pine is just attaining adulthood. Unlike the reds and whites, with their soft fans of needles in threes and fives, jacks produce blunt, short-bristled clusters and cones that recoil on themselves in tight gnarls. The French-Canadian voyageurs regarded the jack as unnatural, as bad luck—a conifer whose cones were mysteriously sealed shut. But jacks are the first conifers to reestablish themselves after a fire. Intense heat melts the resinous glue of their crescent-shaped cones, which open then like blowsy flowers, scattering their seed to the hot winds. The result, write Clifford and Isabel Ahlgren, "is extremely heavy jack pine reproduction, 'thick as hair on a dog's back.'" Jacks are the toughest and most adaptable of northern cone bearers, boreal trees that can thrive on the thinnest sand soils left behind by glaciers. Rangers celebrate jacks' tenacity and homeliness in doggerel—"There, there, little jack pine, don't you sigh. You'll be a white pine by and by"—but the Cutover's first loggers despised them. Their wood is soft and light, unsuitable for timber, unworthy of the loggers' art, useful only for pulping.

Above all else, jacks are survivors.

Seeing the cabin for the first time, I know none of this. I am innocent of the temptation to metaphorize every tree, shrub, lichen. I know only that the landscape seems vaguely distressing and ugly, the forest mournful and neglected—not at all what I have imagined and hoped for. Against the hard white April snow, the forest lacks any beauty I can understand. I see trees with scoriatic bark, rheumatoid branches, the torn flags of last season's leaves. I sense that such trees are the result of damage done here, but I am not sympathetic to their homeliness. Like most city dwellers dreaming of a forest retreat, I am seeking an unblemished North Woods of tall, stately trees. I want no part of these scarred veterans or of the opened earth, the trailer camps back in the trees, the sandbanks riven by ATVs. I am eager to move on without wasting any more time.

The cabin lies at the end of a sand road by a bay still opaque with ice. Far out on its horizon, something black and liquid dips and loops, pouring itself into the ice, reappearing in a skivvying line. With binoculars, the dark coil resolves into an otter. The agent brightens at my new show of interest and quickly piles on other points in the property's favor: bald eagles, bobcat, bear.

I hear her as if from a great distance. Already something else completely unexpected is working in me: a slight, not yet traceable intimation that this ruined land can be my teacher if only I will agree to become its pupil. What surrounds me I can see now only through the eye of convention, but I sense that through the eye of love and knowledge, I may one day find this place beautiful. I am eager to be schooled, to nurse what twitches of hope, of feeling, I can.

There are dangers in reading landscapes and other cultural artifacts as texts. The meaning of any text greatly exceeds the words used to constitute it: this is what intertextuality is about—the excess of cultural baggage we bring to reading something seemingly circumscribed and specific. The references we bring tend to be from other textual systems—films, music, literature—which for all their differences are still a particular kind of human artifact: symbolic representations of real acts.

Treating landscape as text is a dangerous project because land is not merely a representation. It is also a physical palimpsest of complex human, animal, and geologic acts, most of which are not primarily symbolic but written in flesh and soil and rock. While most landscapes are unquestionably cultural, it doesn't follow that theories devised for analyzing cultural representations are particularly applicable to reading them. The Cutover is a deep cultural landscape: even if I look back no further than the arrival of the first documented Europeans, the voyageurs, that still leaves almost four centuries of European, Ojibwa, and Dakota actions on the land to account for and interpret. These woodlands have been fretted by the pathways of peoples west and south, then north and east, then south and west again. If the European settlers' arrival and displacement of earlier inhabitants seems to us now somehow more decisive, more tragic, than the Ojibwa's displacement of the Dakota, it is partly because it is more recent and better documented *as text*. Anguish is kept alive in writing as well as in landscape by both displacer and displaced, heightened by the cultural differences between victor and vanquished.

Suppose I choose to look deeply at the area surrounding the cabin: what do I call such a search? Is it a textual reading? Because it involves the ways cultures shape land, I might instead call it landscape study or a species of cultural studies, with all that the latter term implies about eclectic methods and intentions. Does it matter at all what I call this project? Well, yes: depending on how I conceive it, certain data, certain methods, suggest themselves. My observations might be turned toward the jack pine's life cycle in one case and the history of European-American logging in another.

I ask myself why I find a landscape this damaged so beautiful, or at any rate so touching. Answering this question brings me to the lip of a personal abyss—the eight years I spent under the brand, the whip of AIDS.

I no longer believe there will be time, and time enough, for everything I want to do. That I can control many events. That my culture's standards of beauty and virtue are attainable or even desirable. I know how easy it is to stand outside my own body and watch it strain toward feeling, any feeling, at whatever cost. I've learned to find beauty in places where I never would have searched for or found it before—in an edematous face, a lesioned and smelly body, a mind rubbed numb by pain. Pain. A burned-over district. Mortal lessons: the beauty of a ravished landscape. Now middle-aged, I find mortality doubly my possession, keeper and kept.

The diminishment of this landscape mortifies and therefore disciplines me. Its scars will outlast me, bearing witness for decades beyond my death of the damage done here. Fat-tired ATVs and their helmeted riders lay the land bare, pock and deface it until it runs red and open, as disease has defaced the bodies of my friends. I am learning to love what has been defaced, learning to cherish it for reasons other than easy beauty. I walk after the ATVs, collecting beer cans and plastic leech tubs from the banks of the bass hole, tutoring myself in the difficult art of loving what is superficially ugly. Beauty flashes out unexpectedly. I try not to anticipate its location, try only to trust its imminence.

There are exceptions: curving in a hook southwest of the cabin is a bog that ends in a point forested with a stand of ancient red and white pine, immense and still, grave with age and uninterruption. These pines shelter an eagle couple who wheel over the bog every afternoon. The bog is thick with the improbable feeders who thrive on a peat-acid tea: tamarack, sundews, leathericaf, pitcher plants, bog rosemary, Labrador tea. The pines beyond the bog on the point survived the felling of millions of their fellows because they were too difficult to log out. Crystal Lake is spring fed; no rivers to merrily lead away fallen giants. Thus they stand on the point still, one of the few remaining stands of ancient whites in Douglas County.

There's no more lesson in this than in why some people with HIV survive ten, twelve years while others die after three. These things happen. I have learned to be deeply suspicious of metaphor, resistant to the pretty conceits I once used to explain pain and disaster. When I gaze south toward the black rampart of the surviving pines, I try to resist reading a moral into it—try to abjure the lessons that spin so readily to mind, like files summoned from a whirling disk. The pines have no more intrinsic meaning than the eagles or me. If I choose to read particular lessons in any of us, I must remember that they are *my* meanings, just as the comforts I drag from friends' deaths—heavy, cold, resistant as wet laundry—are not for or by them but for and by myself.

It's common to associate damaged landscape with open dumps, with suburbs shorn of the forests that preceded them, with prairies plowed under for four-bedroom, three-bath strip malls. There's little evidence of such damage here. Other than hillsides altered by the all too aptly named all-terrain vehicles, pines continue to double over in the northwest winds and blueberries to fruit underfoot. Deer flash like glimpsed dreams across the bog, and in late fall, old beater pickups prowl the sand roads, jammed with galvanized kennels and bawling coon hounds, sound as ancient as the cry of cranes. The woods are reputedly full of bear, the sky is thick with waterfowl, the lakes, so clear and deep, filled with muskie and pike. Oak leaves, oxblood in fall, flutter against the navy sky, the bay water is black with cold—natural, natural, all so natural. So *what's the problem?* Why my heart-stopping conviction of measureless damage?

If explaining this is hard, it's because landscape presents itself as an epistemological puzzle. Can we understand a landscape by recurring to what it once was? The sentimental response to this would be yes: merely invoke the "preinvasion" or pre-European forest as a measure of what's been lost, and the job's apparently done. But it's not: *which* pre-European forest do we mourn the loss of? Forests in this sand-skinned country succeed each other with a slowness beyond human scale. Only pollen core samples taken from peat bogs provide a scale of change over forests' time sufficient for tracking how this land has responded to human and other alterations. If the Cutover's most visible recent damage was caused by European-American logging, it's also true that lightning-caused fires have altered these northern forests as dramatically, as conclusively, as loggers have. Or wind: in 1977, a 200-mile-an-hour straight-line wind flattened miles of forest just south of my cabin as low and ugly as any logging operation ever did. The hills down there are covered now with six-foot popple indistinguishable from what succeeds a clear-cut. In the spin of centuries, forest succession barely registers the damage done by European settlers and loggers. So which forest am I mourning? Whose deaths?

Today on my dawn walk, I see for the first time a small meadow obscured all summer by the deciduous undergrowth along the road. Now I crash through the leafless shrubs to look at it more closely. It's perfectly round, knee-deep in frost-stiffened grass. A former beaver pond, silted up, wind- and animal-seeded, moving through the lists of succession on its way to becoming a forest clearing, then a patch of forest. But what kind of forest? Jack pine and black oak? The trees around its edge are birch, suggesting that soil here is deeper, more moist, than in the surrounding pine barrens. So a hardwood thicket, perhaps: a small puzzle for people a hundred years from now, who will wonder at this unexplained ring of deep-soil hardwoods surrounded by dryland jack and oak.

Like that small meadow, the bay outside my door is slowly transmuting, silting up to become a bog. Already it is lapidary with peat eruptions marooning unwary canoeists when the water draws down in midsummer. If the next century is unusually dry and warm, the breakdown of water plants in the bay will accelerate and the bog along the western shore will expand; eventually the bog will dry to meadow. At that point, trees will begin to move in from the edges and form a swamp forest.

Should I call this process damage, should I call it succession? What model—too inappropriate, too human—do I use when I embrace this landscape as altered, imperfect? According to what and to whose sense of time?

I am watching the resident vulture soar on wings like ironing boards, rocking faintly on a thermal. I think about Perry's leg.

Shortly before he died, I got my first look at Perry's dying leg. I'd been uncomfortably aware of it for several weeks—a faintly sweet, overripe smell in the house, an undertone of rot.

He was reluctant to let me change the bandage. "Are you sure you want to do this? It can wait until morning. Are you sure? Are you *very* sure?"

I wanted to do it: It comforted me to think of him going to bed dry and clean when there was so little else I could do for him. I knelt in front of him like a subject before a king and slowly peeled his pant leg away from the soaked bandage. Yards of puke-green gauze, which I unwound and threw into a reeking pile.

How much of the world can I find in something so altered—in a leg no longer smooth, intact, encased in a tan skin, but instead burst open, eruptive, returning to orderless matter?

I am very tempted to touch it, to find out what something so formless-looking can possibly feel like. Are there still nerve endings in this mass of dead and sloughing cells? Does it feel, this leg?

Is there a sense in which this leg can be viewed as a creation instead of only an annihilation? Its world is an entropic one, moist, swirling with energy turned on itself, no longer producing orderly structures. Dermis, epidermis, capillary, vein, artery, ganglion. Instead, hyperbolic replication that guts out needed systems, floods cells, drowning them. The surface looks like deep night sky, dark, light-absorbing, starred with drops of serum winking back my reflection, the room, me kneeling there.

Light gathers up chaos, shapes it. Perry's leg shapes death: here is where it most visibly enters my friend, through this swollen leg. He hauls his death around with him; it comes this way. The leg, or what used to be the leg, midwifes urgent talk. *Talk death*, it urges. *It's present; you can smell it, you can see it.* It creates a faint sweet stench, deep as formalin, as ineradicable, as deeply remembered.

I debride Perry's leg with hydrogen peroxide, much as I would pour soda over a ham or meat loaf. The bubbles wink back at me, catch light; they might be stars wheeling in an unfamiliar galaxy.

Perry talks disparagingly about his leg.

I ask him, "How does it feel, seeing your leg like that?"

"Sometimes I simply can't bear it." As if he can't believe it's his.

"What do you do then?" I ask.

And the curious thing is that as soon as he answers, I forget what he has said. I have tucked away his reply, an unopened valentine, a lost letter. I have tried to remember, have fallen to sleep hoping I'll catch his answer when it bobs unguarded from sleep's deep hole, bursts through the skin of resisting consciousness. But I can't. His reply lies in some shaded place, guarded against memory.

Perhaps he doesn't answer me at all. Soon afterward he says he has developed a high tolerance for pain. And perhaps that is his answer: he has learned to dissociate himself from the slow dying of his body. But that can't be right. Perry hasn't apportioned himself into the comfortingly disengaged blocs of Body and Soul. He knows that the KS festering in his left leg has also laid siege to his lungs, his liver, his esophagus, his soul. None of him is unaffected by what now macerates his leg's flesh. He is turning into something else, rich and strange—a dead organism, human peat. Dear bog.

I rewind his leg's burial sheet.

Content Questions

1. What happened to the land and the economy as a result of the Wisconsin Cutover? (265–266)

2. Why are northern black oak and jack pine dismissed by tree fanciers? What is Grover's attitude toward these trees? (266–267)

3. What makes Grover change her mind about buying the cabin in this "ruined land"? (268)

4. Why does Grover ask, "So which forest am I mourning?" (271)

Discussion Questions

1. Why does Grover describe jack pines as "survivors"? (267)

2. What does Grover mean when she speaks of reading the landscape as text? Why is it dangerous to do this?

3. Why does Grover compare the Cutover to her "eight years . . . spent under the brand, the whip of AIDS"? (269)

4. What is Grover referring to when she writes of "pretty conceits I once used to explain pain and disaster"? (270)

5. Why does Grover "try to resist reading a moral" into "the black rampart of the surviving pines" beyond the bog? (270)

6. Why is Grover uncertain about whether the process of the bay turning into a bog and then meadow is "damage" or "succession"? (272)

7. What does Grover mean when she says that "Perry's leg shapes death"? (272)

8. Why does Grover quickly forget Perry's answer to her last question about his leg?

Gordon L. Miller

Gordon L. Miller (1954–) teaches environmental history and the history of science at Seattle University. His research centers on the history of zoology, with a special interest in the history of herpetology. Miller is the coauthor of *Thirty Walks in New Jersey* (1992) as well as the editor of *Wisdom of the Earth: Vision of an Ecological Faith* (1997) and *Nature's Fading Chorus—Classic and Contemporary Writings on Amphibians* (2000), from which the following essay is taken.

Miller writes eloquently in *Nature's Fading Chorus* of "the dualism that fractures human beings and the natural world." He draws a sharp contrast between this split and the life of "the many species of amphibians which for ages have survived in the face of other challenging dualities" by means of what Miller calls a "both-and" dexterity. Miller joins a long tradition of science writers who have reflected on the "double life" of amphibians as a way of understanding our place in the juncture between nature and culture. Of "Dimensions of Deformity" he says that he "hopes that many readers will find it not just intellectually engaging but also, at least in some small measure, inspiring."

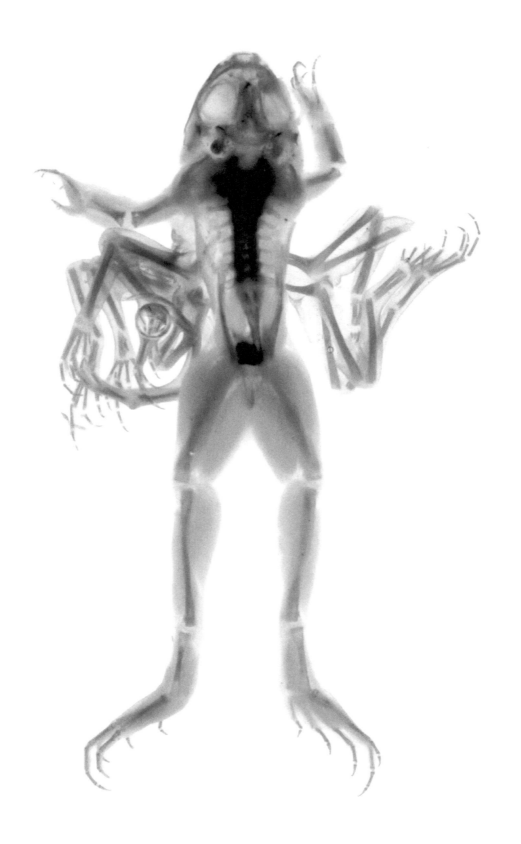

Dimensions of Deformity

The story by now has become almost legendary. In August 1995, a group of Minnesota middle school students discovered a passel of deformed frogs on a nature walk to a nearby field and pond. Recognizing that the percentage of frogs with missing legs, extra legs, or other malformations was apparently much higher than would occur in the normal course of natural events, they suspected that agricultural pesticides might be a factor. Environmental authorities were notified, the media got involved, Web sites were formed, and the world, or at least a significant portion of it, took notice. Since then, deformed amphibians have been found at many and varied sites throughout the United States and at some locations elsewhere. Researchers in both hip waders and lab coats are still busy teasing out evidence and testing hypotheses to explain this apparently variegated phenomenon.

When several scientists reported in the spring of 1999 that a tiny parasitic trematode was the immediate, if not always the ultimate, cause of at least some of the deformities, many members of the herpetological community breathed a collective sigh of relief. Finally, a piece of the puzzle had fallen rather solidly into place. But a whole range of researchers, including those who presented the findings, have emphasized that the puzzle is far from being fully solved. For example, trematodes can account for many cases of extra legs, but not nearly so well for missing legs or various other deformities that comprise the bulk of malformations around the country. For many cases of this type, scientists see chemical pollutants or perhaps increased ultraviolet radiation as more likely culprits. There is also the closely related question of a possible increase in the number of aquatic snails that host the trematodes before they move on to tadpoles. Such snails thrive in lakes with accelerated eutrophication caused by nitrate and phosphate pollution. The patterns in this puzzle are apparently so subtle and intertwined, and the pieces so widely dispersed, that there will be no easy resolution of them into a clear picture of the problem.[1]

It is interesting to notice, however, some of the responses evoked by the trematode reports. Within days, outspoken advocates of free enterprise seized upon the findings and began trumpeting trematodes as an embarrassment to environmentalists who had been suspecting anthropogenic causes for the deformities. One of these champions of commerce and industrial society has proposed that "the hysteria" caused by depicting frogs as poster children in a pollution campaign demonstrates "not the corruptions of capitalism, but the absurd lengths environmentalists will go to [to] manufacture a crisis in hopes of more government control." That writer also believes that what motivates environmentalists "is not a genuine concern for nature, but a hatred of man and his civilization."[2] Conveniently ignoring the facts that the parasitic habits of trematodes cannot explain all deformities, that trematodes may be cofactors with other environmental conditions, and that deformities are only a part of the much larger and still unsolved puzzle of amphibian decline, these evangelists of economic growth have seen this portion of amphibian research as a green light for business as usual.

The most interesting thing about this rush to exonerate humankind in the matter is the general sense of the relation between humans and nature that it implies. Individuals with this perspective would obviously prefer an explanation for deformed frogs that makes no reference to human beings over an explanation that implicates them in the phenomenon. They would prefer a frog that, deformed or not, is just a frog, just a feature of the material world of nature, apparently independent of human life. But the idea of a frog as just a frog, with no nonmaterial link to human life—a purely objective frog—is really a historical invention. It is an invention that has proven to have great practical value, but is an invention nevertheless; which, like all cultural or personal possessions, can become an obstacle when held too dearly or uncritically.

This view of frogs, this view of nature, as essentially alien to humans—*it* as essentially matter, *we* as essentially mind or spirit—is readily evident among many promoters of free enterprise, largely because they unabashedly advocate the dominant ethical and economic system that is a logical counterpart of this epistemology. It is thus not surprising that they often find themselves at odds with environmentalists. But many of the skirmishes between these camps are rooted more in questions of practice than in contrasts of basic epistemology, since a great many members of the green community—sometimes unwittingly, unwillingly, and against their better judgment—also habitually experience nature as distinct from the defining essence of human life. The dualism of subject and object, the apparent independence of we as private selves "in here" from a world of public objects "out there" with the two realms communicating only through the senses, is a part of our cultural inheritance, and all of us, from across the political spectrum, have been in some measure shaped by this epistemological endowment.

It is typically considered simply common sense to see frogs, and nature as a whole, in this dualistic way, but we had to learn, both culturally and personally, to do so. It is difficult to see beyond common sense, even if the spirit is willing, but we can at least make a start by asking how this sense of things became so common. By doing so we will find that throughout much of Western history the "in here" and the "out there" were experienced as joined not just through the senses but also through a supersensible factor common to both, so that the "inner" life of the human self was felt as one with the life of the objects of nature. But we will also find that this dynamic polarity, this play of contrasting mental and material poles, was gradually fractured into the dualism with which we live.[3]

We can witness the emergence of the objectified frog by looking briefly at a few highlights of Western history from ancient Egypt to the eighteenth century. There is a great temptation to see the changing ideas of nature evident in this story as merely changing interpretations imposed by people of the past on a natural world that, at bottom, has always been populated by the same sort of objects we see in it today. But this would be to read our modern mindscape back into historically distant eras, before this mindscape had arisen. In the following sketch, I will resist this temptation and instead will follow the perhaps more demanding, but also more valid and interesting, path of seeing the changing perceptions of nature as indications of the historical evolution of the Western mind. And because our minds are our organs of perception, tracing the evolution of the mind enables us to watch the historical emergence of our familiar world. Evidence for this evolution can be found in many places in the historical record, but I will focus here on a small but pertinent element of it—the history of deformities.

Consider, first, how deformed frogs would most likely have been perceived in the ancient Near East. If such creatures had been discovered in the swamps of Egypt or Mesopotamia in the first millennium B.C.E., where the annual emergence of innumerable tadpoles and frogs with the yearly floods was a manifestation of nature's primordial creativity; they would surely have been taken quite seriously. We can imagine an ancient Ninevite, upon making such a discovery, scurrying to the vast omen literature in the library of King Ashurbanipal, hoping for some hint of the future in the thousands of "if-then" statements carved in stone tablets. He would seek especially a relevant teratological omen, the special type dealing with the import of abnormal births or malformations in humans and animals. On one tablet, he might find help in the statement that "if an anomaly's eyes are brought together on its forehead—the land will be oppressed" or that "if an anomaly's eyes are on its back—the land will decrease in size." And the inscription on another that "if all anomaly's four legs turn toward the rear, and its eyes are on the right—whatever the enemy asks from you, give it to him willingly" might indeed afford the desired certainty.[4] Considering the great cosmological and agricultural significance associated with the lives of frogs, the prognosis probably would not have been bright. If a plague of frogs was an expression of divine disfavor with an Egyptian pharaoh, what would be the meaning of ill-formed frogs—another indication of divine displeasure, or perhaps a hint of divine impotence?

For these ancients, natural phenomena, especially exceptional ones, were practically vibrating with significance, their very bodies echoing with divine impulses and imperatives. They were of interest not so much as entities in themselves, however, but mostly as pointers to something else, as possible indicators of cosmic conditions and as clues about what to expect. If I, as an ancient Mesopotamian, were to find a deformed frog, I would take notice because I would experience it as issuing from a realm beyond itself and as having, because of that fact, reference beyond itself, reference to me and my household or tribe. The frog would not be what we today would call a biological specimen and would study to determine the cause or cure of its abnormality; it would be a communication, a sign, relying for its efficacy, like all communication, on some measure of commonality between the source and the sensitive receiver. The historical evidence indicates, moreover, that for the ancients, this was the natural way of seeing things. It was not that, as we might assume from our modern perspective, they saw a merely material frog and proceeded to attach all sorts of symbolic meanings to it. They apparently experienced the world in this way automatically, without much thought about it. Seeing a frog symbolically would have been "common sense" to them, just as seeing a frog nonsymbolically, we might say "literally," seems common sense to us.

If a misshapen frog had been scooped up a few centuries later by one of Aristotle's students on a walk through the garden of the Lyceum, the pioneering zoologist would have been most intrigued. He, in contrast to his earlier Near Eastern neighbors, would have been less prone to read divine imperatives in the frog and more likely to contemplate its place in the grand order of the cosmos. Given Aristotle's belief that "the craftsmanship of nature provides extraordinary pleasures for those who can recognize the causes in things,"[5] he and his followers would have considered the possible causes of the deformity. And of these "causes," the kind most crucial for understanding biological processes, and the kind most controversial in the subsequent history of science, was the "final cause"—the goal toward which the process is directed, the fully formed frog that is the natural fulfillment of the egg's potential. The Aristotelians noticed that in the great majority of cases, organisms arrived successfully at their intended form, and they thus saw deformities as a failure of this formative pursuit. But it was a failure only in terms of nature's customary performance, not in terms of the multifarious designs of nature in toto.

For Aristotle, nature as a whole was a living organism that not only harbored the creative potential for a great variety of biological forms but also encompassed human life and thought. For him, the forces of nature were also the formative energies of the human mind. A tadpole's transformation into a frog involved the purposive realization of the egg's potential. Similarly, the simple act of beholding a frog, or of thinking a frog, involved the realization of the form of the frog in the person's mind. Seeing, hearing, touching, tasting, smelling the world thus implied a sort of identity or solidarity between the knower and the known, between the human mind and

281

nature. In the very act of perceiving a deformed frog in an ancient Greek garden, then, Aristotle would have felt not only that he was witnessing a curious case of nature's formative work but also that he was participating in this universal process.

Aristotle's ideas about the generation of animals through the purposive "craftsmanship of nature" were elaborated with abandon in the Middle Ages and the Renaissance, as was his idea that gaining knowledge of nature involved not just a process of gathering data but an actual "in-forming" of the mind. For a great many medieval students of nature, frogs, or any other animal, existed primarily to teach people lessons, as is evident in myriad medieval bestiaries. In seeing natural things as whispered words of God, these medieval Europeans are somewhat reminiscent of the ancient Egyptians and Mesopotamians in their interpretation of omens. But the interpretation now, of course, had a Christian cast, with the Book of Nature, like the Book of Scripture, illuminating the heavenly path.

Some medieval naturalists, though, also found natural processes themselves quite interesting. If Albert the Great, that amazing thirteenth-century interpreter of Aristotle and teacher of Thomas Aquinas, had come across a deformed frog in the valley of the Rhine near his home, he would quite likely have looked to the hills and the heavens for answers. Albert, who was well acquainted with the metamorphosis of frogs, thought that, beyond the inner principles emphasized by Aristotle, various local geographical features as well as a rich array of immaterial influences from the stars were also implicated in biological processes. Although he believed that humans were perhaps more susceptible to astral influences than were animals, which he believed were more sensitive to atmospheric changes, he proposed that the conjunction of certain patterns of the planets with particular places on earth could prevent embryos from reaching their proper final form.[6] A deformed frog could thus be an indicator of prevailing cosmic dispositions, conditions also linked to the material and spiritual health of humankind. Throughout the Middle Ages, the Renaissance, and beyond, deformities were typically interpreted as some combination of failed, final causes and unfriendly skies. Perhaps never, then, during this time was a frog just a frog; it was a sign from heaven, an image of a transcendent world that was also the sustaining leaven of human life.

But a sea change was on the horizon, a tidal shift in the history of Western consciousness, and the spirit that was wafting over European culture in the early seventeenth century is epitomized in the figure of Francis Bacon. For Bacon, the study of biological anomalies belonged wholly within the realm of *natural,* not *supernatural,* history. And Baconian natural history could never proceed so long as plants and animals were seen essentially as symbols enmeshed in a web of sympathetic relations, as divine utterances with depths of meaning. On the contrary, he argued that "the world is not the image of God," and that if we could clear the symbolic cobwebs from our minds and remove the scales of tradition from our eyes, the true and unequivocal language of nature would be plain for all to see. So Bacon, on the whole, vigorously rejected Aristotle's teleological philosophy of nature (though traces of final causes still crept into his thought) and the medieval emblematic universe it inspired. The Book of Nature no longer speaks, he said, so it is no use training one's ear to hear a still, small voice. Nature is silent, but clear, and requires simply a reliable reading.

Shorn of symbolism and moral implications, deformities could then fit quite well into Bacon's plan for the advancement of useful knowledge. For in the pursuit of such knowledge by "hounding nature in her wanderings," it was helpful to follow both the highways and the byways because "he who has learnt her deviations will be able more accurately to describe her paths." The more accurate and objective one's knowledge of nature, then, the more successful one could be in applying this knowledge "to the effecting of all things possible" for the betterment of humankind. There were two aspects to this Promethean project, and their linkage is evident in the famous Baconian adage that "knowledge is power." There is the epistemological aspect—that humankind needed a new way of knowing nature—and there is the ethical aspect—that humankind desired a new way of using nature. And these aspects go together like hand and glove.[7]

We thus see emerging a relatively new species of frog—a frog that is just a frog, bearing no transcendental stamp or moral message, a merely material frog. And it seems clear that such a frog, that such a natural world, was linked historically to the very deliberate invention of the new scientific method for knowing and using nature. It is a method that took pains to separate the material world "out there" from the human mind "in here," a perspective that dissolves the solidarity of humanity and nature and stands in such contrast to the ancient and medieval sense that knowledge involves nature re-forming herself in the mind. This method was, of course, developed even more rigorously by Bacon's more mathematical cohorts, Galileo and Descartes, who proposed that nature consists, in essence, of merely what is measurable. Curiously, for these seminal architects of objectivity, even the color, sound, smell, taste, and feel of a frog exist merely in the mind of the perceiver; only the animal's size, shape, weight, and movement persist after the naturalist quits the marshland and goes indoors.

But the objectified frog, at this point, was still but partly liberated from the waters of symbolism. Its full emergence into the modern light of day, so that almost anybody could get a good look, would require much further expansion and assimilation of the new scientific worldview. Bacon's spirit of observation and experimentation stimulated later naturalists such as Thomas Browne and John Ray and was infused into the communal body of the world's first major scientific society, the Royal Society of London, founded in 1660. The Royal Society displayed a lively interest in biological anomalies, but it was the Academy of Sciences in Paris, in concert with the Museum of Natural History, that gave to biological specimens their much more modern feel. Here, from the late seventeenth century, scientific specialists investigated a great many deformities from the perspective of disciplines such as embryology and comparative anatomy. This systematic medicalization of anomalies furthered the movement toward thoroughly naturalistic explanations.[8] The objectified frog was clambering onto the shore. And over the next two centuries, through innumerable field investigations, laboratory studies, and educational endeavors, this new species of frog, by following this naturalistic path, came to rest in full view of professionals and the general public alike. The evolution of the Western mind— the evolution of our familiar world—had achieved one of the most distinctive features of its modern form.

Objectified frogs, whether malformed or whole, can of course be easily eaten, dissected, or ignored with impunity. Aside from the nourishment they have provided through the centuries, especially to the French, they have afforded much valuable biological and medical knowledge, which most likely would not have occurred had they, and nature as a whole, remained immersed in symbolism. The labored invention of the objectified frog, of an objectified natural world, was in essence a positive development. It hardly requires saying that this way of being in the world, having launched the whole grand enterprise of modern science and technology, has had undeniable benefits. But it is also rather painfully obvious, now that the project has played itself out on the planet for four centuries, that it has its limitations.

The main drawback of this mode of perception is its tendency to fragment the world, typically dividing the phenomena of nature into relatively manageable provinces. This is an understandable strategy, of course, but it can lead to some unfortunate provincialism. A six-legged frog would traditionally have been a fascination to anatomists, physiologists, and embryologists. But hydrologists, botanists, and climatologists, not to mention foresters and engineers, probably would have paid little notice. The modern scientific project, as we have seen, also sets up sovereign realms of matter and mind, a divorce that has given many fine philosophical minds epistemological fits and has left even many ardent nature lovers with but faint hope of a thoroughgoing human-nature reunion.

The science of ecology, with its emphasis on relationships, grew out of the recognition that a fragmented science cannot do justice to an actually integrated world. Ernst Haeckel, inspired by Charles Darwin, coined the term for the new field in 1866 to designate the holistic, and scientifically rigorous, effort to understand an organism not in isolation but in relation to the larger household of nature, and ecology thus draws on diverse scientific subfields. Ecologists came to see human beings, too, as elements of ecosystems, a recognition that gave birth, of course, to the modern environmental movement. Now, ecological *science* can get on relatively well without worrying much about that other fragmentation of the world built into the Baconian program, the division between the sentient human mind and the insensate material world. But the broader ecological *sensibility* of environmentalism, with its larger ethical dimension, should, and sometimes does, find this yawning gulf more of an obstacle. In the early 1920s, Aldo Leopold was already realizing that a scientific—even an ecological—understanding of nature was not a firm enough foundation upon which to build a conservation ethic. He remarked that:

> Possibly, in our intuitive perceptions, which may be truer than our science and less impeded by words than our philosophies, we realize the indivisibility of the earth—its soil, mountains, rivers, forests, climate, plants, and animals, and respect it collectively not only as a useful servant but as a living being, vastly less alive than ourselves in degree,

but vastly greater than ourselves in time and space—a being that was
old when the morning stars sang together, and, when the last
of us has been gathered unto his fathers, will still be young.[9]

If Baconian "knowledge" is tied to power over nature, then Leopoldian
"intuitive perception," it seems, is linked to respectful citizenship within
the biotic community.

What truly hinders this sort of responsible citizenship is that for so
many of us today, the "scientific," objective view of nature feels so thoroughly natural, so "intuitive," because we engage in it so automatically,
without thinking about it. Just as the ancient Mesopotamians would have
naturally experienced a deformed frog as a divine omen, and twelfth-
century Europeans might have naturally seen one as a sign from the heavens, so is it second nature for us to see such a frog as just a frog, with no
particular reference to us. But such a frog would never have appeared, and
would not appear to us now, had the story I have sketched in this essay not
occurred and woven its way into the personal history of each one of us. Our
world is populated with objectified frogs because of our objectifying minds.
Thus, they all have reference to us—if not always to our way of living,
inevitably to our way of knowing.

An interesting bit of perceptual entertainment called the "magic eye" has
gained enormous popularity in recent years. It involves holding an apparently nonsensical pattern close to one's eyes, softening one's focus, and
moving the pattern away until—usually after some effort and experimentation—familiar three-dimensional objects stand out rather surprisingly from
the page. The objects are usually a little tenuous at first; it is easy to lose
them if one's focus or perspective changes. But they reappear more readily
with repeated viewing. All of which makes it obvious that the objects would
not appear at all if one were not looking in the proper way, and that they
would sink again into the background if one closed one's eyes.

An incredibly rich world of three-dimensional objects answers to our
opening eyes each morning and meets us at every turn. We are so practiced
in this manner of seeing that we are oblivious to the effort and experimentation that were required in both our cultural and our personal history to
learn to see in this way. We see the world with our magic eyes. And it refers
to us by its very nature.

The vigor with which latter-day Baconians have appropriated some apparent evidence that deformed frogs might have no reference to humankind clearly reveals how the phenomenon of the objectified frog is still so closely linked to the Promethean program of industrial growth. The degree to which humankind is ethically implicated in these frogs is yet to be determined. But the appearance of any merely material frog on the shores of our perceptual worlds always implicates us epistemologically. And our knowing the world in this way, as essentially a material resource, is the license that, when joined with desire, has unleashed untold exploitation— of land, and water, and the habitats of frogs.

The great virtue of ecological *science* lies in its efforts to soften the fragmentizing tendencies of modern science and to see the world whole. With this perspective in mind, even schoolchildren realize that because we share a planet with innumerable other organisms, deformed frogs in a Minnesota field just might have reference to our behavior. But a deeper ecological *sensibility* should also encompass our way of knowing. As Aldo Leopold noticed in the early days of environmentalism, the best foundation for environmental ethics lies in the sense of "a closer and deeper relation" between humans and nature "than would necessarily follow the mechanistic conception of the earth as our physical provider and abiding place."[10] It is possible that we share with the frogs not only a planet but also, at least in some small measure, an essence.

When the early modern philosophers established the great divide between mind and nature, between subject and object, all human beings were, at least theoretically, included on the "subject" side of the line and thus were seen as worthy of ethical consideration. In practice, of course, it has not always worked that way; innumerable individuals throughout history have been treated more as objects than as true subjects. There seems to be no end to the mischief caused by the refusal to grant subjecthood to other human beings.

Or to other nonhuman beings. Suppose that, while not sacrificing the rigorous pursuit of detailed knowledge that vitalizes modern science, we were to recover some sense of nature's depth that was submerged in the scientific wake. Suppose we agreed to bridge the great divide and see nature as somewhat more like us—with some measure of an integrated inner life— than like a collection of mere objects sans *psyche*. A frog with two legs or four would then merit our careful consideration, not only for what it might mean for us but also for what it means to itself. If it were possible for us to consider a frog from the inside—not just in terms of the human project but in terms of nature's project, of which we also are an outcome—we could divine more than just oracles for our way of living. We could discover the ground for a deeper relation in the amphibian's revelations of life on the edge—revelations of life at the boundary of the wet and the dry, in sympathy with the seasons, at the primordial threshold of silence and voice; maybe even of life at the crossing of nature and culture, and of the inherently precarious business of living on both sides.

Notes

1. See S. K. Sessions, R. A. Franssen, and V. L. Horner, "Morphological Clues from Multilegged Frogs: Are Retinoids to Blame?" *Science* 284 (30 April 1999): 800–802; P. T. J. Johnson et al., "The Effect of Trematode Infection on Amphibian Limb Development and Survivorship," *Science* 284 (30 April 1999): 802–804.

2. L. H. Rockwell, "Jumping to Conclusions," *Journal of Commerce* (5 May 1999): 5A; see also M. Fumento, "With Frog Scare Debunked, It Isn't Easy Being Green," *Wall Street Journal* (12 May 1999): A22; B. Doherty, "Amphibian Warfare," *Weekly Standard* (24 May 1999): 16–18. (Mr. Rockwell is president of the Ludwig von Mises Institute; Mr. Fumento is a fellow at the Hudson Institute; and Mr. Doherty is a fellow at the Competitive Enterprise Institute.)

3. I am greatly indebted to thinkers such as Owen Barfield, particularly to his *Saving the Appearances* (New York: Harcourt, 1965), and Theodore Roszak, especially his *Where the Wasteland Ends* (New York: Doubleday, 1972), for insightful explorations of the issues. I have also borrowed from Roszak the term "mindscape" in the paragraph that follows.

4. E. Leichty, *The Omen Series Šumma Izbu* (Locust Valley, NY: J. J. Augustin, 1970), 125, 126, 157.

5. Aristotle, *Parts of Animals*, 645a7f. Quoted in G. E. R. Lloyd, *Early Greek Science: Thales to Aristotle* (New York: W. W. Norton, 1970), 105.

6. Albert the Great, *Man and the Beasts*, books 22–26 (Binghamton, NY: Medieval and Renaissance Texts and Studies, 1987), 440; see also C. J. Glacken, *Traces on the Rhodian Shore* (Berkeley: University of California Press, 1967), 227–229, 265–271.

7. F. Bacon, *Advancement of Learning, Novum Organum, New Atlantis* (Chicago: Encyclopaedia Britannica, 1952), 33, 159, 210.

8. K. Park and L. J. Daston, "Unnatural Conceptions: The Study of Monsters in Sixteenth- and Seventeenth-Century France and England," *Past and Present* 92 (August 1981): 51–53.

9. A. Leopold, "Some Fundamentals of Conservation in the Southwest" (1923), *Environmental Ethics* 1 (summer 1979): 140.

10. Ibid, 139.

Content Questions

1. What is "the general sense of the relation between humans and nature" that Miller says is implied by "the rush to exonerate humankind" in the matter of the deformed frogs? (278)

2. Why does Miller claim that it is so difficult "to see beyond common sense, even if the spirit is willing," when trying to see frogs and nature in a nondualistic way? (279)

3. According to Miller, what kind of information would an ancient Mesopotamian derive from a deformed frog? How would this information differ from what a modern scientist would derive, viewing the frog as a biological specimen? (280)

4. How would the science of Francis Bacon deal with deformities? What does Bacon mean when he says "he who has learnt her [nature's] deviations will be able more accurately to describe her paths"? (283)

5. How does the new scientific method of Bacon, Galileo, and Descartes lead to the emergence of "a merely material frog"? (283–284)

6. According to Miller, in what way is the "objectified frog" an indication of one of the most distinctive features of the modern Western mind? (284)

7. What are the limitations of the invention of "objectified nature," which Miller recognizes as "having launched the whole grand enterprise of modern science and technology"? (284–285)

8. How does ecological science proceed relatively well regardless of the "fragmentation of the world built into the Baconian program"? (285–286)

Application Questions

1. In writing about the attempts to explain the high incidence of deformities among frogs, Miller says that "the patterns in this puzzle are apparently so subtle and intertwined, and so widely dispersed, that there will be no easy resolution of them into a clear picture of the problem." (278) Outline three different possible patterns of explanation for this phenomenon: one that takes into consideration only non-human factors, one that considers only human factors; and one that combines both human and nonhuman factors. Discuss the limitations of each.

2. Describe the deformities of frogs in terms of Aristotle's "final cause." (281) How is this kind of causality related to modern ideas of biological cause?

Discussion Questions

1. What does Miller mean when he refers to "a purely objective frog" as a "historical invention"? (278)

2. What does Miller mean when he says that the skirmishes between environmentalists and advocates of "the dominant ethical and economic system" are "rooted more in questions of practice than in contrasts of basic epistemology"? (279)

3. Why does Miller resist the temptation to see changing ideas of nature as merely different interpretations imposed on the "same sort of objects" we see in nature today? (279)

4. Why is the history of deformities especially pertinent to the evolution of the Western mind and its ideas of nature? What does Miller mean in this context by "mind"? (280)

5. What does Miller mean by ecological *sensibility?* In what way does this sensibility have an ethical dimension?

6. In what way does an objectified frog have reference to "our way of knowing"? (286)

7. In his example of the magic eye, is Miller suggesting that one way of seeing nature has no special value over any other way?

8. What does Miller mean when he says that the world we see with our magic eyes "refers to us by its very nature"? (286)

9. What distinction is Miller making between being ethically implicated and epistemologically implicated in the appearance of deformed frogs?

10. Is Miller suggesting that a "deeper ecological *sensibility*" might lead to yet another conception of the frog? (287)

11. What does Miller mean by recovering "nature's depth"? (287)

Comparative Discussion Questions

1. How might Vernadsky, Commoner, or Lovelock respond to Descartes's method for knowing and understanding reality?

2. Compare Thoreau's experience of Mt. Katahdin with Grover's experience of the Wisconsin terrain. How are their reactions similar? How are they different?

3. Are Clements's superorganism, Vernadsky's biosphere, Thomas's "organized, self-contained" living creature, and Lovelock's Gaia the same thing?

4. In what ways does Leopold's "The Land Ethic" reflect the influence of Marsh's ideas in "Man and Nature"?

5. To what extent does Leopold, Thomas, or Lovelock lend credence to Tansley's use of the term *ecosystem?*

6. When Leopold speaks of particle X's role in the "common task of hoarding sunlight," and Thomas of the earth as "marvelously skilled in handling sunlight," are they talking about the same photochemical processes?

7. Boulding and Commoner both recommend economic systems that are radical departures from that of modern industrialized capitalism and consumerism. In what ways are their alternatives similar to or different from each other?

8. Both Hardin and Commoner suggest that the solutions to environmental problems are not technical solutions. Do they mean this in the same way? How might Commoner respond to Hardin's emphasis on population control as a significant remedy for environmental problems?

9. Is Dillard's recognition of "intricacy" a recognition of Gaia? Why or why not?

10. Compare Lovelock's and McKibben's attitudes toward genetically engineered species. How are they similar? How are they different?

11. Compare McKibben's, Williams's, and Grover's responses to damaged or human-altered landscapes. How might different views of these landscapes influence a determination of value, policy, and management?

12. How does Snyder's analysis of the language used to describe nature compare with McKibben's assertion that the traditional idea of nature is ending?

13. Both Snyder and Grumbine offer definitions of the terms *wild* and *wilderness*. In what ways are their definitions similar and different? For these two writers, can *the wild* and *wilderness* be lost, or are they always present in some way?

14. McKibben says that we "don't choose our friends from among the terminally ill" and that "there is no future in loving nature" because it is ending. Would Grover agree with him about where we choose our friends? Would she agree that it is pointless to love nature because it is ending?

15. Do Clements and Grover use the term *succession* in the same way? If not, what are the differences?

16. Both Grover and McKibben speak of meaning and look for it in the landscape. Are they talking about the same thing?

17. Compare Grover's view of damage and recovery with Miller's view of deformity and normalcy. Where do these views overlap and where do they diverge?

18. Many of the writers in *Keeping Things Whole* advocate a holistic approach to science, while at the same time recognizing that the reductionist approach continues to yield important results. Is there an optimal balance between these approaches and can they complement one another?

19. The writers represented in *Keeping Things Whole* come from an array of disciplines: natural science, social science, literature, and philosophy. If you were designing a short course for a general public of nonspecialists and wanted to impress upon them the most central concerns, problems, and insights of environmental science, which three selections might you use, and why?

Bibliography

For further reading

Allaby, Michael. *Basics of Environmental Science,* 2d ed. London: Routledge, 2000.

Botkin, Daniel B. *Discordant Harmonies: A New Ecology for the Twenty-first Century.* New York: Oxford University Press, 1990.

Bowler, Peter J. *The Norton History of the Environmental Sciences.* New York: W. W. Norton, 1993.

Daly, Herman E., and John B. Cobb Jr., with contributions by Clifford W. Cobb. *For the Common Good: Redirecting the Economy Toward Community, the Environment, and a Sustainable Future,* 2d ed. Boston: Beacon Press, 1994.

Eisenberg, Evan. *The Ecology of Eden.* New York: Vintage Books, 1999.

Gleick, James. *Chaos: Making a New Science.* New York: Penguin Books, 1988.

Malthus, Thomas R. *An Essay on the Principle of Population.* 1798. Reprint, edited and with an introduction by Anthony Flew. New York: Penguin Books, 1983.

Milbrath, Lester W. *Learning to Think Environmentally: While There Is Still Time.* Albany, NY: State University of New York Press, 1996.

Nash, Roderick Frazier. *Wilderness and the American Mind,* 4th ed. New Haven, CT: Yale University Press, 2001.

Thomashow, Mitchell. *Ecological Identity: Becoming a Reflective Environmentalist.* Cambridge, MA: The MIT Press, 1995.

VanDeVeer, Donald, and Christine Pierce. *The Environmental Ethics and Policy Book: Philosophy, Ecology, Economics,* 2d ed. Belmont, CA: Wadsworth Publishing Company, 1998.

Wilson, E. O. *The Diversity of Life,* college ed. with study materials. New York: W. W. Norton, 1999.

By and about authors represented in this collection

Descartes
Descartes, René. *Discourse on Method and the Meditations.* Translated by John Veitch. New York: Prometheus Books, 1989.

Thoreau
Thoreau, Henry David. *The Maine Woods.* New York: Penguin Books, 1988.
——. *Walden.* Introduction and annotations by Bill McKibben. Boston: Beacon Press, 1998.

Vernadsky
Bailes, Kendall E. *Science and Russian Culture in an Age of Revolutions: V. I. Vernadsky and His Scientific School, 1863–1945.* Bloomington, IN: Indiana University Press, 1990.

Clements
Clements, Frederic E. *Plant Succession: An Analysis of the Development of Vegetation.* Washinton, D.C.: Carnegie Institution of Washington, 1916.

Tansley
Tansley, A. G., and T. F. Chipp, eds. *Aims and Methods in the Study of Vegetation.* London: The British Empire Vegetation Committee [etc.], 1926.

Leopold
Leopold, Aldo. *For the Health of the Land: Previously Unpublished Essays and Other Writings.* Edited by J. Baird Callicott and Eric T. Freyfogle. Washington, D.C.: Island Press [for] Shearwater Books, 1999.

Boulding

Boulding, Kenneth E. *The Image: Knowledge in Life and Society.* Ann Arbor, MI: University of Michigan Press, 1956.

Commoner

Commoner, Barry. *Making Peace with the Planet.* New York: New Press, 1992.

Thomas

Thomas, Lewis. *The Medusa and the Snail: More Notes of a Biology Watcher.* New York: Viking Press, 1979.

Dillard

Dillard, Annie. *Teaching a Stone to Talk: Expeditions and Encounters.* New York: Harper & Row, 1982.

Lovelock

Lovelock, James. *The Ages of Gaia: A Biography of Our Living Earth.* New York: W. W. Norton, 1988.

McKibben

McKibben, Bill. *The Age of Missing Information.* New York: Random House, 1992.

Snyder

Snyder, Gary. *A Place in Space: Ethics, Aesthetics, and Watersheds.* Washington, D.C.: Counterpoint, 1995.
——. *The Gary Snyder Reader: Prose, Poetry, and Translations, 1952–1998.* Washington, D.C.: Counterpoint, 1999.

Williams

Williams, Terry Tempest. *Refuge: An Unnatural History of Family and Place.* New York: Vintage Books, 1992.

Grumbine

Grumbine, R. Edward. *Ghost Bears: Exploring the Biodiversity Crisis.* Washington, D.C.: Island Press, 1992.

Miller

Miller, Gordon L. *Wisdom of the Earth: Visions of an Ecological Faith.* Seattle: Green Rock Press, 1997.

Acknowledgments

All possible care has been taken to trace ownership and secure permission for each selection in this book. The Great Books Foundation wishes to thank the following authors, publishers, and representatives for permission to reprint copyrighted material:

Death of a Pine, from A YEAR IN THOREAU'S JOURNAL, by Henry David Thoreau. Copyright 1992 by Princeton University Press. Reprinted by permission of Princeton University Press.

Man and Nature, by George Perkins Marsh, from MAN AND NATURE: OR, PHYSICAL GEOGRAPHY AS MODIFIED BY HUMAN ACTION, edited and annotated by David Lowenthal. Copyright 1965 by the President and Fellows of Harvard College. Reprinted by permission of the Belknap Press of Harvard University Press; Cambridge, Mass.

The Biosphere, from THE BIOSPHERE, by V. I. Vernadsky. Copyright 1998 by the Far West Institute. Reprinted by permission of Springer-Verlag.

The Climax Concept, from "Nature and Structure of the Climax," by Frederic E. Clements. Reprinted from THE JOURNAL OF ECOLOGY, Vol. 24, 1936, by permission of The Ecological Society of America.

The Ecosystem, from "The Use and Abuse of Vegetational Concepts and Terms," by A. G. Tansley. Reprinted from THE JOURNAL OF ECOLOGY, Vol. 16, No. 35, 1925, by permission of The Ecological Society of America.

The Land Ethic and *Odyssey,* from A SAND COUNTY ALMANAC: AND SKETCHES HERE AND THERE, by Aldo Leopold. Copyright 1949, 1977 by Oxford University Press. Reprinted by permission of Oxford University Press, Inc.

The Economics of the Coming Spaceship Earth, by Kenneth E. Boulding, from THE ENVIRONMENTAL QUALITY IN A GROWING ECONOMY, edited by Henry Jarrett. Copyright 1966 by Kenneth E. Boulding. Reprinted by permission of the author.

The Tragedy of the Commons, by Garrett Hardin. Reprinted from THE JOURNAL OF SCIENCE, Vol. 162, No. 1243, 1968. Copyright 1968 by the American Association for the Advancement of Science. Reprinted by permission of the author.

The Closing Circle, from THE CLOSING CIRCLE: NATURE, MAN, AND TECHNOLOGY, by Barry Commoner. Copyright 1971 by Barry Commoner. Reprinted by permission of Alfred A. Knopf, a division of Random House, Inc.

The World's Biggest Membrane, from THE LIVES OF A CELL: NOTES OF A BIOLOGY WATCHER, by Lewis Thomas. Copyright 1971, 1972, 1973 by The Massachusetts Medical Society. Reprinted by permission of Viking Penguin, a division of Penguin Group (USA) Inc.

Intricacy, from PILGRIM AT TINKER CREEK, by Annie Dillard. Copyright 1974 by Annie Dillard. Reprinted by permission of HarperCollins Publishers Inc.

The Recognition of Gaia, from GAIA: A NEW LOOK AT LIFE ON EARTH, by James E. Lovelock. Copyright 1995 by J. E. Lovelock. Reprinted by permission of Oxford University Press.

The End of Nature, from THE END OF NATURE, by Bill McKibben. Copyright 1989 by Bill McKibben. Reprinted by permission of the author.

The Words Nature, Wild, *and* Wilderness, from "The Etiquette of Freedom," from THE PRACTICE OF THE WILD, by Gary Snyder. Copyright 1990 by Gary Snyder. Reprinted by permission of North Point Press, a division of Farrar, Straus and Giroux, LLC.

Water Songs, from AN UNSPOKEN HUNGER: STORIES FROM THE FIELD, by Terry Tempest Williams. Copyright 1994 by Terry Tempest Williams. Reprinted by permission of the author and Pantheon Books, a division of Random House, Inc.

The Politics of Wilderness and the Practice of the Wild, by R. Edward Grumbine, from PLACE OF THE WILD, edited by David Clarke Burks. Copyright 1994 by Island Press. Reprinted by permission of Island Press.

Cutover, from NORTH ENOUGH: AIDS AND OTHER CLEAR-CUTS, by Jan Zita Grover. Copyright 1997 by Jan Zita Grover. Reprinted by permission of Graywolf Press, Saint Paul, Minn. "Cutover" first appeared in *New American Nature Writing 1996*, edited by John Murray. San Francisco: Sierra Club Books, 1996.

Dimensions of Deformity, by Gordon L. Miller, from NATURE'S FADING CHORUS, edited by Gordon L. Miller. Copyright 2000 by Gordon L. Miller. Reprinted by permission of Island Press.

Art Credits